Ice
Fishing

By the same author

For Mireille Fortune Skory,
with affection

A Jim Capossela Outdoor Book

Ice Fishing

A Complete Guide, Basic to Advanced

Jim Capossela

with Drawings by the Author

The Countryman Press
Woodstock, Vermont

The Countryman Press, Inc.
Post Office Box 175
Woodstock, VT 05091

Library of Congress Cataloging-in-publication data

Capossela, Jim
Ice fishing / by Jim Capossela : with drawings
by the author.
p. cm.
"A Jim Capossela outdoor book."
Includes bibliographical references and index.
ISBN 0-88150-234-0
1. Ice fishing. I. Title
SH455.45.C37 1992
799.1"2--dc20 91-45934
CIP

3948730/

Printed in the United States of America
10 9 8 7 6 5 4 3 2 1

Acknowledgements

I would like to thank Harry Wirtz, who composed the pages of this book and was chiefly responsible for its design. On the editorial end, Carl Taylor provided invaluable comments and helped to steer the project. Steve Grooms contributed an excellent chapter to the book, as well as several nice photos and general editorial support. I have to thank my best ice fishing buddy, John Zelyez, who posed for the camera ad nauseum (always cheerfully) but who still refuses to remove that silly looking hat. Appreciation, if not compensation, is due to John's wife, Loretta (my cousin, whom I allowed him to marry) who is sick and tired of all this fishin' and huntin' but who may let us go to the Adirondacks next winter anyway.

Other persons or companies who helped and to whom I am grateful include but are not necessarily limited to: Angela Aiello, The Berkley Company, Pam Brundage, Jay Cassell, Jim Crowell, Feldmann Engineering, Charles Guthrie, H. T. Enterprises, Minnesota Department of Natural Resources, Diego Padro, St. Croix, Tom Schlichter, Tackle Marketing, Tackle Test, UMM Holdings, Alice Vera.

Contents

(Continued)

(Continued)

Illustrations

Preface

IT HAPPENS ABOUT THE same time every day, all winter long. I'm standing near shore with my gear collected around me. It's 4:45 and I've just left the lake to the horned owl and the moon. I look up and down the frozen far shoreline and it is serene, stark, beautiful. I glance back one last time to where I've been fishing and say out loud, "God, let me do this one more time—just one more time."

If you feel that way about ice fishing, you've come to the right book.

Or, if you'd *like* to feel that way about ice fishing—or anything else for that matter, if you never have—you've also come to the right book.

Ice fishing is pure magic. But why?

There is no form of matter on earth that so defies us one day and then so fully yields to us the next as does water. It would be hard to express this better than Harold F. Blaisdell did in *McClane's New Standard Fishing Encyclopedia:*

> The general character of ice fishing differs so greatly from that of conventional forms of angling that the unique qualities which account for its widespread popularity are worthy of identification. Perhaps the greatest single source of fascination is the drastic change in the relationship between man and water brought about by the dramatic appearance of the ice itself. The waters which now lie hidden beneath the frozen surface immediately become a dark, sealed-off mystery and thus pose a tantalizing and compelling challenge to the fisherman. Yet at the same time the latter is suddenly accorded an intriguing advantage: he can walk about boldly on a surface which is normally immune to any such approach.*

But the magic of ice fishing goes beyond that fact that we are temporarily being allowed to transgress a basic law of physics. There are other things.

I hate being alone at a party. I hate anyone being near me when I'm deer hunting. Yet I can both love and hate companionship on the ice. The activity simply lends itself to either, and you can pick and

*A. J. McClane, *McClane's New Standard Fishing Encyclopedia* (Henry Holt and Co., New York, N.Y.. 1980)

choose at will by just grabbing your bucket and moving to another cove or another lake.

"Hey Billy, I heard you got a nice 4-point up over on Shedd's property."

"Yeah, I took a big spike off of Walden Mountain on the last day, too."

"Hey Cappy, how do you want your eggs?"

"—over well done—yeah, there weren't diddly for steelhead in the main river this year, so we went up to the Black. Took a ten-pounder and an eight."

"This coffee's cold."

"I wonder why. It's two degrees. Somebody fire up that Coleman Stove."

"I got out on White Pond December 6th. Unbelievable. That's a month earlier than usual. They say it was the coldest December ever."

"I shot two grouse in those oak woods across the street there last November. Saw a lot of scrapes, but there's too many guys in there for gun season."

"Damn job. I couldn't get out at all for bird season. Did make one run for flounder to Moriches Bay. We took a half a pail on the incoming out by buoy 42."

"This coffee tastes like flounder. Who made this coffee, anyway?"

And so the gibberish goes, the livelong ice fishing day. It is redolent of the feeling that, "Heck, we may not catch anything today, but we all had a few successes in the season past, didn't we?"

Who can enjoy ice fishing?

Bring your lover and dine on duchesse potatoes and cajun style perch cooked on the ice. Bring your kids, both boys and girls, and watch them have a ball chasing flags, falling in the snow, ice skating, laughing, and tackling the dog. Bring your dad, and your grandad— and anyone else you know who can put up with a little bit of cold to feel absolutely whole and healthy and exhilarated.

Magical? When else could you get truly and honestly excited over a twelve and a half inch perch? Or a fish simply biting (the flag going up)? Or a phone call from a buddy who "just wanted to let you know that there's already two good inches of ice on that back cove on Muscoot."

Yet in spite of the oftentimes social nature of ice fishing, I must admit that there is no better place to be alone than out on some frozen lake.

And now I'm back out on just such a lake. I've been writing dutifully for two days, as that's how I make my living, and for my diligence the spirits of field and forest have granted me another day at my favorite place. I'm sitting on a bucket and a snow squall is blowing in from the northwest. First the bridge goes, then the big maple on the point, then my farthest tip-up, and in a few minutes, I will be all alone with my jig pole and the one tip-up I can still see. It is simple—the pines, the snow, the ice. It is pure—the enduring of nature's harshest for the privilege of being able to kill one's own meal. And it is childlike—the present moment is the only moment.

But wait, there's a flag on the near tip-up! I set my jig pole down across the top of the bucket and run to it. The snow grows thicker and thicker, painting my wool coat and my hood and my face a pure white.. Now, the passing commuters, if they do look, see only a desolate, snow-blown lake. I have vanished from their world, and stepped into a far better one.

CHAPTER 1

Finding Good Ice

THE MOST OBVIOUS PART of ice fishing might seem to be finding ice to fish through. Nothing could be further from the truth! There are places where good ice can be found amazingly early in the season and there are places that never freeze up. At locations in between these two extremes, ice will come — and go — on what seem to be pretty random dates. It isn't random at all, though. Here are the main factors affecting ice formation and thickness on any given body of water:

1. Distance from or nearness to the ocean (which has an effect on the next item)
2. Air temperature
3. Depth of the water
4. Exposure to the wind
5. Angle and amount of sunlight (determined by the surrounding topography)
6. Currents, and the speed of those currents

Air temperature is the primary determinant, but latitude certainly isn't the only factor determining air temperature. Both coasts of North America are warmer, at comparable latitudes, than inland areas. Thus the average annual temperature curve (isotherm), when depicted on a weather map, shows a distinct dip in the middle of the continent. For example, Chicago at about 42 degrees north latitude is much colder than Provincetown at the same latitude.

There are many more localized differences, too, altitude being one factor. For example if ice hasn't formed yet where you live, you may be able to drive only a short hour to a hilly area to find good ice. Drive two hours to a mountain range and you might find a good six inches even though your neighborhood ponds are still ice free. This could be the case even if the mountains are to the south of your home. The greater the altitude, the greater the differential. The ponds in your neighborhood might still be at 42 degrees F (6°C)* while a fishable pond at 3,000 feet is already locked in.

There are some surprising differences on a still more local level. There is a community only 20 miles north of me that has often been called "the icebox of the county." It's commonly five degrees colder than villages very close to it. Its particular geographic location simply makes it a cold spot, and the ponds up that way are usually the first to freeze.

Large, open waterways transfer heat to the surrounding land, so to find good ice you'll often have to move farther from them. The best example I can think of is Long Island, New York. By its latitude, it should afford some ice fishing, but because of the warming effect of the waters that surround it, good ice is a reality in only some winters. And what ice does form doesn't last very long.

This type of negative influence (negative to the ice angler) occurs to a much lesser extent inland. For example, let's say you live along one of the country's great river systems. Let's assume, too, that the river runs north and south. Here, the winter isotherm could curve upward away from the ocean and along both sides of the river. You may have to move inland from the river to find good ice.

WHY LAKES DON'T FREEZE UNIFORMLY

Now let's focus on a single body of water. If you're still green on the ice, you may be amazed at the variability in ice thickness from one part of a lake to another. By understanding these next factors you'll not only be able to find ice earlier and later, you'll be safer at any stage of the ice fishing season.

*All Celsius figures in this book are to the nearest whole number

Three and a half inches of brand new black ice. It's a great time to ice fish, but exercise extreme caution.

The first is depth. Deep water in general will take longer to freeze than shallow water. It has to do with the wind.

Let's say a good cold snap comes along in late November and the temperature goes below 20 degrees F (-7°C) for five nights in a row. Simultaneously, the daytime air temperatures never squeak past 35 degrees. There has to be ice, right? It's not that easy. In the shallower backwaters of your lake, you probably will see a little ice, perhaps even a couple of inches. But this early in the season, the deeper, open part of the lake will resist icemaking to a degree that some find amazing. As early December rolls around, the coves start to freeze, but in spite of days of bone chilling weather, the deepest parts of the lake remain stubbornly ice free. Why? The reasons are discussed fully in Chapter 9.

You can't do anything about this process, but you can seek out those places where the forces that prevent ice formation are minimized.

Depth and wind have to be considered together.

First, the larger the lake the less likely that any part of the lake will really be able to escape the wind. Oh, it's true that there will be frozen bays on — for example — Lake Ontario, the main part of which never freezes. But on these very large lakes, depth may not be that much of a factor. The very protected bays and lagoons may be frozen and that may be about it.

But what about small to medium size lakes? There are a number of factors to consider here.

One is the prevailing winds. If, for example, the prevailing winds are from the northwest in winter, as they are where I live, you may find the first ice forming on those sections of the lake in the lee of that wind. This could be true even if the deepest water is hard to the northwest or lee corner of the lake. Conversely, the southeast arm of the lake may be so riled by the wind that it freezes very late, even if it is relatively shallow water.

Where I live, we fish long, twisting reservoirs with many arms and bays. Those sections of the reservoirs on an axis with the N/NW winds are tough to freeze. Those arms that are perpendicular to the prevailing winds freeze much more readily. On all of the lakes and reservoirs near me, shallow coves very protected from the wind — for example those with steeply rising hills all around them — are apt to be the first places to freeze and the last to thaw.

That leads us to the next important factor: degree of openness to the sun.

In our hemisphere, the sun passes to the south in winter. Its lowest point in the sky, as measured at twelve noon, is on the winter solstice, December 21 or 22. The farther north you go on the continent, the lower the sun stays in the southern sky until you get to the arctic where the sun is totally out of the sky for a period of time in winter.

STUDY THE TOPOGRAPHY

Want to get out for some of that very productive early season ice fishing? All the factors discussed in this chapter must be considered, but one good bet will be a southerly part of a lake to the south of which the land rises to block the sun much of the day. I know a cove of a lake near me that fits this description perfectly. Its axis is east–west and it's nestled down between two steep ridges. I never got around to clocking how many hours of direct sunlight this cove gets in winter, but the southernmost edge of it gets none. Consequently, last winter this rim of the cove still had 10 to 12 inches of good ice even after weeks of freakishly warm weather had completely opened most of the other lakes in the vicinity.

Steep topography around a lake or a part of a lake is almost always good news. As just stated, a hill behind the southerly part of a lake will help the most, but if the east or west sides of the lake are bordered by fairly steep hills, it will also help, since morning and/or afternoon sunlight will be blocked off. Thickly growing tall trees, especially along the southerly edge of a lake, can help to keep ice. This is most true where the trees are found in combination with a rise in the land.

What the land does on the north rim is least important in terms of the angle of the sun, although it can be a significant factor if the wind is blocked.

Along the lines of what we've been discussing, there are some very particular places that make ice remarkably early and keep it often astonishingly late.

Little pieces of a lake can be cut off from the main lake by train tracks, roads, and sometimes natural or manmade hummocks. In reservoirs, in particular, these little isolated "ponds" are usually connected by a culvert or pipe to the main lake; fish can (and will) move back and forth between the main lake and this offshoot piece of water. They're usually shallow, and by virtue of their small size, not prone to wind-induced wave action. In short, they're natural ice makers, and may be safe to stand on six weeks before the big waters lock up solid. Best of all, such ponds can be extremely productive.

Some time back, we found two such semi-detached ponds behind a set of train tracks that skirt the edge of a large water supply reservoir. One was alive with small, but keepable crappies, plus bluegills. In early March, the people at the tackle store looked at us funny when we showed up to buy bait and said we were going ice fishing. A disgustingly warm January and February had opened up most area lakes weeks earlier.

The next chapter approaches this same topic from the opposite perspective: where the *thin* ice will be. Both chapters should be considered safety-related, however.

CHAPTER 2

Safety on the Ice

IN THE TONY CURTIS MOVIE about the life of Harry Houdini, there is a compelling episode where the great escape artist is locked inside a large crate and dropped through a hole cut in the ice over the Detroit River. I believe he is also handcuffed, or in a strait jacket, or whatever. He gets out of the box quickly enough and swims towards the surface, but he can't find the hole. He's forgotten about the current! He finds air pockets to breathe and eventually does get out, many hours later. Everyone but his faithful assistant has given him up for dead.

It's not known for certain if Houdini ever "came back" as he said he would, but it's pretty certain that you won't come back if you fall through the ice at the wrong time and in the wrong place. Forget about surviving a fall through ice into a moving river. It can take no more than six feet of water and an old bluegill pond to put you on the other side of the Ouija board.

Some people say ice is unpredictable. It is completely predictable. It will always act at any given moment exactly the way the laws of physics dictate that it must. However, ice is unpredictable in that no human being can assess it, all the time, with complete accuracy. There are too many variables. This makes an important point: It's impossible to guarantee that you'll never fall through the ice.

With that sobering thought in mind, you can set out to tilt the odds against it ever happening.

WHICH ICE IS SAFE?

I really don't like equating ice thickness to safety because it tends to oversimplify something that is not simple. Yet there must be a starting point:

Less than 3 inches	Stay off this unless you have extensive ice fishing experience.
3 inches	Safe for a few scattered anglers if the ice is clear, black, new ice unadulterated by layers of snow, slush, or periods of thawing and refreezing.
4 inches	Safe for a larger group, if the ice is unadulterated as just described.
5 inches or more	Generally safe for anglers on foot.

The above was not taken from any safety bureau or other agency or pundit. Rather, it is based on my own 30 years of ice fishing experience.

If you choose to drive a vehicle onto the ice, the only thing I can say is that you should do so only with the utmost thought and consideration. In my home state of New York, the ice varies from almost non-existent (on Long Island) to extremely thick in most winters (the Adirondacks). In the coldest parts of America's ice fishing belt, including the Adirondacks, vehicles are routinely driven on the ice, and indeed, they are necessary to haul out and later haul back in the shanties employed to keep fishermen warm. If you live in an area where this tradition prevails, you may well have the savvy needed to take the bold plunge. Yet in many fringe areas, where the weather just doesn't get super cold, I have seen hot-rodders streaking across what I considered to be very marginal ice for that activity. Fifteen inches of ice is enormously strong, but weak areas can occur for a myriad or reasons. Springs can weaken the ice. Currents can weaken the ice. Heavy vehicles all parked together can weaken the ice. Pressure ridges can weaken the ice. Carp wallows (where carp mingle under the ice) can weaken the ice. Opposing shock waves caused by vehicles in operation can weaken the ice. If open water is nearby, wave or wind action can weaken the ice.

Every year a number of cars and trucks go down, and survival rates in this situation are low. Don't become one of these morbid statistics.

There are all kinds of ice. Clear, black, new ice of sufficient thickness is not only comparatively strong but almost always provides the best fishing opportunities. New black ice will crack as you walk across it. This is not dangerous if the ice is of sufficient thickness. Ice at this stage will also rumble, a little more so at four to eight inches than at less than four inches. With the rumbling comes cracking not related to your presence. People call these expansion cracks. They are actually contraction cracks (though expansion or upward bending of the ice might be witnessed in the form of an upthrust "pressure ridge"). Ice will contract and expand just like any other solid. On very cold nights, the ice will contract as its surface temperature falls down to below 32°F (0°C). If the day is warmer than the night, usually the case, the upper part of the ice will expand as its temperature rises back towards 32°F. Rumbling and cracking are most closely associated with ice between four and twelve inches thick, but they are not criteria I use in assessing ice safety. I should point out that thin ice which cracks out of weakness is very much dangerous. Only experience will tell you the difference between normally occurring cracks (contraction or otherwise) and real, menacing cracks.

Oftentimes with new ice, the ice around shore is thinner than what you find just a bit farther out. This is especially true (a) on the north side of a lake, where the sun hits directly, (b) where there are jagged rocks, that act as a heat sink, and (c) if the bank is sloped. More often, though, shore ice will be better in early season than the ice farther out. You may find six inches of marbled white ice in a sheltered cove surrounded by shoreline while the main lake is still wide open. Out where it's windier and deeper, wave action will continually "turn over" warmer water so that the surface has a hard time freezing. This leads us to another great truth about ice safety: The larger and more irregularly shaped the lake or reservoir, the less likely it will freeze uniformly. In fact, almost no large, irregular lakes freeze uniformly. Shallow, wind-protected areas will freeze first. So will sections that get little sun. Other parts of the lake may not freeze for another month — or the entire season.

Generally, small ponds will freeze at fairly uniform rates. Inlet and outlet areas, springholes and spring seeps, and heat-absorbing objects can throw curveballs into even the most innocent looking pond, though.

These Adirondack Mountain pike were taken in late season. Late ice — like early ice — can offer excellent fishing. Just be aware of the particular dangers that exist at the book-ends to the season.

I am very wary of new or relatively new ice that's covered with snow. Of itself, a little dry snow doesn't hurt. It's just that I can't see what's up ahead. I just mentioned contraction cracks. All new, black ice has these. I like them because as I proceed out from shore, I can gauge ice thickness by looking at a crack in its vertical dimension. New snow wipes this out. Still, if the black ice underneath a little powdery snow is of sufficient thickness, I will proceed out with extreme caution.

As a general rule, when I'm walking on ice and there are patches of snow here and there, I avoid these patches. Many people say that snow insulates the ice and slows the thickening process. I recently checked this with a cold region scientist who confirmed that it is true. In any case, a good rule to follow is to avoid or at least be wary of any patch of ice that for any reason looks different or peculiar.

Next to experience, perhaps your best tool in judging ice is an ice chisel or "spud" as it is usually called. You need this item, even if you have an auger. Test the ice at the shore. How many chops did it take to go through? If you've determined that it's actually safe to step onto the ice, use the bar to poke at the ice ahead of you as you walk. Keep testing it. Go slowly. Fish a hole near shore for a little while as you observe the lake and get into tune with it. Now walk out another ten yards and chop another hole. Remember: New ice will very possibly be thinner over deeper water.

It's important to note that a larger lake freezes not only at a non-uniform rate, but also in what appears to us to be a random pattern. Why is there good ice here, open water just out there, marginal ice off to the side, and yet more good ice just around the point? The factors that combine to create this often disturbing early season mosaic are many.

Lakes with complex currents and certain other features can be treacherous. We mentioned areas wide open to the wind. Also watch out for pipes that run under causeways. On either side of the causeway by the pipe the ice may be thin. Inlet areas are always suspect, because of the moving water. Yet sometimes, outlet areas are just as bad. An outflow from a lake creates a suction that in turn sets up a current uplake (sometimes far uplake!) of the outlet point. These currents can keep the ice thin all winter. The edge where water flows over a dam is always bad ice.

Take note, sometime, of where a goose or a swan has just relieved itself. Come back six hours later and those droppings may already be two inches down into the ice. Come back three days later and they may be almost through the ice! All objects on the ice absorb heat, and that heat melts the surrounding ice to varying degrees. Large objects absorb more heat than small objects. Dark objects absorb more heat than light objects. Bird droppings, a leaf, a small twig or your own bait bucket will not create dangerous ice. Docks, boats frozen into the ice, rafts frozen into the ice, and similar large objects will absorb a lot of heat and the ice for several feet around them may be unsafe.

I keep learning new things about ice and ice safety. This past winter we were on a 60-acre pond near last ice. It had been warm, but this particular pond is in a hollow and holds ice very well. The shore was a little bit dicey, but we easily glided out onto nearly six inches of ice.

As I often do, I stood there a few yards out from shore and studied the lake. I had my spud bar in my hand. I started working my way out when I spotted a patch that just didn't look right. I tapped at it lightly with the spud. The spud went right through! A small patch of leaves, a few feet square, had been blown out onto the ice and had absorbed enough heat to have melted halfway through the ice and weakened it greatly. We found several other patches like this, and each was treacherously thin.

OTHER HIDDEN PERILS

Where boat docks or houses line a lake, beware of submerged water pumping systems designed to keep the area of the boat house ice free. Often regulated by timers, these churning water systems can sometimes create a hazard well out from shore.

If a lake or reservoir is used for drinking purposes or irrigation, there may be considerable intake and outflow, yet the structures performing these tasks may be hidden beneath the surface. When a reservoir is heavily "tapped," the entire body of water can become like a moving river. Ice may never form, or at least safe ice may never form. It's the same with narrow, twisting reservoirs formed upon rivers. The upper parts of these reservoirs may be more river-like than lake-like. The net result? Possibly, weak ice.

Besides drinking and irrigation, impoundments can also be used for hydroelectric power generation. If a lake is known for water level fluctuations, for any reason whatsoever, be especially careful. Ice heaved up at an angle onto shore can tell you that a drawdown recently occurred. Here, the shore ice in particular can be treacherous.

We mentioned above the incidence of light, powdery snow on top of relatively new ice. While this is not ideal, there is a worse scenario. When snow falls onto new black ice, two bad things can happen. If it gets warm, the snow will start to melt, forming a layer of slush on top of the still black ice. Or, if there's still some open water adjacent to the new ice, a good wind can blow it up under the snow layer, also creating slush on top of the new ice. Either way, the slushy snow insulates the new ice, slowing the thickening process. I don't like this kind of ice.

Here's something even worse. It gets cold that night and freezes the top of the slush. Now you have a crust, a layer of water or slush, and then perhaps a marginal amount of black ice underneath. Every step you take you crash through the crust, into a layer of slush, and you never really know what's under that. I am petrified of this kind of ice — stay off it.

Even though ice can thicken in many different specific ways, the preceding is a pretty good scenario for early ice formation. Lets now move into mid-season ice.

After a couple of good, cold nights, the snow/slush/water/ black ice layers will all fuse into one solid layer of ice. Now, though, it will be what I will call white marble ice. The key thing here is how cold it gets. Remember, you may only have had three inches of good black ice before the snow came. That's very marginal ice, so what's on top won't help unless it's solid.

Poke at this solidified ice with your spud. Has it indeed all fused into one good layer, or do you see soft pockets or distinct layers? If it's iffy, and the weather is real cold, time is on your side. Wait another few days till it's one solid layer of five or six inches.

At this stage, chances are a small pond will be comparatively safe. (Remember our master premise: There is no 100% safe ice.) However, a large impoundment should still receive much respect at this stage. That good looking five to six inches of white ice may only be 2½ inches in the channels. Here it pays to know your lake. What part of the lake generally freezes last? If you want to fish this area, work out towards it slowly. Your spud may again come in handy — you can thump the ice ahead of you as you go. You can't do this with an auger. Then, too, with a manual auger there's a lot of direct, downward pressure right next to where you're standing. You just can't do without that spud.

As the white ice thickens to six to ten inches, your concerns diminish but never disappear. One thing I never do is assess ice strictly by human activity. Snowmobilers who don't ice fish go screaming across a frozen lake thirty times faster than you do with your little spud bar poking ahead of you. Have they done any testing? Do they really know how the ice is just around the point? Tragically, some don't know and they become statistics. All snowmobilers should be ice fishermen first.

In any case, I never assume a lake is safe because there are a lot of people out on it. Frankly, there are some stupid people. Last year, a plane landed on a lake I was fishing. All that convinced me of was that the section the plane landed on was probably safe to walk on. I didn't take anything else for granted.

But now it's late February, lets say, and even the channels and inlet areas have more ice than you really want to cut through. Then a freakish warm front sneaks in on a south wind one night and the mercury hits the high fifties or even low sixties. Time to panic?

Not really. It takes a lot to melt a foot of good ice. You may be amazed at how long good ice persists in the face of a mid or late winter warm-up.

But spring cannot be denied. In a normal year in most areas, that good, thick white ice will start to "honeycomb" by early March or sooner. Day by day it will lose thickness and simultaneously grow weaker. After rain, snow and many warm and cold spells, it will be pocketed, layered, weakened. In many lakes, at least, the ice will be more uniform than early season ice. I'd say that's most true of regularly shaped lakes where the surrounding topography is such that sunlight hits most of the lake about the same. In larger reservoirs, the ice may be just as unpredictable as it was in early season. Channels, in particular, will open up first.

While shore ice may be the best ice in early season, it is usually the worst ice in late season. As the land absorbs heat from the ever higher sun, the shore ice will melt first and become unsafe even when there may still be a good ten inches just ten yards out. If you pick your access and egress points carefully, you may still be able to enjoy some good ice fishing in comparative safety.

As a matter of fact, from a fishing standpoint, the next best thing to first ice is last ice.

YET ANOTHER PERIL

If a heavy fog or a snowstorm sets in, it's entirely possible to become lost on the ice. This can be extremely dangerous if it's a large lake with open sections, or ice that tends to shift in large flows. Quite a few people get in trouble in just this way each winter. The lucky ones make their way to shore or are lifted off the ice by helicopters. (On some lakes, Erie for example, there are routine helicopter patrols of the ice.) The unlucky ones you read about with your coffee the next morning. A compass is a simple gadget that, on a big lake, can yield some piece of mind. A map of the lake would also be useful, since you can make a bearing on a shore point and at the same time avoid sections that you know or think to be open or unsafe.

COPING WITH THE ELEMENTS

There are still other dangers lurking on a frozen lake besides the ice you stand on. The first is the elements you will have to deal with.

An entire chapter in this book is devoted to staying warm on the ice, and all of that should be considered safety-related. If you die of hypothermia, you're just as dead as if you fell through the ice and drowned. There has been much good material published on the subject of hypothermia or lowering of one's body temperature; on the different stages of the malady; and on the indicated action at each stage. Studying up on this subject would be a good project for the ice loving angler.

It's true that I've been cold many times, and might technically have been considered hypothermic on some of these occasions. But it only scared me once.

It wasn't while ice fishing. I was trolling a big lake all day long in early April, out of a cold, metal rowboat. At 4:30 p.m. I met my buddy on shore. He'd taken an eight pound brown and said he felt good. I was so cold that he had to take the car keys out of my pocket. I was shivering violently and was definitely in the early stages of hypothermia. Thirty minutes in a heated car stopped the shivering, but I felt cold for the rest of the day. It wasn't until a few years later that I realized I had indeed experienced hypothermia.

It is insidious. You may deny it to yourself. Worst of all, your mental faculties can be dulled, so you might not even clearly recognize the symptoms as they progress.

Any prolonged shivering is to be taken very seriously. So is any loss of dexterity. If you couldn't remove something from your pants pocket on a bet, you'd better do something to get warm.

Interestingly, the coldest weather is not necessarily when most hypothermia occurs. When it's below freezing, most people head out soberly prepared. But when it's in the upper thirties, forties, and even low fifties, one's guard can be let down.

If you do take a dunking in very cold water, ice or no ice, you must take immediate steps to prevent hypothermia. Quite obviously, the best thing is to avoid the dunking at all costs. But having a dry set of clothes in the car, along with a good-sized bottle of hot liquid, can be good insurance. Fishing with someone in winter is also highly advisable.

Frostbite is of course the other half of the two-headed winter dragon. It takes extreme exposure plus some lapse of time to freeze your extremities to the point where amputation becomes necessary. But frostbite can dog you for years and years, and it's something to avoid.

Just listen to your body. You might be a mentally tough individual, but if you stubbornly stay out when your fingers or toes have lost all feeling, you're not being tough, you're being stupid. Don't push it. It's not worth it.

FALLS ON THE ICE

One of the worst and yet most common kinds of accidents is falls. The result of a fall can range from no effect at all, to a bad bruise or broken finger, to a broken hip that can prove to be devastating to an older person. Falls are something to be taken seriously.

Start by wearing boots that provide good traction. Lug soles generally perform quite well on ice. Flat-bottomed rubber boots or pacs (even if textured) will usually perform less well. Next, get yourself a set of creepers. Creepers are traction devices that strap onto your boots. They always feature some kind of little spikes that dig into the ice and help to keep you from falling. A good many tips regarding the purchase and use of creepers may be found in Chapter 4.

The worst fall I ever took was on an icy embankment right in front of my country cabin, in February. It was irony at its worst. For two days I had gone up and down that embankment as I left the house to go to the store, go ice fishing, get gas, and so on. Then, the morning I was leaving, I had to make several trips down to the car with an array of gear. I decided that it might be smart to put on my ice creepers, so I dug them out of my ice fishing gear and strapped them on. On the very last trip out of the house I got a little bit overconfident with the creepers on and took a bad fall. Now I've plopped on the ice dozens of times without injury or even bruises to speak of. But this time two things worked against me. First, the slope sent my body moving in two different directions at once so I couldn't do much to protect myself. Second, I had a guitar case in one hand and I really wasn't able to break my fall. Worst of all, though, the side of my rib cage came down on the edge of that very hard case.

The ice was covered with a dusting of snow and I realized, too late, just how incredibly slick it was.

I was in agony, and drove the two hours home and right to my doctor, who I told with certainty that I had broken ribs. There were none, though, thank God. I'd torn some flesh from one of the ribs. I had to "sleep" in an easy chair for two nights and the pain was intense. The injury still bothers me from time to time.

Perhaps you can learn a few things from this, as I did. First, a light dusting of snow on top of smooth ice is like graphite — it's the worst of all possible situations. Second, when something is in your hands, you not only cannot effectively break your fall, but you may fall on the object. That will almost certainly be worse than falling on

A slit tennis ball (left) can be used to cover the sharp edge of a spud. With manual augers, be sure to use the safety cover provided.

smooth ice. Finally, don't put so much faith in your creepers that you get careless. They are by no means foolproof.

If you're getting on or off a lake and the bank is sloped, hand things up or down to your buddy. Especially when you're proceeding down a slick bank, try to have your hands free. Don't be afraid of sliding your gear down ahead of you. It won't get damaged.

POWER TOOLS

Don't walk with a power auger that's turned on. If you fall, you really could hurt yourself. Keep the covers on all auger blades when the auger is not in use.

If you've never used a power auger, try to have someone cut a few holes in front of you. Approach this new process as you would any other one where potential danger exists. Don't force the auger. Let it do its job. If you have to force it, something is wrong.

Be careful of children using power augers. Their lesser height could very well make safe operation of the implement almost impossible.

SHANTY HAZARDS

Probably the biggest potential hazard here is driving to or from your shanty — or driving a vehicle on the ice in the first place. I understand, there are cold regions where driving out on the ice is no more unusual than shaving in the morning. But if it's so wonderfully safe, why do I have these gruesome newspaper clips before me? This current winter, December was very mild, causing thin ice in the state of Maine. Several people went down with their vehicles. All died. Almost every year, a snowmobiler in my home state of New York loses his life after crashing through the ice.

Official sources list 10 inches of ice as safe for a car or light truck. Don't even think about driving out on less than this, but regardless of ice thickness, always investigate, beforehand, where weak ice might occur. Follow established travel routes where they exist, and fish with people who know the ins and outs of ice, if you don't. Be aware of the menacing fissures and/or pressure ridges that develop on some large lakes.

Once you get to the shanty, realize that there are new safety concerns. Shanties can and have caught on fire, killing their occupants. Be careful with heat sources and never lock a shanty from the inside (illegal in most states anyway).

Above all, don't asphyxiate yourself. This year, in Crookston, Minnesota, two men died from carbon monoxide poisoning inside their shanty on Lake of the Woods, one of North America's most popular ice fishing lakes. It is believed that a strong wind may have blown fumes down the stovepipe and back into the shanty, where the men had apparently fallen asleep.

Make sure ventilation is more than adequate. In such a small space, this is a critical consideration. Especially if it's a sleepover shanty, make sure everything is in order before sack time. Make sure an overnight snowfall can't block up your ventilation point. Have, in fact, two means of ventilation.

A WOODSMAN'S MAXIM

Heres a tip that should help you as you're walking through the woods to or from the lake. It seems to me that this old saw is especially relevant in winter, when objects lying on the ground are apt to be ice-covered:

Never step on anything you can step over.
Never step over anything you can step around.

CHAPTER 3

Primary Equipment

IF YOU LIVE IN AN AREA where good ice forms every third year and then only gets to about five inches maximum, you aren't going to grease the local tackle shop for a $250 power auger. Conversely, if you live where the ice in mid winter is always two feet thick or more, you'll never become much of an ice fisherman without a power auger.

There are actually three main types of cutting tools for ice fishing: spud, manual auger and power auger. Here are my general recommendations as to who needs what:

Average ice you cut	Implement needed (minimum)
less than 6 inches	spud
6 to 12 inches	manual auger
12 to 18 inches	sharp manual auger will suffice
more than 18 inches	power auger

Before somebody jumps on me about this, let me add a few qualifications. You certainly can cut a foot or more of ice with a sharp spud. The problem is, I believe the pounding kills your chances with some gamefish, especially shallow water trout. Also, the hole gets smaller and smaller towards the bottom and is usually left ragged when a spud cuts through thick ice. The tendency here is to settle for a hole that is functionally too small. Similarly, you can cut more than 18 inches with a very sharp manual auger. Last year, I saw a fellow cutting 24 inches on a lake we were fishing for pike in early March. But he was after panfish only, and was using a four or five inch auger. He cut that two feet surprisingly well, but he was young and strong and obviously had good sharp blades on his cutting tool. I'm strong enough, but I really don't want to work up a sweat on a bitter day. Over 15 inches of ice and I'll always use my power auger when it's legal to do so.

ICE SPUDS

Let's start with the most basic of those tools: the ice spud, AKA ice bar, ice chopper or ice chisel. I don't think you need one with a cutting edge that is too wide. The blade on my store-bought one is only 2½ inches wide and I like it fine. It's the sharpness, not the width, that matters most. You'll see both homemade and store-bought spuds that are as much as six inches wide but I just don't think it's necessary. A spud must have a beveled edge like a chisel, and you can easily sharpen this edge with a flat file. The blades on a manual auger are usually very hard steel and are brutal to sharpen; but there's no excuse for having a dull spud.

As to length, the 65 inches that mine is is about right. If you're taller or shorter than my 5'10½", make an adjustment up or down accordingly. A spud, to be effective, should have some real heft to it. On the other hand, it doesn't have to weigh 30 pounds.

Because I'm very particular about my gear and how I transport it, I customized my spud so that it breaks down into two pieces. It seemed like a good idea, but the metal threads at the joint inevitably started to rust so that now I wouldn't be able to take it apart unless I put it in a vise, if then. I just live with it in the one-piece form. Actually, I'd like to make it three-piece, so that I can slip it into a bucket or the pack basket. Until I devise a method of joinery that is without problems, that scheme will have to wait.

A good sharp spud will cut eight inches with little trouble. Keep the file in your sled or bucket so it's always available for touch-up. Use a slit tennis ball over the edge so it can't hurt anyone between trips.

I have to admit, because of its potential for spooking fish I use a spud mostly to open old holes and test the ice.

MANUAL AUGERS

There used to be two primary types of manual augers: spoon and corkscrew. The spoon type came first in my area but started giving way to the corkscrew some 15 years ago. Now, it's extremely rare for

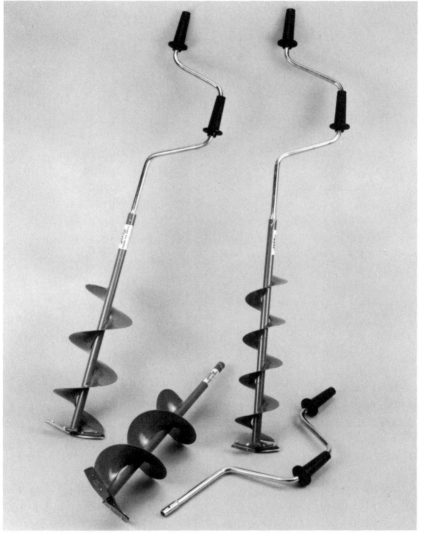

Corkscrew manual augers come in different cutting widths. The most popular design allows for break-down into two pieces.

me to see someone using a spoon type auger. I do not see them for sale any longer.

Corkscrew augers come in different cutting widths, and what one you choose can be of paramount importance. In studying the several catalogs I have before me right now, I see corkscrew augers offered in these widths (in inches): 4, 4½, 5, 6, 7 and 8. I had a 7-inch and I sold it because cutting even 8 to 10 inches of ice with it was a real chore. My friend had an 8-inch auger and that's even worse. When I finally bought a replacement, I opted for a 6-inch. I plan to eventually get a 5-inch bottom for it, for those days when I'm strictly after panfish. That's an important thing to know, by the way. When you buy an auger, make sure it's the type that comes in two pieces so that you can add a different bottom. It's a lot cheaper than buying two separate augers.

What's the smallest size hole you can get away with if you're after hefty gamefish? In 95% of the cases, I'd say 6-inch is fine. Unless you were consistently fishing for very large pike, very large trout or you were spear fishing, the 6-inch should do it. For panfish, five inches is fine most times. Only outsize crappies or the odd gamefish can burn you. The problem I have is that the "odd" gamefish comes nosing around a little bit too often. Many times I've had heavy fish smash my tiny panfish jig or jig 'n' bait, and if they don't actually snap the line — which has happened — then the small hole is there to foil me. I almost always feel comfortable with a 6-inch hole, though.

I strongly recommend that you steer clear of the 7-inch and 8 - inch models. A quick diversion into geometry will show you vividly that every time you jump up an inch in auger diameter you dramatically increase the amount of ice you have to cut. As the ice thickens in mid winter, that geometric progression is doubled and tripled, and pretty soon you're so soaked with sweat that you haven't a prayer of making it through the day.

A 6-inch manual auger is enough. If you absolutely need a bigger hole, go power.

In the popular catalogs, you'll see two main types of corkscrew augers: two-piece and folding one-piece. The two-piece design features a top and bottom that simply screw together. Once you've cut a few holes with it you have to put it in a vice to take it apart, which essentially kills the two-piece feature. The folding model seems to make sense but reliable ice fishing friends report having problems with this design.

They say that the specific design of the folding type makes for more work. Also, one friend says he has snapped two augers of this type.

It's true, there are some off-the-wall auger designs, some of them strays from the Eurasian continent. I have seen some of these in various printed pieces, but nowadays, virtually all the manual augers I see on the ice are of the corkscrew type. If you're one of those people who always has to do something different, you might want to take a trip to Finland and see what kind of weird-looking auger you can bring back to impress your friends.

I have a spud, a 6-inch manual auger and an 8-inch power auger, and I can't imagine life with any one of these missing. A spud is always necessary, for tapping early ice to check its thickness and to open up old holes when they exist. The manual auger I like when I'm after trout, but the ice isn't thick enough yet to warrant the power auger. I also like having the manual auger for those times and places when the noise of a power auger is not desirable (i.e. a suburban pond at 6 o'clock in the morning). You should know that power augers are actually illegal on some bodies of waters, for example, certain reservoirs, and that's yet another reason why I feel I have to have a manual auger.

POWER AUGERS

And now for some specific discussion of those labor saving power ice cutters. There are two main types, electric and gas. The electric type operates off a snowmobile battery, or, to be more specific, any 12-volt battery. A big attraction of the electric auger is that it does not create noxious fumes inside a shanty. I have not used the electric type yet.

I bought an 8-inch Jiffy brand gasoline power auger and I like it a lot. Since you have the power, there's no reason I can see for buying the small diameter ones. On the other hand, why get the nine or ten-inch model? It's more hole than most ice fishermen in most places will ever need, and these really large holes become very definite menaces. In warm or rainy weather, this already large hole will keep on expanding and before you know it, it's big enough for a small child to slip through. Not only that, but very large holes have the nasty habit of eating tip-ups every so often. Further, they pose a menace to vehicles operating on the ice.

Because of the danger, I believe augers that cut holes larger than eight inches ought really to be banned. I admit I've never heard anyone else express this concern. I also admit that where the ice gets extremely thick, the wider hole is an advantage and is less of a menace.

Gasoline-operated power augers are standard equipment where the ice gets very thick.

Whatever brand you choose, after cutting width the most important consideration is horsepower. Common sense should tell you that if you constantly have to brute your way through 24 to 36 inches of ice, the higher horsepower engines will be desirable. If the ice in your area is typically marginal for the power auger, you may be able to get away with the lowest horsepower model. Be advised, certain friends of mine who live in the north country advise against getting the lowest horsepower models. They claim that these just don't have the guts (that's not the word they used) needed to hold up to heavy use.

My Jiffy model #30 kicks out 3 horses (85cc) and I have used it without difficulty on ice of up to about two feet. I can't say this appliance is light. It weighs a cumbersome 35.6 pounds but I can carry it one-handed if need be. Lighter power augers are now available, and I sometimes wish I had one.

As I explain in Chapter 6, a toboggan is a great way to carry gear and when you're talking about something as heavy as a power auger, the toboggan makes even more sense. Where snowmobiles or ATV's are used, a large sled-box that is pulled out onto the ice can haul the power auger and whatever else there is.

Just to look at some other choices you have, Jiffy makes, in addition to their Model 30, a Model 76, which is two horsepower and 49.2 cc's. It weighs 28.4 pounds in the 8-inch size. Eskimo makes a model 8900 that's 2 HP and 49 cc's, and is available in either 8-inch or 10-inch. Eskimo also makes its newer model 9000, which has a 3 HP engine and is also available in either 8-inch or 10-inch. Strike Master is yet another popular maker of augers, both manual and power. The overall industry trend is definitely towards lighter machines.

These air-cooled engines require the proper fuel mix. If it calls for 16:1 gas to oil give it that and not something close. People I know who have 40 years experience servicing air-cooled engines tell me that the right mix can make all the difference in an engine's performance.

A few further tips on power augers should be scribed here. First, they don't stand up on their own. At home, hang or support it in such a way that it won't come crashing down. On the ice, cut a hole part way through, if the ice is at least 8 or 10 inches, and use that hole to prop up the auger. Personally, I like to lay it down on its handle. There's not much bad that can happen to a power auger, but if it falls over from a standing position, expect trouble.

For very thick ice, power auger shaft extensions are available.

Check with the manufacturer of your unit. Without an extension, mine will cut about 38 inches. I never face ice thicker than that so I don't need the extension. Diehard ice anglers in the upper midwest and in Canada routinely use shaft extensions. They are available in 6-inch and 12-inch lengths, and 12-inch is the more popular size. Extensions can be stacked if necessary, but few anglers ever have to contend with more than 50 inches of ice.

Keep the guard on at all times when the auger is not in use. About every 500 holes, the blades should be sharpened. This should be done by the manufacturer, according to the instruction booklet that came with my auger. At the end of the season drain the gas tank. At the beginning of the season, check the spark plug and change it if it's fouled.

TIP-UPS

Items for transporting your ice fishing gear are covered thoroughly in Chapter 6, and we won't duplicate that material here. Let's move on to the other two primary pieces of ice fishing equipment: tip-ups and jig poles. This discussion will be fairly brief since other chapters deal with the customizing of this gear and the more refined uses of it.

A standard subsurface tip-up. The angler forgot to clear around the hole. (see Ch. 15)

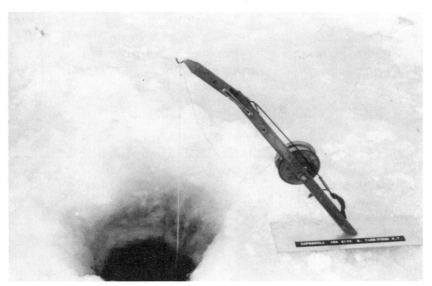

A homemade topwater tip-up. This one is unusual in that it is made completely of metal.

A tip-up is a mechanical device that is almost always baited with some kind of live bait and is so constructed that it can be left to itself propped in or suspended over a hole cut in the ice. A jig pole, on the other hand, is usually hand-held by the angler, although it certainly can be set down onto the ice or over a bucket from time to time. Most often, an angler uses a lure on a jig pole, though live bait or a combination of a lure and bait can be used.

When my companions and I discovered the extraordinary effectiveness of jigging, we got into a mindset where we would leave the tip-ups home. We even started calling them such derogatory names as tip-downs. It was true, the tip-ups would sit like statues some days while 95% of the fish we'd take would fall to jigging. As I learned more about ice fishing I started to see that there was a place for both methods. Perhaps a third of the time I sally forth with only my jig poles. But on the other days, I set out the tip-ups in the best pattern I know how and then cut my holes for jigging. While there are days when only the jig poles produce, there are also days when the fish want strictly bait and the jig pole never gets a bend in it.

It is the thread of ingenuity and craftsmanship that runs its way through ice fishing that explains at least part of my fascination with it. "Homemade" has a natural, sweet ring to it, and it rings all the sweeter when you've just iced a prize fish on a tip-up you've crafted yourself. But whether you decide to make or buy your tip-ups, you should know the two main types: topwater and underwater.

A topwater tip-up is one where the spool that holds the line remains above the ice. An underwater tip-up is one where the spool is actually in the hole and submerged.

No matter what its particular design, a topwater tip-up presents an obvious dilemma: When the air is cold enough to freeze up the hole, the line gets frozen up along with it. This may very well prevent the flag from going up on a take, and it also will be an encumbrance if the flag does pop and you now must frantically clear the hole to retrieve line and play the fish. On a really cold day, you'll have to chop the line out; the heel of your boot won't suffice. In the next chapter, hole covers are discussed and these gadgets can partially or completely thwart the problem just described.

But why use a topwater tip-up in the first place, when more often than not the holes will be freezing up? For one thing, topwaters may be all you have. Among all the homemade tip-ups I've seen, most have been of the topwater variety. For another thing, you may feel that when you're fishing in very shallow water, the topwater jobs — which are totally out of the water — might be less likely to disturb the fish. I used to feel this way, too, but I seem to have no problem taking chain pickerel and occasionally other fish when I'm using my subsurface tip-ups in very shallow water. I do paint the bottom arm of the tip-up black, and I do use black spools and black line. Perhaps that helps. In any case, I rarely use topwater tip-ups nowadays. I've refined my subsurface devices to the point that I'm very satisfied with them and that's certainly a big reason why I drag my topwater models out less and less frequently. I do have five beautiful, handmade topwater models that I tote on rare occasions just to admire them. They're made of a combination of aluminum and magnesium — all metal, even the spools. When a south winds blows in early March, I'll bring these out and let them help me kiss the ice fishing season goodbye.

Since I can't really endorse topwater tip-ups, I present no plans for the construction of them. Nonetheless, photos showing a few different topwater designs are presented in this book.

Relatively few people make subsurface tip-ups, a design which accounts for about 80% of all the tip-ups I see on the ice. Like most of the boys (and girls) out there, I bought my subsurface tip-ups right off the shelf. But unlike most of the others, I went to work customizing my tip-ups until they began to function precisely right. How I do it is gone over in Chapter 5.

How do you choose your tip-ups? Where I live and fish, more and more wintertime anglers are selecting the new, high quality tip-ups that cost twice as much as the standard wooden tip-ups, but that work twice as well. One good example is the Polar tip-up made by H. T. Enterprises.

The people who designed this tip-up are quite obviously students of the sport. These inventors, it seems, took the problems inherent in traditional tip-ups and attacked them one by one. As near as I can tell, they solved each and every one of those problems.

Standard wooden tip-up	Polar tip-up
1. Flag often hard to see.	Fluorescent material used for flag.
2. Spool often doesn't turn smoothly, especially if the line is being pulled by fish at an oblique angle.	Spool turns smoothly regardless of the angle of line to the spool.
3. Little room for adjustment of flag-trip mechanism.	Four basic settings for this, and more possible.
4. Somewhat time consuming to wind up.	Protruding tang on top makes line winding extremely easy.
5. Prone to being blown over in a very brisk wind.	Lies flat on ice. Cannot be blown over. Has wedge-shaped bottom so it won't freeze in.
6. You can't see if a fish is running without looking down into the hole.	You can easily see a shaft spinning if line is going out.

About the only shortcoming of this tip-up is that its low profile makes it hard to see on the ice. But the bright orange flag is extremely visible.

The Windlass wind-activated tip-up made by H. T. Enterprises.

As I stated earlier, I am very happy with my customized wooden tip-ups and that's why I haven't switched to one of these new generation tip-ups. But alas, recently I saw a new model of the Polar tip-ups constructed with a wooden rather than a plastic base. They were so beautiful that I had to order five for the upcoming season. I plan to rig these up for walleye fishing. They can be set very sensitive and should serve in this capacity well.

If you'd rather stick to the five to seven dollar wooden tip-ups, here are a few tips for selecting them.

You don't need the extra long ones. In fact, you don't want them. They're clumsier to carry and store, and offer little practical advantage. About the only advantage I can see is that the flag, once it does pop, flies higher in the air and is seen more readily. Other than that, there is no apparent compensation for that extra bulk. The long ones, when I did own them, did not fit inside my sled and they may not nestle into your gear either. They also fall out of buckets more readily.

Watch out for shoddy workmanship. Do the spools turn relatively freely? Are the screws and nails tight and centered properly? Does the flag-trip mechanism work just right? Do the arms of the tip-up fold up the way they're supposed to? Although the price of these wooden tip-ups may not vary too much, the quality can vary greatly. This is still a cottage industry product. Tip-ups are made by hundreds of small-time craftspeople. Make sure yours were put together by someone who was "put together."

In recent years, I have seen subsurface tip-ups of the standard design but made of hard plastic rather than wood. With the ones I saw, the plastic was black. In fact, a prominent guide I ice fished with recommended these. The only problem I foresaw with them was that I would not be able to "tune them up" as I could with the more malleable wooden ones.

Mention has to be made of the wind-activated tip-ups. I tried to like these, I really did. But I think any measure of a piece of equipment is how much you use it, and I observe that my wind tip-ups stay at home on the shelf.

Like all topwater tip-ups, you have the problem of line freezing up in the hole when it's below 32 degrees F (0°C). A hole cover might alleviate this problem, but I have others that won't go away.

Cleverly engineered, the wind tip-up I have has a range of different adjustments that allow you to set the wind-catching "fan" to match current wind conditions. This would be fine if the wind blew at a steady pace through the day, but it almost never does. I find that when the wind changes velocity significantly I usually have to readjust the wind tip-up. On days with very heavy wind, wind-activated tip-ups are troublesome. On days with no wind (rare), they're just expensive tip-ups.

The idea of using the wind to keep the bait moving is an excellent idea. Certain types of bait just sit there like statues all day. If you're captivated by the idea, try one or two of these devices. They're expensive and very bulky but you might very well like them better than I do.

ICE JIGGING RODS

Jig rods are a critically important part of any successful ice fisherman's armory. Notice I said "rods." To go out with just one would be rare indeed for me. I'd rather have several rods rigged with different lures than have to do a lot of knot tying on the ice. They're inexpensive enough to make this feasible.

Commercially made jig rods come in a wide variety of lengths and designs, and are made for both conventional reels and spinning reels. I have personally seen them in lengths from about 20 inches to at least 48 inches, and the industry trend is now leaning to the longer models. I use jig poles ranging in length from 24 inches to 42 inches. My buddy Jimmy always brings out the seven-foot spinning rod that he uses for seemingly every fishing situation, fresh water

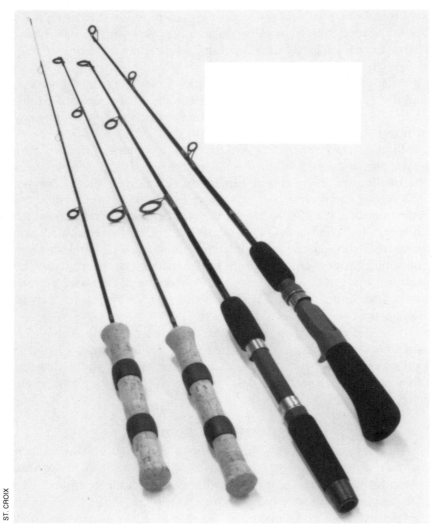

There are now hundreds of different models of jig rods to choose from. Here are four in the Arctic Angler line from St. Croix.

A jig pole with its own built-in stand. A normal jig rod can be simply laid over the top of an open bucket.

or salt water, summer and winter. I ask him how in God's name he could use such a long, heavy pole for ice fishing but the more I fume the more he uses it. He says it's just fine, but last year we were fishing a semi-private little pond known as Nuclear Lake and I demonstrated to him exactly how ineffectual his heavy stick was out on the ice.

The lake had lots of super large yellow perch, real humpbacks. It took me about six or seven holes to find them, but when I did I quickly collected six or eight huge ones. Each fish would easily make a meal for one person. Jimmy was standing right next to me, but he just wasn't feeling the bites with that heavy pole. It was one of those days when the perch were just mouthing the jig. You didn't feel so much a hit as you did a sensation at the end of the line. With my ultra sensitive 30-inch graphite rod I was able to do business with those finicky perch. Jimmy never made contact once, and believe me, nothing in fishing is more frustrating than to have someone using the exact same tactics catch fish right next to you while you go fishless. I'm certain, though, that next year Jimmy will still be out there with his seven-foot, all purpose spinning pole. Some people you just can't change.

Fishing tackle manufacturers have seen the blossoming of ice fishing and have gone after that new market with vigor. As an example,

Berkley has their "Northern Lites" line of jig rods, several of which I've tested and can endorse. H. T. Enterprises offers an astonishing 144 models of jig rods.

Both conventional and spinning jig poles have their place, but this discussion is relegated to Chapter 14. You should look that chapter over carefully if you're contemplating buying one or more jig poles for the next ice fishing season.

As with wooden tip-ups, jig poles are made (actually wrapped) by countless craftspeople, each of whom does his or her best to strike up a business arrangement with the local sport shop (often on consignment). Thus, like tip-ups, jig poles can vary greatly. One thing to watch out for is jig poles that are too clubby. Look to the lighter ones, which are essential for panfishing and desirable in most other cases. To phrase it another way, buy a pole that's just a little bit lighter than what you think you need. Also look for ones that have larger than normal guides. These guides will be less likely to clog up with ice.

I do have two or three poles that are homemade. In each case I cut about 20 inches off the tip of an old bait casting pole and joined the tip back to the handle. This required a little ingenuity, but in each case I was able to devise a strong joint that held. These no-cast bait casting jig poles worked fine for me for years, and I still use them, especially when I feel I need a heavier jig pole. But by now, I've been pretty much spoiled by the modern, graphite jig rods that are so much more sensitive and nice to fish with.

Still popular with panfish lovers in some areas is the peg rod. The ultimate in simplicity, this rod has two little pegs (usually wood) at the bottom of the rod where a reel would normally go. The fishing line is merely wrapped around these pegs in handline fashion. When a fish bites, you simply haul him up like a tuna. If it's too deep for that, you handline the fish in. I don't use peg rods, since I prefer to have a "real reel" on all my jig poles. But if I did use them, I would do so only in very shallow water for small panfish.

There are a lot of fine points to jig poles and jigging, and many of these are discussed in Chapters 13 and 14.

CHAPTER 4

Ancillary Gear

YOU'RE ENTERING ANOTHER dimension, a dimension of not only sight and sound, but mind. It's a journey to a wondrous land, whose boundaries are those of imagination. There's the signpost up ahead. Your next stop...

As you step out onto the ice for the first time, you can almost hear Rod Serling's voice with the Twilight Zone music in the background. "This is a strange scene," you say to yourself, as you look at these people voluntarily freezing themselves to death as the wind howls and driven flakes of snow cut the flesh like countless little chisels.

Then you eyeball the equipment you see scattered about you: The paraphernalia of the sport is every bit as strange as the practitioners. You wonder, for a second, whether you're really weird enough to get involved in this off the wall activity.

Once you do, though, you find that while the gear, like the people, is a little weird, it is at least not voluminous. In fact, once you have the primary gear described in the preceding chapter you'll have few additional expenses. This is in stark contrast to many other forms of outdoor sport, where the primary equipment is only the beginning of a very tall pile of bank withdrawal slips. All in all, ice fishing is very much a poor person's sport.

A small but absolutely essential item is a skimmer, shown in the photo. This is used to remove ice chips from the hole. I have two: a large one (5½-inch diameter) that stays on little brackets on my sledbox; and a smaller one (4½-inch diameter) that I use from day to day. I recently painted the smaller one black so that I can spot it better on the ice. Don't buy a skimmer with either a plastic handle or a plastic basket. You need an all-metal one to help free up the holes from time to time.

A gaff is very useful for landing large fish, although a relatively small percentage of ice fishermen carry one. I've lost a couple of very large trout at the hole so I now always have a gaff on the ice. Some fish, like pike and chain pickerel, are shaped in such a way that you can grab them behind the head and, except with very large, toothy pike, get them up through the hole very easily. If you'd rather skip

A skimmer is necessary to clean out the chips after you've cut a hole. On a below freezing day, you'll have to go around continually and skim the holes.

the gaff and give the fish more of a chance, that's fine, but you may very well lose that trout of a lifetime on some fateful day, since trout cannot be easily grabbed.

I got sick and tired of wondering just where my gaff and skimmer (especially skimmer) were when I needed them. I finally made my "Ice Fishing Belt" to deal with this problem. See Chapter 5.

THE BUCKET BRIGADE

When those 5-gallon buckets became popular for ice fishing some years ago, enterprising minds began to go to town on them. I've now seen two or three that were customized nicely enough to pry a few more dollars out of your sportsman's billfold. One is called the Sit-N-Fish, which features a padded seat and a divided storage compartment at the top for tackle. This surely would be useful, but with the seat in place you surely could not tote lengthy items like tip-ups and jig poles. See p. 38.

There is further discussion on storage buckets in Chapter 6.

Bait buckets and their construction are not beneath discussion. Understand, first of all, that the smaller the bucket you carry the less bait you can keep alive. There's a finite amount of oxygen in a given quantity of water and you just can't cram four dozen extra large shiners into a gallon of water and expect them to be alive and kicking after you've driven from your retirement home in Pensacola to Lake of the Woods, Minnesota.

A battery-run aerator can save the day when, for some reason, you have to bring a lot of bait to where you're going, or you're going for more than a day. The Mino-Mizer is a popular brand that costs about $16 and that has proven its worth. It claims to run 70 to 80 hours on one 6-volt battery, but I have never kept track of this. For $4.99 you can buy a converter that allows you to use your Mino-Mizer with a 12-volt battery. For $9.99 you can buy an attachment that lets you plug it into a 120-volt wall outlet. This system is excellent for the ice fisherman who makes overnight trips away from home.

You also have an increasing number of other aerators to turn to, but be advised that some of the cheaper ones have proven to be very ineffective. "You get what you pay for" seems to be quite accurate in the realm of minnow bucket aerators.

My own bucket is made of ⅞ inch thick Styrofoam, supported by a wire frame that completely surrounds the bottom and sides of the

The Sit-N-Fish fisherman's bucket. It has a little tackle storage tray built in at the top.

Styrofoam. I bought it from Herter's, a now defunct tackle company, about 20 years ago, and it's beat up but still working fine. Styrofoam has some advantages and disadvantages versus plastic or polyvinyl buckets. On the plus side, the water inside will freeze more slowly in Styrofoam. Another plus is that delicate bait like alewives will keep better because Styrofoam is softer. On the other hand, because the water inside will stay warmer, the minnows will have to make a greater adjustment when first dunked into the frigid lake water. All things considered, I still prefer Styrofoam. Get one that's large enough. Mine holds 2½ gallons of water. There are now large, perforated minnow bucket "inserts" that can be used in conjunction with a 5-gallon bucket.

Always have a little dip net to extract the minnows. Your bare hands deserve better than to be repeatedly immersed in cold water. Don't leave it in the water from trip to trip. It will rot out.

In the preceding chapter, I briefly mentioned hole covers. These are used to keep your holes from freezing up. There are now commercially made ones, for example the Ice Guard which currently costs less than $5. It is made of hard rubber. You certainly could make your own. I recommend that you try ½-inch marine plywood. You will have to cut some kind of slit for the tip-up or, at the minimum, the line from the tip-up if it's a topwater model. When cutting your hole covers, you will of course need to make them wide enough to cover the size hole you typically cut, with a little overlap built in. The Ice Guard is small enough that it will fit into the bottom of a white bucket. Since these Ice Guard hole covers nest together nicely, a great amount of space is not taken up. Keep this consideration in mind if you make your own.

The ice guard also prevents light from entering the hole. This helps or hurts the fishing, depending on who you talk to.

IMPORTANT FOOTWEAR

Ice creepers, mentioned in Chapter 2, help keep you from falling on slippery ice. I suspect that these devices are more frequently used in the southerly portion of ice fishing country since, up north, con-

A simple rectangular wooden box mounted on a child's sled. It will hold plenty of tip-ups, and all the smaller stuff, too.

sistently heavy snow cover makes for good traction. I know creepers can be extremely important in my region where minimal snowfall and other factors combine to create often treacherous conditions.

Young ice is usually the culprit. Take four inches of smooth, black ice, dust it lightly with snow and you'll be doing the hard water shuffle most of the day. A little bit of rain on top of smooth ice will also give you some unwanted dance instruction. If the mercury slips up above the mid-thirties, water from the melting ice will lie on top and that too can make for a slippery day. It all depends on the texture of the ice at the moment.

In any case, four or five times a year I find ice creepers to be a Godsend. From cottage industry basements above the 42nd parallel they spring forth, ice creepers of myriad design but none that you would call comfortable to wear on your feet all day.

A very simple design is one that has two triangular spikes and fastens to your foot via a rubber strap that is pulled over the instep and then just placed on a cup-shaped hook. These are extremely easy to put on and remove, and that's why I like them. Unfortunately, they do start to dig into the sole of your foot after a few hours, causing discomfort.

Another kind is similar but the fastening mechanism consists of a two-part buckle that snaps together over the instep. Still another design employs strong nylon straps and buckles. It seems to me that the strap type would be the most difficult for half-frozen fingers to manipulate.

Full sole creepers are more comfortable, but cost $20 instead of $5. They're also more difficult to put on and remove. That can be extremely frustrating when your hands are numb, the straps are all iced up, it's five o'clock and you'd really like to drive yourself home. Fiddling around with any kind of strap-buckle arrangement in the cold of early morn is equally confounding. Before you even march out onto the ice your fingers feel like carrots, and you start to wonder if you really shouldn't have taken someone to the shopping mall instead.

OTHER ESSENTIALS

Sunglasses are essential on the ice; the glare can be fierce. We've all heard of snow blindness and while I've never had it, I have suffered some effects from glare off snow and ice. Cheapie sunglasses, which are about worthless and may even have a negative value, should never be considered. Buy only quality sunglasses.

Lures for ice fishing are inexpensive, very inexpensive when compared to most other categories of fishing lures. Which lures to use is gone over in other chapters, especially Chapter 14. Here we'll look at ways of storing jig lures.

I have two boxes. One is a Plano Mini-Magnum #3213, which has two sides and lots of nice, small compartments. I tote all my split shot, hooks, and other small hardware and some of my lures in this box. My other box was designed for fly fishermen but it works well in storing tiny jig lures. On one side of this box are a bunch of metal clips where I can hold several dozen small panfish jigs. I customized this side of the box somewhat by gluing in a piece of foam rubber at the top, which holds more small lures. The other side of this hinged fly fisher's box has little compartments concealed by a plastic lid. In these compartments I store ice flies and certain other lures. Virtually all of my small stuff is housed in these two boxes.

If you customize your tip-ups in the manner I suggest in Chapter 5, you will have at least 10 or 15 extra interchangeable spools. I keep these in my sled-box and snap on the ones I want at the start of a day's fishing.

Depth sounders are necessary since more often than not you'll want your bait to be just off bottom, and you can't find bottom without a sounder. Most of these feature a small "alligator clip" that has been molded into a sinker-shaped hunk of lead weighing about an ounce. Any store that sells ice fishing gear should have these, and they cost about $1.50 each.

You could make your own sounders, if you have a little bit of lead, a melting pot and some ingenuity. I'm sure someone sells molds for depth sounders but I haven't come across them yet. You could fashion your own mold and then purchase some alligator clips in an automotive parts store. Since sounders are inexpensive, it's questionable whether you'd gain much from this enterprise.

You'll lose a few sounders. Carry extra ones.

LINE MARKERS

Line markers are also necessary. A line marker is a device that you affix to your line to set a particular depth. The idea is that once you've caught a fish, you can simply lower the rebaited line so the line marker is right at the spool and then you know you're at the same depth.

I've seen many types of markers. Most were not good. For

Two ice fishing essentials: a depth sounder (left) and a line marker — here, a poultry marker, discussed in the text.

example, some anglers thread their line through two holes of a button and then slide the button up and down the line as necessary. This can fray the line, though, and it's not the quickest solution when you have five or more tip-ups to work with.

A small split shot could be used, but would frequently have to be attached to my dacron running line. I'm very protective of that line and I'd rather not crimp a potentially damaging split shot onto it. Dacron is known to be easily damaged when it's pinched.

Some anglers have the horrendous habit of putting knots in their line to mark the depth. The idea is that later they will take the knots out, but, of course, by the end of the day they are too cold to do so. After several trips, their running lines are all knotted up and silly looking. It almost looks like their kids got a hold of their tip-up spools and decided to do some kind of creative sewing project with them.

I have a better kind of marker: poultry markers, available at farm supply stores. I half-hitch the line twice or three times around one coil of the double-coiled round marker, slide the line around 180 degrees, and it usually stays there for the day, or until I decide to move it. It cannot damage the line, it is easy to put on and take off, and it does slide up and down the line easily for when the vertical adjustment necessary is only a minor one. This marker works perfectly on my heavy dacron, acceptably well with medium weight mono, but poorly with fine mono. I've not yet found a good marker for very light monofilament. The best bet is probably just a tiny split shot.

I carry a second type of line marker: an inexpensive fly tyer's hackle pliers. I wouldn't call it absolutely essential, but I use it in the following way.

When I'm baiting a tip-up, I lower the bare hook to the bottom with a sounder. I pick the sounder up two feet, or whatever distance from the bottom I wish to be, and then, topside, mark that spot by clipping on the hackle pliers. Now I know that I won't lose that spot if, for example, the line being pulled by the heavy sounder should slip through my fingers. Then I retrieve the sounder, bait the hook, lower the bait, and wind any excess line onto the spool up to the hackle pliers. I then hitch on my line marker and unclip the hackle pliers, and set the tip-up into the water.

I keep the hackle pliers in the same pocket all day. I keep the sounder in the other pocket all day. I always know where each is, without rummaging. I remove any loose change or other things from my pants pockets before starting to fish, so I can quickly grab the object I want.

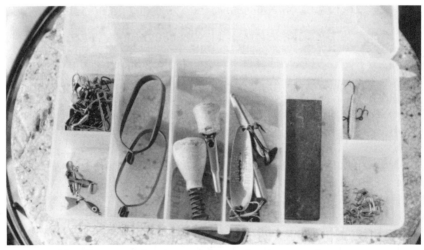

Hackle pliers used by the author are in the second compartment from left. In third compartment from left are two types of depth sounders: spring type (rarely seen now) and alligator clip. A couple of functional plastic boxes are needed to tote the small things all ice fishermen need.

I consider a hook disgorger to be essential. One time I tried to unhook a pike without using a disgorger and that's why I consider a disgorger to be essential. I usually use a pair of six-inch-long hemostats or surgical pliers, which lock in one of three positions. I leave these clipped onto a pocket flap on my coat. (Your depth sounder can also be clipped to an outer garment for easy accessibility.) Not all fish are as well dentured as pike, but there isn't a fish that swims that doesn't have some biological part in or around the head that will cut you. Then, too, the hook from the lure or bait can cut you, if you try to bare hand it out of the fish. Remember that in winter you will have less dexterity. This means that you are more apt to hurt yourself. Use a disgorger.

Don't stick a five-inch hemostat six inches down the mouth of a big pike that has swallowed the bait. One inch of bloody finger will result. Use as long a disgorger as you need so as not to expose any portion of human flesh to the jawbone of a toothsome fish. We carry extra long, extra strong ones for pike.

With a really big pike or musky, that's thrashing for all it's worth, cut the steel leader with cutting pliers. You'll need that second arm later in the day.

Bobbers figure heavily in ice fishing. There are dozens of models you can now choose from, and some of these have been designed with the ice fisherman specially in mind. I can think of five different types that I've used on the ice: the standard plastic red and white bobber; slip bobbers; extremely sensitive balsa bobbers designed after ones used in northern Europe; extremely lightweight foam bobbers; and spring bobbers that attach to the tip of your jig rod. When you use a bobber in winter it's in conjunction with a jig rod. Thus, most of the discussion on bobbers is in Chapter 14.

Now that portable ice fishing shelters have become so popular in recent years, the subject of heating those shelters bears scrutiny. Most plywood shanties have a heat source, often a propane, kerosene or — infrequently — wood stove. With a portable shelter you may well skip the heater. But if you do choose to use one, what type will it be?

Some ice fishermen have turned to the "infra-red" heaters which can crank out as much as 30,000 BTUs/hr. (two burner model). Some of these devices even double as cooking units. They are fueled by bottled propane gas, either canisters or large tanks. In a portable shelter you'd use the canister type, most likely. In any case, one of their virtues is that they begin heating your shelter instantly. Some now have a safety fuel shut off, in case the flame goes out. Kerosene and especially wood take longer to get going. This speed factor can be especially beneficial when you're only out for a short jaunt and want to get right down to business with minimal fussing over stoves. The larger units are often used in shanties.

Especially if you use a portable shelter, there are safety factors to consider. Follow closely the recommendations of the manufacturer when it comes to using any type of heating unit inside a shelter. If you are apt to fall asleep inside your shelter, intentionally or unintentionally, you must be certain that there is adequate ventilation.

A few more tips related to heating and safety inside of ice fishing shelters may be found in Chapter 7.

Most jiggers carry some kind of natural bait, dead or alive, to add further appeal to the jig lure. Mealworms, maggots, mousie grubs, and so on, are usually sold (where I live) in small plastic containers. These are a nuisance since the lids come off and the containers get easily crushed. Some smart ice fishermen have begun to use those little belt-worn cans that a stream fisherman uses to tote worms in. They work well, but the grubs or other bait will freeze on a very cold day. Conversely, if you keep a small plastic container (one with a secure closure) inside a pocket and close to your body, it will be virtually impossible for your bait to freeze up. Whatever way you tackle this problem, if you have live bait like grubs and want to keep them alive from trip to trip, bring that bait inside at day's end and keep it in the refrigerator until your next excursion. (If your spouse is squeamish, that next "excursion" might come sooner than you think.)

Sooner or later you're going to lose a tip-up flag. It will tear, or more commonly, the clip holding it on will get knocked off the spring that pops up into the air. I had some trouble finding little clips that effectively hold tip-up flags onto the spring. I finally found some in the Dickey ice fishing tackle catalog. You get 12 clips for less than a dollar. Spare flags can also be seen in some of the ice fishing catalogs, and these too cost little.

ODDS 'N' ENDS

Tip-up lights are great to have if you do a lot of after dark fishing. Such a device attaches to your tip-up and when the flag goes up, a circuit is made and juice from the device's battery or batteries makes the light go on. Crappies, walleyes and smelt are some of the winter species that can bite very well after dark, and if you pursue these good eating finfish, the tip-up lights are useful. The ones I've seen cost between $5.95 and $8.95 — significant when you consider that here in New York we are allowed five tip-ups (15 on waters like Lake Champlain and Lake Ontario).

A simpler and less expensive alternative does exist: little bells. Take a small bell and find a way to attach some kind of little clip to it. Keep several of these in your sled-box. When you find yourself out in the cold night, against all rational argument, take your little bells and attach them to the springs of your tip-ups. If you're strictly all thumbs with hammers and such, you can actually purchase bells rigged up for ice fishing. I see in this catalog that you can get 6 for $4.75. I use the bells as opposed to the lights, and I carry a flashlight so I can also visually check for flags.

My buddy Zeke got to like his bells so well that now he leaves them on all the time. Over a frozen lake, the sound of the bell carries remarkably well. When you're preoccupied you can easily miss a flag going up, but you can't miss that ringing bell. Who knows — maybe someday bells on tip-ups will be like telephone answering machines. Everyone will have them.

Over the past two seasons we took some especially impressive largemouth bass that we had to return since bass may not be kept in winter in our region. We weighed them on small, combination scale/ruler devices of questionable accuracy. I really would like to know what those bass weighed. I don't, so I ordered a more expensive and more accurate scale for the upcoming season. Especially in this age when many anglers voluntarily return trophy fish, a good scale would seem to be a nice thing to have along on the ice.

On a large lake, bring a compass, for reasons discussed in Chapter 2.

A contour map can certainly help you find the fish. Other chapters get into this subject. Suffice it to say here that you should avail yourself of whatever contour maps you can get your hands on. Even ones that are not terribly accurate, which defines most of the contour maps I have, will usually be helpful.

You may want to have a few tools along on the ice, or at least back in the truck. An alin wrench may be necessary to tighten the blades on your manual auger or the head on your power auger. A small screwdriver set, for example a driver with different size bits, can be extremely useful. Screws can loosen up on jig reels or rods, augers, or even on your homemade sled-box. A pair of adjustable pliers would be just as useful to have along. Among other possible tools, you would certainly want to have a flat file to touch up your spud when necessary. I've hit more than one rock while trying to chop through ice in shoal areas. The file comes in handy.

I've had a problem with my power auger sometimes running a bit too rich. This led to a fouled spark plug and some hard starting. Of course the best thing is to get the auger adjusted correctly, but just in case something goes amiss, carry a spare spark plug and the socket and ratchet necessary to change it.

Most tip-ups employ wing nuts in one way or another. Make sure these are tight before starting to fish, but carry a few spares just in case.

In the local sport shop, you may see a small sharpening stone selling for about five bucks and advertised as being for auger blades. Don't waste your money. These little stones are worthless. Send your blades in to be sharpened or better yet, follow the directions in Chapter 15 for sharpening the blades yourself.

If you live in the heart of the ice fishing world, you may well use a truck, car, ATV, snowmobile or other vehicle (possibly with a storage sled towed behind it) to transport your ice fishing gear. Common sense says that if you fish where vehicles are consistently used on the ice, it will be very cold in winter and you certainly don't want to get stranded out there. It may be that the pizza place delivers on some lakes (there is such a thing as perch pizza), and that Sal's towing service will even come out to get you. But it's still desirable to be self sufficient, so if you do use a vehicle on ice you must be sure you have things like spare tires, jacks, or whatever other items your particular vehicle might require. A tow-cord with a hook would be good to have since getting bogged down in snowdrifts is a common affair.

I've described elsewhere how my sled-box stays in the truck for the winter and serves as a master tackle box. I just rummaged through it and here are the items I came across that have not already been mentioned in this chapter:

1. Rubber bands, assorted sizes
2. One strong knife and one small fillet knife
3. Plastic utensils, for eating

4.   Duct tape
5.   Masking tape
6.   Can openers, both types
7.   Small plastic bags and ties
8.   Small wheels of 4, 6, 8, 10 and 14 lb. test monofilament, for leader material
9.   Egg shells (we chum with these)
10. Matches in a waterproof case
11. Instructions and parts list for the power auger
12. A rigid plastic cup
13. A folded wad of aluminum foil

Most of this I do not transfer to my little knapsack at the start of the day. But in the course of the season, a lot of it sees some use. Much of this stuff is only used when we cook out on the ice.

As the ice fishing boom builds to a crescendo, the wheels of entrepreneurs keep on spinning. In some instances, a really interesting new item comes along. In many cases the "you can't build a better mouse trap" truism holds forth.

A combination tip-up/hole cover? Yup, there it is, right on Page 125. An electronic sensor that transmits a signal to a belt-worn pager (good God!) when a fish strikes your tip-up? It's yours for $39.95 (extra transmitter only $17.95).

Then there's the electronic fish finder that tells you the depth, the bottom configuration (in three dimensions), the exact species you're looking at on the screen, and probably, what's on HBO tonight.

Ah, the wonders of modern science!

CHAPTER 5

Customized Gear

"IT'S GOOD ENOUGH. I'LL MAKE DO WITH IT."

It was probably something you heard your grandparents say quite often. Your parents probably said it too, from time to time. You probably say it less often. And your kids — well, that's another matter altogether.

I'm here to tell you that, in ice fishing, you can make do. Those beautiful old hand-crafted tip-ups, that fiendishly well engineered sled-box, those cleverly improvised jig poles — with only these you can have a marvelous day out on the ice and want for nothing.

Both of my grandfathers dug ditches. One dug grave ditches and the other one road ditches. They worked hard to make life better for their families. My parents had it better, but they still knew how to make do. My father worked in a factory for 44 years. He likes to fish and hunt but seldom buys much for himself. My mother also knows how to sacrifice, to make do, to appreciate the little things.

These people shamed me with their ability to work hard and give up things for the sake of others. But they never spoiled me, and everything important I know I learned from them. I learned to make do, but even more important, I learned to see beauty in things that cost nothing but are still priceless.

I came up the hard way in ice fishing. I started out cutting holes with implements that looked like state evidence in a murder trial but were actually dull enough to put you to sleep. That I still have ten toes is no small wonder, since as kids we cut up to 16 inches of ice with these axes, tire irons, and what not. I must have been 20 before I graduated to a spud, and 22 before I graduated to one that actually cut. That second one weighs about 18 pounds and was forged by a blacksmith decades ago. I used it for 14 years before my parents gave me a hand auger as a birthday present.

All that time I never even thought to buy a tip-up, a bait bucket or a jig pole. Old-timers from my home town passed on, one by one, and since they knew the Caposselas liked to fish and hunt, we were bequeathed much of their gear. They came from the make-do generation, and I still cherish the ice fishing gear they left me.

I ice fished for 15 years before buying a tip-up and 25 years before buying a power auger. I don't make any apologies for the gear I have bought, but I can tell you that every trip I took in those early years was happy, even if the gear was a little bit dull, or bent, or wobbly. You *can* make do.

CUSTOMIZING YOUR TIP-UPS

It's true that jigging is the main game of most of the better ice fishermen I've met. Yet tip-ups can have their day in the sun, too, and there are things you can do to them to greatly improve their effectiveness.

I was never satisfied with the way my off-the-shelf tip-ups performed. The problems were several, both in regard to ease of operation and fish catching qualities. Perhaps the single thing that disturbed me most was the inability to change spools. I knew there had to be a way to rig interchangeable spools, and after rummaging around in some hardware stores, I finally found that way.

In Chapter 3, the difference between topwater and underwater tip-ups was explained. This discussion will focus on wooden underwater tip-ups.

It's very true that with each passing season more and more fishermen are replacing their wooden models with the well engineered plastic and metal tip-ups of modern design. In spite of this, the wooden tip-ups will be around for a while, and they are more cooperative in terms of the customizing that is possible.

Most tip-up spools are fastened to the bottom arm of the tip-up with a nail. This can be pried out very easily. Now, for each tip-up you have, purchase the following:

1. One fully threaded round head bolt
2. One self-locking nut of an interior diameter to fit the bolt
3. One wing nut, also to fit the bolt
4. One spool of the type I will discuss

The bolt must be long enough to pass through the spool, the little bushing that sits next to the spool on most tip-ups, the self-locking nut, and the leg of the tip-up. It then must stick out enough so that the wing nut can easily grab it. The bolt I use is three inches long

The author's customized tip-up spools. Note the self-locking nut that sits between the bottom arm of the tip-up and the bushing that sits against the face of the spool. Use little stick-on labels to mark what line(s) you have on the spool.

by ⅛ inch in diameter. Those numbers could vary somewhat depending on the tip-up and the spool. The bolt should be thick enough so that the spool does not wobble when spun on it. In other words, the diameter of the bolt should be just very slightly smaller than the diameter of the hole in the tip-up spool.

The key to this set-up is the self-locking nut. After passing the bolt through the spool and the bushing, thread on the self-locking nut. Tighten the nut so that the bushing is nearly up against the spool but not so tightly that the spool is prevented from spinning easily. A self-locking nut will not back off because it features a soft core that the threads of the bolt cut into. Rigged this way, you have a complete unit consisting of spool, bolt, bushing, and self-locking nut that will not back off. Just pop the unit through the hole in the tip-up's bottom arm and put on the wing nut. You're in business. To change it, just remove the wing nut, detach the entire spool unit and snap in a new one. It takes about ten seconds to do this. Keep as many spool units in your sled-box as you think you need. For example, I have about 20 spool units rigged up and with me since I fish for many different species. As explained in Chapter 15, I rig up my spools with different weight and type leaders, and each morning I snap on the ones I want that day. All this means that I almost never have to change line out on the ice. Ice fishing is a survival game, and the less you have to do with your hands the better.

The usual tip-up features a nylon or hard plastic bushing, referenced above, that positions the spool without restricting its ability to spin freely (it must spin completely freely). Be sure to save this little bushing when you remove the factory spool. You will almost certainly have to cut it to compensate for the extra space taken up by the self-locking nut. I used a plasterboard knife for this purpose. If it's a metal bushing, you might have to use a hacksaw.

A tip-up spool has a little tang which protrudes and serves to tip the lever that in turn makes the flag go up. Before you do anything to the bushing, and even before you buy the hardware, determine what position the spool must be in so that its tang can in fact trip the flag mechanism. As it happens, on the spools I bought the tangs were too long. I had to cut them down with a knife blade in my saber saw.

The nail that holds the factory spool in place may not quite go through the bottom arm of the tip-up. If that's the case, you must drill out this hole. This hole should match exactly the diameter of the bolt you are using. If it does, the spool will not wobble as it spins.

Another thing to remember is that a self-locking nut should only be used once. If it's removed and then put back on, it may loosen up, another reason to size the whole thing up before you start tinkering.

I never cared for the little aluminum spools that come with most wooden tip-ups. The reason is threefold: (1) they're too shiny, (2) they're too light in weight, and (3) they hold too little line. The fish may or may not care about the shininess, but I frequently fish with only a few feet of line down and I just don't want that shiny spool in the nose of some gamefish. It is true that in very shallow water fishing a topwater tip-up might be a smart choice. But I avoid topwater models since they're big trouble when the mercury is below 32 degrees F (0°C). Instead, I use a black plastic spool and go on the assumption that the fish are not bothered by it.

The weight of the spool might be more important than you think. How much line the spool holds also might be more important than you think. This is all explained in Chapter 15.

After much searching I finally found a tip-up spool that I like. It is black plastic, 2⁵⁄₁₆ inches in outside diameter and it holds a lot of line — 400 yards of the line that I like to put on it. They are available from National Sports Supply and currently cost about $1.50 each.

I affix little self-stick labels to the outside of the spool. The spool has little ridges that divide the outer surface into four pie-shaped sections. I place a label on each section. The labels are ¾ inch x ½ inch and are available in office supply stores. The Avery brand labels I purchased have never come loose in the water.

I use indelible ink to write down what line is on the spool. A pen called a Sharpie has proven to be truly indelible. For example, on one label I might write 12 # OM Back 12/91 (OM is an abbreviation of the brand name while Back stands for backing). On the second label I might write 50 yds. 45 # DAC 12/91. On the third label I might put 18″ ANDE step 20# 12/91. And on the fourth label I might put 12′ XL 6# 12/91. I thus know exactly what line is on that spool and when it was put on. If something fails, I at least know what line I was using when it happened.

The plastic spool I use is itself a bit heavier than the standard factory aluminum spool, but with about 400 yards of line wound on it, it's much heavier. For the implications of this, see the discussion in Chapter 15.

Some people like to use really large tip-up spools. I guess I've seen ones up to about six inches in diameter. I believe these people have become enamored with the very heavy "ice fishing lines" that look like fly lines and are coated so they are very thick, freeze-proof and tangle-proof. I don't use these expensive lines, but perhaps they do require a very large spool arbor. Then, too, perhaps the anglers using these humongous spools have learned what I learned a long time ago: A heavy spool trips the flag a lot better than a light one. Yet I cannot see any practical reason for turning to these jumbo tip-up spools. They take up a lot of space no matter where you store them, and they are much more expensive to buy in the first place.

The length of a tip-up is of some interest. The extra long ones present the flag in a higher position, but I see no other advantage to them. The length I prefer is 22 or 23 inches. That's mainly because this is the largest tip-up that will fit inside the two side compartments of my ice fishing sled-box. If you carry your tip-ups strictly in buckets, you should know that the longer tip-ups will be more likely to fall out.

Most underwater tip-ups are very similar in design, while topwater models, many of which are homemade, vary much more. Whichever kind you are inclined to use, you can usually tinker around with the flag tripping mechanism to make it work more smoothly. I don't know how many times I've had another fisherman come up to me and say, "Jeez, I had a fish on, but the flag didn't go up." This is intolerable to me, and with my customized tip-ups, it almost never happens. Leastwise if it does happen, it's probably a skanky old perch five or six inches long.

Sometimes, bending the post that the end of the flag spring sits on can make the flag trip more or less easily, depending on what you want. This adjustment can help to compensate for variations in bait size and wind velocity. There are two main types of trip mechanisms: the kind where the spring is actually knocked off the curved tip of a wire, and the kind where the spring is pushed off a bent post. Between the two, I like the bent post design. Not only does it work more dependably, but it offers a little adjustability that the first design does not offer.

The way most underwater tip-ups are made, they do not sit squarely on the ice. This is because two legs sit at one level and the other two sit at a different level — the difference, of course, being the thickness of one leg. To make the tip-up more stable on smooth, snowless ice, tack little squares of wood onto the two arms that are suspended just above the level of the other two.

Most tip-up flags are red. This is not the most visible color against most winter backdrops. The best is the "blaze orange" used in hunting garments. Black is also a good color, especially when there's snow. My friend Richie uses black flags on his tip-ups and calls them his Jolly Rogers.

The wood of a store bought tip-up seems to last indefinitely and I've never felt the urge to varnish it or anything of the sort. I do paint the bottom arm black. This, again, is an attempt to make my rig as invisible to the fish as possible in shallow water. In fact, with the black spool and the black bottom arm of the tip-up, I often see nothing when I look down into a hole. This bothered me because when a flag goes up I like to see whether the spool is spinning. Now, I've painted the little tang on the spool white. If line is paying out, that little bit of white going around and around is quite noticeable. Not all the photos in this book will reflect all the things I discuss, since I'm still refining my gear.

It's been pointed out to me that black is probably not the least visible color to a fish looking up...that some mid-range grey would show up least against the bottom of the hole and the bottom of the ice. This theory impresses me enough that I may paint the bottoms of my tip-ups medium grey next year.

TWO BUCKETS IN ONE

In recent years, the 5-gallon white bucket has become the basic on-ice tackle box for most fishermen in my region, where shanty fishing is not the rule. You've seen them and maybe even used them yourself. They're the ones that joint compound and other things come in, and they're useful for all kinds of fishing. I still bring my trusty sled-box but most often I leave it in the truck and only take what I need from it. On many short outings, I may sally forth with only a spud bar and a bucket with some jig poles and odds and ends crammed into it. But on almost any day, it's nice to have a spare bucket out there. I wondered, Without tying up my

Two white buckets that can be carried as one. The special brass latch in the center makes it possible.

second arm, how can I carry two buckets out onto the ice? The answer seemed to be nesting buckets, one inside the other, and both carried with only one hand. I devised just such a thing.

I found a special kind of brass latch that makes the whole thing work. It's shown in the photo on the preceding page and you should bring this to the hardware store and show it to the people there to see if they have it. The latch holds the two buckets together, but I did not attach either part of this two-part latch directly to the bucket. Rather, I first bolted on small pieces of wooden paneling to provide a more stable and flat base for the latch. To attach the pieces of panel, I used solid brass bolts, and each one goes through the wood, through the bucket's wall and then is grabbed on the inside of the bucket with a nut.

The latch itself consists of an arm, a circle, and then a second circle that spins around and locks the latch together. It is difficult to describe, but the photo should make it clear. You could use two latches, 180 degrees apart on the bucket. I have found, though, that one is enough. Each part of the latch, by the way, attaches to a bucket (through the wood first) via a wood screw.

If you placed two white buckets inside one another and sat on them all day long, you might never get them separated. That has already happened to me. To prevent this from recurring, I so positioned the latches that the inner bucket does not and cannot slip into the outer bucket as far as it conceivably could. What stops it from going down beyond the point of no return? The piece of wooden panel. The panel not only serves as a base for the latch but it serves to suspend the inner bucket high enough so that it cannot get jammed down into the outer bucket.

During the day, it's great to have that extra bucket. For one thing, you can use it for a seat if you're jigging or just taking a break. It can be a depository for a heavy garment that you have to take off beneath the midday sun. It can be used to bring your fish back to the truck. The way my buckets nest together, there is about a six-inch space between the bottom of the inner bucket and the bottom of the outer bucket. This is usually enough to bring back a nice little mess of fish.

I found an even sneakier use for it, though.

When I'm ice fishing, I like to keep a very low profile. If I'm out trout fishing and other people start chopping holes near me and the water is relatively shallow, I know I'll have to move or go fishless. One day a few years ago I was having a very hot day with 15 trout, 10 perch and one bass caught (though not all kept). I didn't especially want them flopping on the ice to attract attention to the good spot I'd discovered, so I did the following.

First, I bored an extra hole with my auger. Then I snapped the top, single loop of the stringer on which my fish were hung to the bucket's metal handle. After this, I slipped the stringer with the fish into the hole, completely covered the hole with the bucket, and folded the bucket's handle fully down to the side of the bucket. Finally, I pushed a little snow up against the side of the bucket so there was absolutely no evidence that a stringer was attached to it.

Sure enough, by and by some guy came out for a look-see.

"Nothing," I said, as I prayed that the man would not notice the slight wobbling of the bucket as the stringered fish pulled and yanked.

"Not a thing?" he pressed.

"Nah, nothing," I said, and then tossed in a bit of vitriol aimed at the conservation department, stocking policies and life in general.

"Chrisamighty, just what do they do with our license money?"

"It's a damn shame," I answered, as the man slowly moseyed off.

A HOMEMADE SLED-BOX

There aren't too many sporting devices, homemade or otherwise, that can lay claim to serving five distinct and different functions. But my unique ice fishing sled can. It's a sled, tackle box, chair, rod holder and table all in one! You can make one at very little expense, perhaps with materials you already have in the garage.

The accompanying drawings and instructions should make it clear how to construct the box. These are the exact dimensions and features I used in making my box. You can copy this design more or less exactly, or adapt it to fit your particular needs.

First, be sure to use exterior, not interior, plywood. You could, of course, substitute a more expensive wood, such as highly rot-resistant cypress or redwood lumber, but regular plywood will suffice and will be stronger. If cost is a factor for you, use whatever's lying around the garage.

Use ⅝ inch thick plywood for all components except the lift-out tray and the tray supports, which can be ½ inch plywood. As the sled will be out in the weather, try to use a non-rusting metal such as alu-

The author's sled-box shown with the "caboose" (bait bucket transporter) in the down position.

minum, brass, or galvanized steel for metal parts. It's most important that you measure the ice fishing gear you already have, especially tip-ups, before finalizing dimensions.

There are several key design features. First, each side of the sled was cut so that the front juts out and curves up like a real sled. Note that the sides extend all the way from the top to the bottom. This is for strength. For even more strength, and to make it glide better when the ice is snow-covered (which is usually the case) the bottom of each side is built up, left and right, with strips of ⅝ inch plywood which are bolted on. Thus the sled's runners are a full 1⅞ inches wide where they contact the ground. These features make this box so strong that I can literally jump up and down on it. I've often thought of screwing segments of skis to the bottoms of the runners. This would make the sled glide through the snow even better, and would protect the bottoms of the wooden runners very well. But the skis would also add more weight, and my sled-box is heavy enough already.

How you divide up the inside of the box will depend on the type and size of the gear you will be toting. As you can see, I first divided mine in half horizontally. I then divided the bottom half vertically

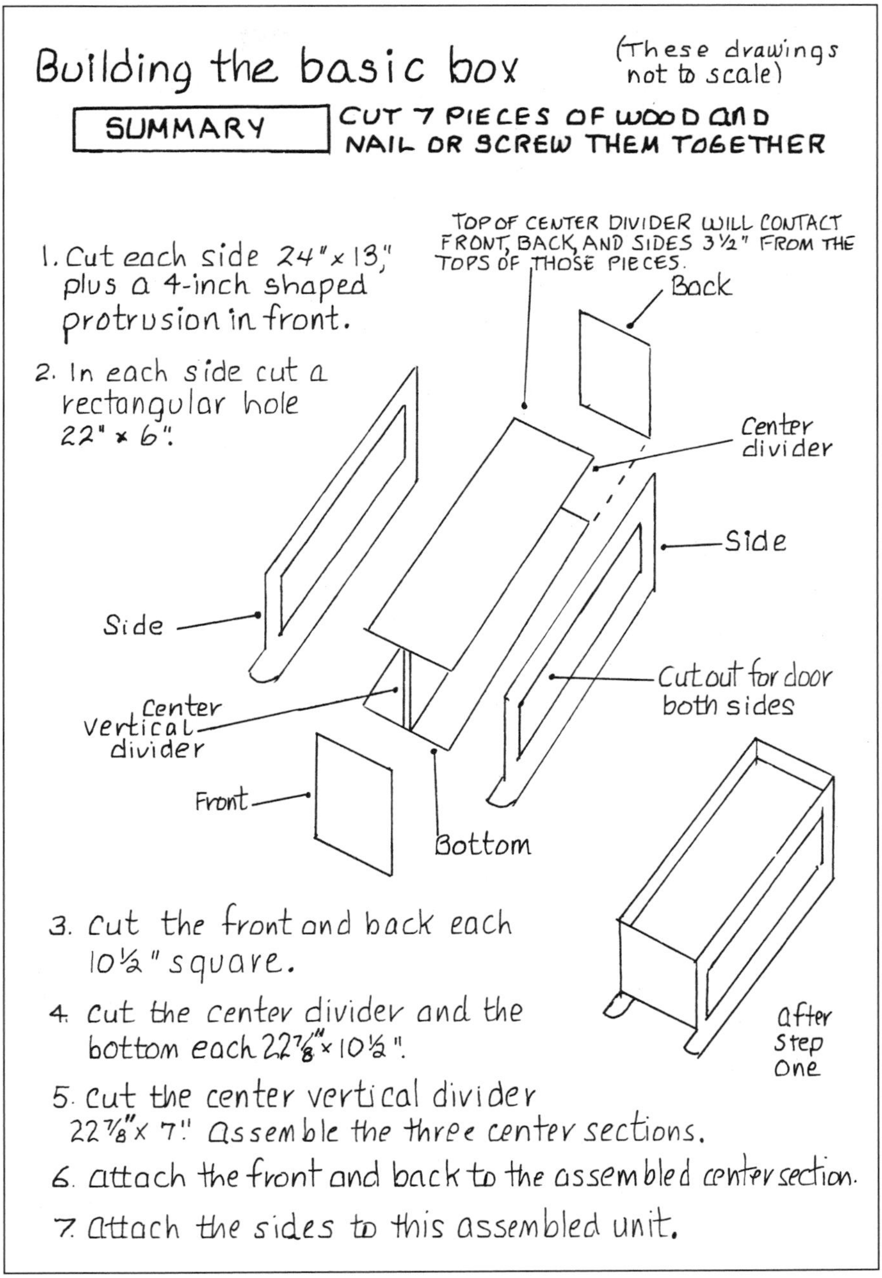
Building the basic box
(These drawings not to scale)
SUMMARY
CUT 7 PIECES OF WOOD AND NAIL OR SCREW THEM TOGETHER
1. Cut each side 24" x 13," plus a 4-inch shaped protrusion in front.
2. In each side cut a rectangular hole 22" x 6".
TOP OF CENTER DIVIDER WILL CONTACT FRONT, BACK, AND SIDES 3½" FROM THE TOPS OF THOSE PIECES.
Back
Center divider
Side
Side
Cut out for door both sides
Center vertical divider
Front
Bottom
3. Cut the front and back each 10½" square.
4. Cut the center divider and the bottom each 22⅞" x 10½".
5. Cut the center vertical divider 22⅞" x 7." Assemble the three center sections.
6. attach the front and back to the assembled center section.
7. attach the sides to this assembled unit.
after Step One

Fig. 5.1 Building a sled-box — step one

Adding the bottom support strips

| SUMMARY | CUT 4 PIECES OF WOOD AND ATTACH THEM TO THE BOTTOM OF THE BOX |

Bottom view

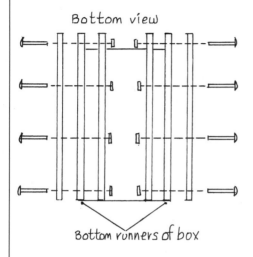

Bottom runners of box

Back view
after
step two

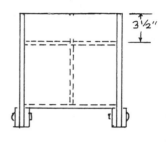

3½"

1. Cut 4 strips of wood, each one 28" x 3".

2. Shape the fronts to match exactly the protrusions on the sides of the box.

3. Use clamps to hold the support strips in place. Use 2 clamps on each side.

4. On one side, drill 4 ¼" holes as shown.

5. Repeat on the other side. Use 2¾" round-head bolts to attach support strips to runners.

Fig. 5.2 Building a sled-box — step two

Compartmentalizing the top section

SUMMARY DIVIDE THE TOP COMPARTMENT, WIDTHWISE, IN HALF. DIVIDE AREA "A" BY ADDING TRAY SUPPORTS (WHICH WILL SUPPORT A REMOVABLE TRAY).

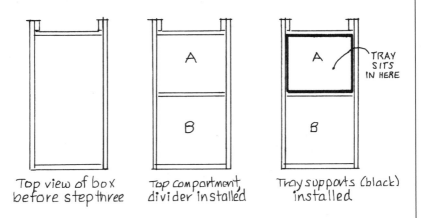

Top view of box before step three

Top compartment divider installed

Tray supports (black) installed

A

TRAY SITS IN HERE

B

1. Cut the top compartment divider 10½" x 3½".

2. Nail or screw this divider to sides of box to create two equal-size compartments, "A" and "B".

3. Cut 4 tray supports, each one 1¾" high. Their length will be to fit the inside dimensions of compartment "A".

4. Attach these to the walls of compartment "A", using small nails.

5. Make a removable tray to match in size the inside dimensions, top part, of compartment "A". Divide this tray any way you wish or skip that.

LIFT-OUT TRAY

Fig. 5.3 Building a sled-box — step three

Final construction steps

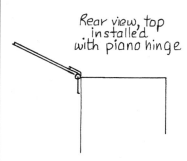

Rear view, top installed with piano hinge

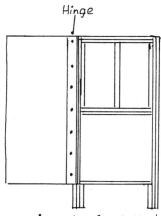

Hinge

Top view, top installed

1. Cut the top to match exactly the perimeter of the top of the box.

2. Using 5/8" wood screws, mount the top with a piano hinge as shown. Points of screws will probably protrude. Grind or file these off.

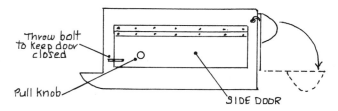

Throw bolt to keep door closed

Pull knob

SIDE DOOR

3. Cut each side door 1/16" less all around than the hole allowed for it. Mount flush with a piano hinge. Add a pull knob and throw bolt to each door.

4. Cut the bait bucket transporter ("caboose") 11 5/8" x 9 1/4." Mount to back of box with a piano hinge. Small hook'n'eyes can be used to hold caboose in up position.

Fig. 5.4 Building a sled-box — step four

Adding the rod holders; embellishments

SUMMARY ADD THE ROD HOLDERS AND A ROPE PULL

Pipe segments   Metal strapping

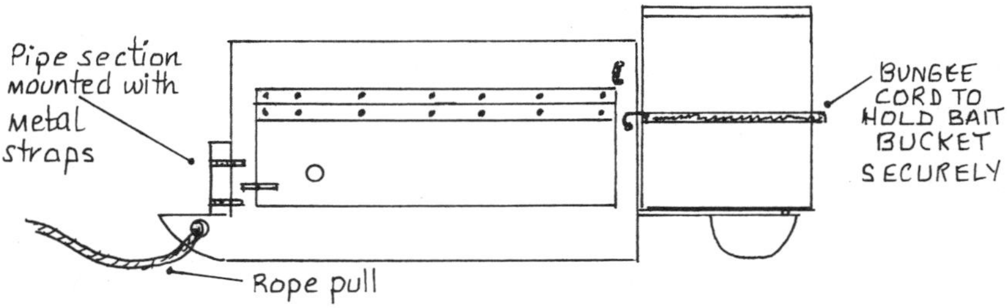

Pipe section mounted with metal straps

BUNGEE CORD TO HOLD BAIT BUCKET SECURELY

Rope pull

1. Obtain two galvanized pipe sections, each one 4½" long by 1½" in diameter. Sand or file off any rough edges.

2. Affix these segments to the front of the box, one to a side, using metal strapping. Each will carry one jig pole.

3. Drill ½" holes in the fronts of the runners. Through these tie a rope pull.

4. Add screw eyes near the back of the box, one to a side. These are fastening points for a bungee cord.

5. Add an I.D. label. Add decals, painted scenes, etc.

Fig. 5.5 Building a sled-box — step five

from front to rear. These two bottom side compartments nicely carry ten tip-ups, five on each side, plus a gaff and any other long items. I divided the top half with a center divider from right to left. Then on one side I eventually added two nesting trays (themselves compartmentalized) which can carry hooks, lures, and other small gear. Thus my box has a total of eight compartments ranging from small to large.

The top of the sled should be fastened with a full-length piano hinge. Hinges can always be mounted in several ways, just make sure you mount it in such a way that the top opens at least 180 degrees. Also, be sure the top is both wide enough and long enough that it fits the perimeter of the box exactly. This, again, is for strength.

With this construction, when the top is closed the box substitutes for a chair. This is nice for those in-between-flag periods, and also for jigging. I made the seat a little softer by gluing on a piece of vinyl, which is extremely tough and hasn't ripped after a lot of hard wear. Any local shop that specializes in car upholstery and convertible tops should be able to spare you a small piece. Alternatively, you could affix a soft, foam rubber cushion, but this would be less durable.

Many ice fishermen, myself included, like to cook on the ice. "A bad day of fishing is better than a good day at work," some say. At no time in your life will the prospect of going to work tomorrow be more onerous to you than when you catch the aroma of fresh fish fillets, sautéed in butter, wafting across the ice.

But to cook, it really helps to have a little table. Here we come to the next feature of this sled. In the open position, the top of the sled serves as a small table. All I add are two slip-on support sticks, one at each corner, otherwise the top would open a little more than 180 degrees and be uneven and unsteady. These supports, which can be metal or wood, should be always kept inside the sled-box so you have them when you need them. The bottom side compartments store them nicely.

Whatever food you're preparing, hot or cold, the little table comes in handy. And of course you can still get at all your gear because the box is open. What if it rains or snows, you ask? No — my gear in the open sled doesn't get wet. I carry a piece of very heavy plasticized cloth to cover the open box when it's rainy or snowy.

The two rod holders, each one capable of carrying a jig pole, are easy to add. The wide front face of the runner supports the holder.

Actually, the sled serves a few other less necessary but still helpful functions. The "caboose" is something I added on later. This is just a little fold-up shelf upon which a bait bucket can be set. With little runners of its own, the shelf, when not in use, folds up and is held tight against the sled with small hook-and-eyes.

Every ice fisherman needs an ice skimmer, and this constantly used item should be always at the ready. Although not shown in the drawings, I affixed to my sled-box two spring clips that hold a large skimmer tightly in place. When I don't drag out the box, I use the small skimmer that rides on my belt (see below).

Even if you use treated plywood, the box will last longer and look better if you finish the wood with varnish or paint. I painted mine with some leftover, exterior glossy white. Use what you have hanging around the garage, but try to make it oil-based. Put your name and address somewhere on the sled.

My sled-box is heavy and for that and other reasons I now usually use a flat toboggan to transport my gear from truck to lake and back again. But on those occasions when we want to have a little cook-out on the ice, I always bring the sled-box topped with a vegetable crate in which I keep the stove, pots and pans, and food.

A CUSTOM ICE FISHING BELT

You've just walked over to your most distant tip-up, a good 75 yards away from all the others. The hole needs skimming, but where's your skimmer? You thought it was dangling from your pants pocket, but it's really over by the ice shanty, a hundred yards distant. You can just make it out, sparkling in the sun.

You mumble as you start walking over to it, but on the way a tip-up near shore springs up and you run to it instead. The fish feels like a heavy one, probably a big old pike, and you look around anxiously for the gaff. It's over by the hole you just went to! You lose the fish at the hole, and then glumly walk over to the bait bucket with the idea that you'll bait the shore tip-up then go skim the other hole. But on the way, another flag springs up! You get to it, and since it's a cold day, it's filled with ice. This was a tip-up you set for trout and you wonder whether this is the flag you've been waiting for. You glance around quickly for the skimmer. It's by the far tip-up! No, it's by the shore tip-up! And where's the gaff? You left it by the tip-up that needs bait! Or is it over by that middle tip-up? By the time you clean out the hole with your bare hand, a good minute has passed. The gaff won't be needed. The fish on the trout tip-up has gotten away.

Three flags and nothing to show for it. It feels like an Abbott and Costello routine.

How would you like to have these two critical items always with you at every hole on every trip? All you have to do is think like a surf fisherman.

Surf casters wear a belt that serves two primary functions: It holds a gaff safely, and it holds a stringer to keep fish while the angler is still casting in the suds. Some also hold a knife. I took this concept and made it work for the type of gear you need when ice fishing, namely the skimmer, gaff and knife. What I came up with was a belt that I could also use for surf fishing, a real plus since I do like to surf cast and had never bothered to make a belt for that express purpose. My design was inspired by and strongly modeled after one created by Mike Campanelli, of Long Island, New York, who presented the plans for his belt in *The Fisherman* magazine. You'll need:

1. One army issue pistol belt, the one with rows of parallel holes located all along it. (Width will be about 2⅜ inches. Get the old fashioned soft cloth type, not the more rigid type with plastic buckles.) Look in army surplus stores.
2. A 7 x 4½ inch piece of stainless steel sheeting.
3. 24 inches of stainless steel welding rod.
4. A brass tankball guide (used in toilets) which some hardware stores will have.
5. One stainless steel eyebolt, ⅛ inch in diameter.
6. Two stainless steel round head (un-notched) bolts, ¾" long.
7. One brass snap clip.
8. A 4-inch length of surgical tubing.
9. 6 inches of brass chain.
10. One "quick-release" snap clip.

The drawings and instructions should clearly show how to assemble this belt. I'll add just a few more comments here.

The gaff simply dangles from the eye bolt. Note that the eye bolt is so installed as to rotate freely. This will allow the gaff, which rides on the eye bolt, to swivel in conjunction with the movements of your body, making the whole unit more comfortable. If you do

Forming the metal frame

SUMMARY CREATE A RECTANGULAR FRAME OF SHEET METAL SUPPORTED AROUND ITS PERIMETER BY A BENT ROD

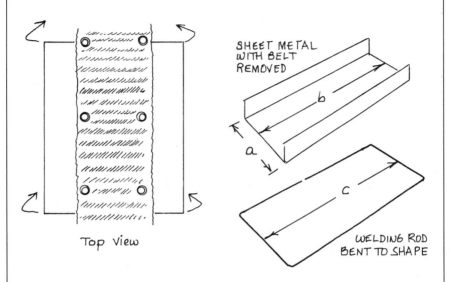

SHEET METAL WITH BELT REMOVED

b

a

c

Top view

WELDING ROD BENT TO SHAPE

1. Lay the pistol belt over the sheet metal. Bend each side of the metal up 90.° Dimension "a" should be slightly larger than width of belt.

2. Bend the welding rod so that it fits within the bent piece of sheet metal, but "c" must be 1" greater than "b."

3. Place the bent rod inside the sheet metal. Bend the upturned edges down over the rod on both sides. Tap down with a hammer.

✳ Note: See p. 66 for a list of materials and key dimensions

Fig. 5.6 Making an ice fishing belt — step one

Modifying and preparing the fittings

| SUMMARY | DISASSEMBLE THE TANK BALL GUIDE; SHORTEN THE STEM. CUT THE EYE BOLT. |

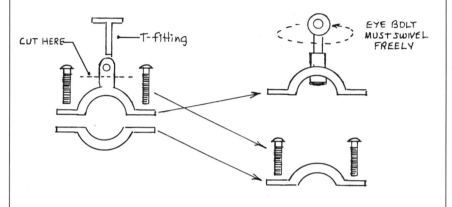

CUT HERE

T-fitting

EYE BOLT MUST SWIVEL FREELY

1. Disassemble the tank ball guide unit. The T-fitting will not be used in this project, the other four pieces will be.

2. Cut the stem on the top clamp below the set screw hole, as indicated by the dotted line.

3. Insert the stainless steel eye bolt into the cut off stem of the top clamp. Cut off the bottom end of the eye bolt so that there are just enough threads to hold a nut with a few threads still protruding. Peen this end of the bolt to lock on the nut.

4. The two brass bolts of the tank ball guide will be used in conjunction with the bottom clamp.

Fig. 5.7 Making an ice fishing belt — step two

Finishing the plate

SUMMARY | FASTEN BOTH CLAMPS THROUGH THE METAL PLATE

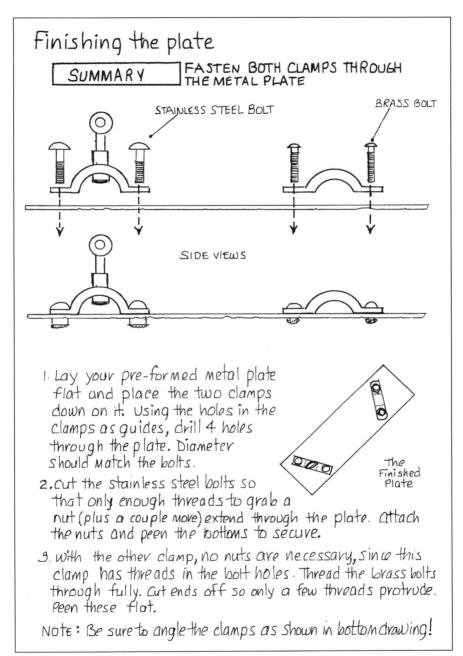

STAINLESS STEEL BOLT

BRASS BOLT

SIDE VIEWS

1. Lay your pre-formed metal plate flat and place the two clamps down on it. Using the holes in the clamps as guides, drill 4 holes through the plate. Diameter should match the bolts.

2. Cut the stainless steel bolts so that only enough threads to grab a nut (plus a couple more) extend through the plate. Attach the nuts and peen the bottoms to secure.

3. With the other clamp, no nuts are necessary, since this clamp has threads in the bolt holes. Thread the brass bolts through fully. Cut ends off so only a few threads protrude. Peen these flat.

The Finished Plate

NOTE: Be sure to angle the clamps as shown in bottom drawing!

Fig. 5.8 Making an ice fishing belt — step three

Completing the belt

SUMMARY ATTACH THE GAFF POINT PROTECTOR. ADD THE SNAP CLIP AND QUICK-RELEASE SNAP.

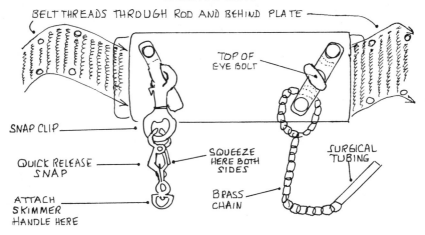

BELT THREADS THROUGH ROD AND BEHIND PLATE

TOP OF EYE BOLT

SNAP CLIP

QUICK RELEASE SNAP

ATTACH SKIMMER HANDLE HERE

SQUEEZE HERE BOTH SIDES

BRASS CHAIN

SURGICAL TUBING

1. Onto the left clamp, attach the snap clip. To this attach the quick-release snap.

2. The handle of your skimmer attaches to the bottom of the quick-release snap. When you wish to use your skimmer, just squeeze and the quick-release snap will come off the snap clip.

3. Affix the brass chain to the right clamp. Affix the surgical tubing to the other end. Bits of wire may help to accomplish this. The gaff rides on the eye bolt. The tubing covers the point of the gaff.

Note: It matters not whether the gaff (eye bolt) is on right or left. This is strictly personal preference.

Fig. 5.9 Making an ice fishing belt — step four

A somewhat unusual subsurface tip-up. When a fish takes, a magnetic contact is broken, and the inner part of the center tube springs up.

end up using the belt part-time for surf fishing, this swiveling feature will allow the gaff to move with the pounding of the waves.

The surgical tubing is essential for safety, and it also helps to make sure the gaff won't fall off the eye bolt. When the need for the gaff arises, simply flick off the tubing and remove the gaff from the eye bolt. After a few tries, you'll be able to do it without looking.

The brass snap clip that attaches to the clamp without the eye bolt will be findable in any marine store if your hardware store doesn't have it. If you do go surf fishing, just detach this snap clip with the skimmer attached to it and snap a surf fisherman's stringer in its place.

For ice fishing purposes, snapped on to the brass snap clip is a quick release snap. This type of snap releases under the pressure of a simple squeeze on the device. It snaps back on quickly. The skimmer attaches to the bottom ring of this clip. You might want to bend the handle of your skimmer so it can't come off the bottom of the quick release snap. Not all skimmers will have handles that will mesh with this design. You may have to buy a different skimmer, or modify the handle on the one you already own.

Look for the quick release clip in stores that specialize in fly fishing equipment. Many anglers use such a clip to fasten their landing net to the back loop of their fly vest.

Remember that the belt is designed to go over your outer garments, no matter how bulky those might be. Make sure the belt you purchase is long enough to do this. It should probably be at least four inches longer than your normal waist size.

An ordinary sheath knife will slip over the belt if the sheath has a loop that's large enough. If not, you'll have to either buy a larger sheath, or make one to fit the belt.

I have to say, it's nice to have the knife on the outside where it's readily accessible. If you normally wear a sheath knife on your pants, you probably already know how difficult it is to get to when you have numerous layers of clothing on.

CHAPTER 6

Transporting Gear

HERE ARE ONLY A FEW of the bad things that can happen if you pay any less attention to how you carry your ice fishing gear than to what you carry:

1. Your minnow bucket will tip over as you're walking out and now you have to furiously cut a hole to replace the water so the minnows don't die.
2. Even after you do, the colder water will probably stun the minnows and they will all float to the top. If you're lucky, they'll acclimate and come back to life.
3. Also as you're walking onto the ice, your fishing sled will tip over, likely spewing part of its contents into the snow. You'll numb your hands ferreting it out, and you'll still lose something.
4. Your power auger will fall off its vehicle, bending the choke adjustment lever.
5. The white bucket will tip over, most likely the one with your sweater and gloves. Without question, the ice will be slushy that day.
6. As you're dragging your gear through the woods to get to the

lake, some items not under control will fall off, into the snow, never to be seen again. Probably it will be your gaff — you know, that nice homemade one that's been in the family for 600 years.

7. The jig rod bucket, if it's not balanced or is too shallow, will tip over either breaking the tip on the pole or bending the handle on its reel.

These are only a few. There are innumerable others, as per the Laws of Murphy.

I'm a firm believer that what has worked once will work again. Having been born the organized type, I'm also a firm believer in systems. My system for organizing and transporting my ice fishing gear revolves around one basic desire: I want to carry as little onto the ice as I can get away with on any given day.

THE BUCKET AS TACKLE BOX

Most ice anglers I see use the 5-gallon white buckets, and these certainly are useful. But this past year I picked up a 7-gallon pail and I like it much better. Because it's about five inches higher, it holds the tip-ups and jig poles more securely. Also, the 7-gallon pail is much more comfortable to sit on, for an adult of normal size. A commercial

A 7-gallon pail (left) is not only more functional, but much more comfortable to sit on than a 5-gallon pail.

detergent called Zep came in the 7-gallon pail that I procured from a custodian friend.

An excellent gear-toting vehicle for an ice angler is a child's flat toboggan, the bigger the better. Mine measures 68 inches long by 19½ inches wide and is shown below (larger one).

In years past, almost everyone you'd see out on the ice in my area would have a little homemade sled or box. Throughout this book we'll call it a sled-box, since that's what it often is: some kind of box mounted on or imitating a sled (the designs are infinite). I made one nearly twenty years ago and it's so rugged that it's still in near-perfect condition, even though I used it constantly for about ten years. Plans for building it are presented in the preceding chapter.

You'll still see anglers, especially old-timers, pulling behind them these wonderfully crafted little buggies, but I use mine infrequently now and with good reason. I find that rarely am I parked immediately next to the edge of a lake. Usually there's at least a little walk through the woods, and it seems there's always some obstacle like an incline, heavy brush, fallen logs, open water near shore and what not. My particular sled-box is quite heavy, and I dislike lifting it over and around these obstacles. Moreover, the sled does not accommodate very well odd-shaped objects as do the buckets I use in conjunction with the toboggan. For example, a bulky down vest

A child's toboggan is an excellent vehicle for transporting your gear. If you have a power auger, definitely get the larger size.

or a heavy sweater can be stuffed into one of the buckets, but there's really no room in my sled-box for such objects.

WHAT TO TAKE WHEN

Because ice fishing is so demanding physically, there's no room for allowing the transportation of your gear to make things even tougher. Here, then, is a summary of the gear I carry, and how I carry it, in various circumstances. Although it's not listed, I always have the spud in the truck for when I need to test the ice, or open old holes. With very minimal ice, I will cut with the spud rather than the hand auger.

Short jaunt, early ice, no bait	— Two nesting buckets with jig poles and misc. gear, plus my hand auger. (In all these scenarios, the second of the two nesting buckets is used to bring fish back.)
Full day fishing, mid season	— Pack basket with tip-ups — Toboggan on which goes: Hand or power auger 2 nesting buckets Minnow Bucket Note: If toboggan is large enough, you can even fit the pack basket on it.
Full day fishing and we want to have a cook-out	— Homemade sled-box which carries tip-ups and all gear, including minnow bucket. — Wooden box which sits on top of sled-box and carries all food and cooking gear, plus stove — Hand or power auger, possibly on a toboggan

The nice thing about the toboggan is that it's light and you can just toss it onto the ice from shore. Then you load your gear onto it as you remove that gear from the car. This can be especially beneficial when the ice by shore is rotten or open. Did you ever try to "toss" or even coax a relatively heavy sled-box over bad shore ice?

The pack basket is also invaluable. No matter what your system for the day, the pack basket frees up both hands. Personally, I like to carry my tip-ups in the pack basket.

Hard plastic buckets, a pack basket, a flat toboggan: Get these items and I guarantee that the rest of your system will fall in around them. On the other hand, if you custom built your old trusty ice fishing sled-box 52 years ago and have used it on every trip for all that time, keep using it! I think the important thing is that you do have some kind of a system that you're comfortable with and can depend on time after time.

Let's assume that I've sold you on the flat toboggan. You've found a nice big one in the toy or department store, and upon getting it home you're delighted that all the gear you normally want to bring out on the ice fits on top of it. Now, how do you keep that stuff from tipping over or falling off the toboggan? If the ice is smooth, it should all ride nicely with nothing tipping over or off. But if the ice is bumpy, you'll have to take some measures.

I described it before as a "flat" toboggan, but of course it isn't completely flat. The sides curve up a little, and so does the front. It's this configuration that allows it to do its primary job as well as the one we're describing here.

The toboggan will likely have little plastic handles that a child would hold onto when gliding down a hill. These can be fastening points for bungee cords. The cords can be used to help batten down any gear on the toboggan that seems like it might tip over or fall off. If you need additional bungee cords, you could drill holes in the upturned sides of the toboggan and use these as fastening points.

In the first few paragraphs of this chapter, I didn't tell you quite all the ways you can lose things. While ice fishing, the answer, my friend, may be blowing in the wind, but so may your gear be if you don't watch out. Usually you can do a few quick steps and retrieve whatever the wind has decided to gobble up for a snack. But what if open water looms only 50 or 100 yards away? I remember we were on slick black ice one time on a big reservoir where the coves were all frozen but the main lake was a patch quilt of open water and unsafe crinkle ice. We were busy with flags when a gust caught my buddy's 2-gallon vinyl bucket. It blew across the lake at a furious pace but Jimmy was preoccupied with a fish and didn't go right after it. I saw

A little folding seat, a pack basket, and an unusual turn-key corkscrew auger.

the bucket go a good hundred yards out of the corner of my eye, but the next time we looked up it had simply vanished. In it were a bunch of lures, a skimmer and a knife. We never saw it again. It was getting dark and misty, and the ice — with plenty of open spots — was too scary to allow us to go after it.

I've also seen gloves and hats blown away, usually to be retrieved, but often uselessly wet.

No matter how you tote your minnow bucket, the potential exists for its top being snatched from you. I have a beautiful and irreplaceable wire-framed Styrofoam bucket made by the old Herter company. I am not about to let the top to this bucket blow away on me. Through the top, I drilled a quarter-inch hole and through that hole I placed a solid brass eye bolt. A brass nut and lock washer go on the inside. To the eye of the bolt is fastened a six-inch length of wire (use stainless steel or copper) with the other end of that wire fastened to the wire frame of my bucket. When a big wind comes up the top may flutter but will not sail across the lake.

STOP TANGLES BEFORE THEY START

A critical aspect of moving your ice fishing gear from home to lake is avoiding tangles. Let me repeat what I've said elsewhere in this book: Ice fishing can be an extremely tough sport physically. You have to minimize your problems. The fewer intricate tasks you have to do on the ice the better. At the same time, the fewer times you have to remove your gloves the better. Stop tangles before they even start.

Keep rubber bands on your tip-up spools when coming and going. When you take the band off to start fishing, double it over and place it on an arm of your tip-up. You'll still lose some so carry extras. Use the wider ones if you have them; or better yet the very wide ones with the little tabs for easy removal. Many fishermen dig the hook point into the line to keep the line from unwinding. This mindless practice will ruin any line. A better way to secure your hook on the spool is described on p. 189.

One of the biggest problems I've had in the tangle department revolves around my jig poles. I like to carry several poles in a plastic bucket and they seem to inevitably tangle with one another. Specifically, it's the lure on one pole that tangles with the line of another pole.

I started experimenting with Velcro. I made strips to secure the lure tight to the rod so it couldn't catch anything else in the bucket. Soon after, I heard of manufactured gadgets called "lure wraps" and these serve the same function. I strongly recommend that you make or purchase some of these. Getting out on the ice on a five degree day and seeing all the jig poles jumbled up like spaghetti is only a notch above getting poked in the eye with a sharp stick.

What about small gear: hooks, lures, split shot, flickers, rubber bands, extra flags, and so on? My sled-box is compartmentalized and holds all this small stuff (in their own little boxes) just fine. However, since I rarely bring out my sled-box these days, I have to take whatever gear is needed for the day and place it either in the plastic buckets or the pack basket. I hate lots of small objects loose and begging to get lost, so I started rummaging around some army surplus stores. The gear you come across in these stores is almost always inexpensive, functional, and extremely durable. I finally found an old Swiss Army knapsack. I removed the shoulder straps but left on the two little spring clips the pack had. All my small gear, plus a bit of lunch or snacks, goes into the knapsack. The clips enable me to snap the pack onto the outside of the bucket to free up the inside of the bucket for other things. I take the army pack every day, except on those few days a season when I drag out the sled-box.

SOME IDEAS ON CLOTHING

In Chapter 8 I talk at length about keeping warm on the ice. Your overall system ought to include some provision for carrying clothing as well.

I like to have three or four pairs of dry gloves in the truck all winter long. I normally wear a pair and if the car is not too close to our chosen spot I'll take another pair in a Zip-loc bag. The gloves I happen to like are unfortunately not water resistant, that's why I like having the extra sets in the truck.

The layer system is the approach I recommend, but what happens when a little noontime warm-up prompts you to remove a layer or two? Where will you put that sweater, sweatshirt, pullover, down vest or coat? Again, those plastic buckets just can't be beat. If the weather is foul, bring a few 13-gallon plastic bags to keep the clothing dry when you take it off. Even if the weather is nice, shadows fall early in winter and you may very well want to put one or more layers back on before it's time to call it a day.

Whatever clothing I'm wearing for the day, I definitely do plan on the transporting and storing of it. I don't make a big deal out of it, but I do spend a few minutes thinking about what I'll take, what I'll wear to start the day, and how I'll store whatever I might need to put on or take off. Again, it doesn't hurt to keep a complete extra set of dry clothes in the truck. Just put it there and leave it. The day will come when you'll be glad you did.

COMMERCIAL ICE BUGGIES

To get back to the concept of a sled-box and its use in transporting your ice fishing stuff, it should be mentioned that there are a few interesting commercially made ones. Unless you live in a really big ice fishing area you're not likely to see these on the shelves of sporting goods stores. However, you should find them in the winter catalogs of such mail order companies as Cabela's, Gander Mountain, Bass Pro Shops and others.

Among the buggies I've seen advertised there are at least a couple of noteworthy features. One such buggy is called the Ice Shuttle and currently sells at $89.95. It's one of the nicest combination storage box/portable ice shelters that I've yet seen. It's a three-sided shelter with a polyethylene fabric on a frame that pops up. It has a nice padded seat and a place to put your minnow bucket. It also has a nice roomy storage compartment.

Ice fishing camp! This shows some of the contrivances ice anglers use to transport equipment. Front, two milk cartons have been placed on a small toboggan. Center right is a homemade wooden box mounted on runners. To the left and behind that is a vegetable crate mounted on a toboggan. Behind that is a commercially made buggy. At the rear is a Sit-N-Fish bucket, also shown on p. 38.

Another buggy I saw advertised offers no protection from the elements but does have a place to put a small heater. It also has room for a substantial amount of gear. If you're convinced that a sled-box is the best thing for you, but you're not especially handy, one of these ready-made buggies might be an answer.

Where it's good and cold, a popular contrivance for transporting a day's worth of fishing gear is a large box that is pulled out by, most typically, a snowmobile. This is really just an oversized sled-box. More and more these days, a vehicle-towed trailer or homemade box in the north country is likely to have stuffed into it some kind of portable shelter. The box may also tote a small propane heater, a power auger, gasoline, food, extra clothing, miscellaneous small gear and possibly even a "cooler" for the fish (which can help prevent fish from freezing). In other words, a serious amount of gear for a long day under severe conditions.

Such a box should have runners that effectively negotiate the snow. It should be of a shape that enables your particular gear to fit neatly. It might well have a hitch for a ball and hitch arrangement. Some cautious anglers make sure the box's closure system allows for a padlock.

A good substitute for such a vehicle-towed box is a new product called a Snow-tote, put out by U. S. L. Products, Inc. (see Appendix). It's really just a big, strong toboggan but it has molded-in tie-down ports and from the photo I have of it, looks to be very rugged. It can be pulled by a snowmobile or ATV, but it could be hand-pulled as well.

It's certainly possible that, even if you fish out of a true shanty that is left on the ice, you may want to tote a fair amount of gear with you. But if the shanty is large enough, and well designed, it will allow for the storage of a lot of stuff. The celebrated overnight shanties of some lakes will not only store your gear but feed you, sleep you, and take care of your toiletries. For more insights on the fascinating shantytown subculture, see the next chapter.

CHAPTER 7

Ice Fishing Shelters

By Steve Grooms

THEY GO BY MANY NAMES: ice shelters, bobs, shanties, ice houses, dark houses, shelters and fish houses. By common usage, "shanty" usually refers to a homemade plywood shelter. Commercial shelters made of fabric are usually just called "shelters" or "ice shelters." In this chapter, we'll call plywood ice shelters "shanties," and we'll call the commercially made fabric ice shelters "portable shelters." When referring to shelters in general, we'll call them "shelters," "ice shelters," or "ice houses."

Whatever they're called, shelters are increasingly popular. There are two basic reasons for using a shelter, namely comfort and fishing efficiency.

Nobody likes being cold, and ice fishing outside a shelter can be mighty cold. Keeping warm is the basic motivation for building or buying an ice shelter. But comfort relates to fishing success, too. The comfortable angler stays on the ice longer and fishes with better concentration than the poor schlub shivering as he or she sits in the open on a bucket.

The smelt fishing is hot here on New York's Lake Champlain. Here, as on other large North American lakes, little shanty cities spring up in winter. Some even have names — and mayors!

Efficient fishing is the second basic reason people use ice shelters. It is convenient to leave tip-ups, jigging rods, floats and other equipment in an ice house rather than transporting all that gear out to the ice every time you fish. A well-designed shelter has shelves and drawers so gear is easy to find and put into use.

The shelters of serious fishermen are designed to help catch fish. They might have sonar units with transducers mounted on articulated arms so they can give true readings. They usually have several set lines (like rattle reels) mounted over the holes. Considerable ingenuity has gone into inventing set lines that signal a fish bite with an alarm, flag, light or — in one case — an LED panel that flashes the number of the particular line that has just been moved by a fish. A good shelter, like a good boat, allows an angler to operate efficiently.

Yet there are reasons for not using shelters. The first and most obvious is cost. While shelters aren't terribly expensive, they aren't free. Typical costs run from $200 for a two-person portable shelter to $800 or higher for the more deluxe commercial shelters and home-built shanties. Ice fishing is generally the least fussy and expensive form of angling. Some anglers want to keep it that way.

A second problem is vandalism. Shanties left on the ice are vulnerable to malicious vandalism and theft. It is virtually impossible to protect unattended shanties against thieves with crowbars and bolt-cutters. This problem seems to vary enormously by region.

Then, too, an ice shelter might be more trouble than it is worth to some anglers. In many states or provinces you have to license any shelter left on the ice. Plywood shanties require a certain amount of maintenance each year, plus the effort of moving them out and bringing them back. For some anglers, these tasks are a pleasant annual ritual; for others, they are a headache.

Perhaps the strongest argument against semi-permanent shanties that are left in place all season is the loss of fishing mobility. Few summertime anglers would be content to fish the same identical spot and nowhere else all year, yet that is just what many ice anglers do. Throughout the ice season, fish schools move. If you are fishing from a heavy shanty that is a hassle to move, you have traded comfort and convenience for fishing effectiveness. How badly that limits your fishing depends on what species you fish for and on what lake. But if you are serious about fishing, you should put a higher priority on the mobility of your shelter than on roominess and creature comforts.

HOME-BUILT OR STORE BOUGHT?

In the past, if you wanted a shelter you built yourself a shanty. Now, quite a few companies offer well-designed portable shelters. Which is better for you?

If you like to fish with several partners, you'll probably prefer a plywood shanty. Similarly, if you like to stay on the ice all night long, a well-insulated plywood shanty offers you enough space for a heater, sleeping bags, bunks and plenty of food.

For toasty warmth and roomy comfort in the coldest weather, a plywood shanty can't be beat. They are substantial. You can lean against the walls. You can hang lanterns or mount set-line reels anywhere you want in them. You can build tackle lockers and shelves for greater efficiency in a plywood shanty.

But most shanties are heavy, which means they can only be safely used when the ice is thick. A typical plywood shanty might weigh from 400 to 700 pounds, and some are much heavier than that. On some lakes, you can count on having thick ice several months each winter. Other lakes never develop enough ice to support a heavy wooden shanty.

If you fish alone or with one partner, a tent-type portable shelter might suffice. Such small shelters are easy to keep warm; usually body heat, a lantern, or a tiny propane heater will do the trick. Some portable shelters are even large enough for four anglers to fish from at once.

But the most important advantage of portable shelters is — of course — portability! They are easy to get on the lake and off again. They can be moved around on the lake to chase the best fishing, which means you can easily fish four or five locations in a day rather than just one. Whereas you might need a 4WD vehicle to move a plywood shanty, a portable shelter can be stowed in the trunk of a passenger car.

And you can drag a portable shelter on a sled over ice to locations where you couldn't safely drive any kind of vehicle, even a snowmobile. This portability is particularly useful if you mean to fish a lake covered with a great deal of snow. The "first ice" and "last ice" seasons can feature great fishing and a relief from the hubbub of internal combustion motors, but only a light portable shelter can be used at these special times.

Price is usually not much of a consideration. A quality portable shelter and a well-built homemade shanty cost more or less the same. People who think they can build a shanty cheaply are often surprised at how all the "little" stuff — hinges, wiring, locks, etc. — adds up. You might be able to build a shanty cheaply if you have access to free or inexpensive materials, but that isn't the usual situation.

BUILDING YOUR OWN

The two central issues when designing a plywood shanty are size and portability.

To decide how big your shelter should be, consider how many people — realistically — will be using it at once. A shelter with a 4-foot x 8-foot floor is only big enough for a pair of anglers. Four anglers need a shelter something like 8 feet by 8 feet. Remember, too, the bigger your shelter, the more heat you'll need to make it cozy.

Right from the start you need to consider how you'll move your home-built shanty around. Once it is on the ice, a shelter can usually be dragged about on runners (some anglers like to face their runners with metal for durability and easier travel). But unless you live on or very close to the lake, you can't just drag the shanty. To get there, you need wheels.

A full-sized pickup truck has a bed big enough to take a 4 x 8-foot plywood sheet, so some shanties are built to that floor size. Others are

A snowmobile or (as shown here) an ATV is a popular way of getting back and forth to one's shanty.

built with a 4 x 8 floor, but with walls moved out to a more generous dimension above the height of the pickup walls (just like a camper topper that fits over a pickup). These shanties obviously aren't very roomy, but they can be lifted onto a truck and driven to the lake.

The most popular way to move a larger plywood shanty to the lake is to jack it up and run a flat-bed trailer underneath. The process is reversed when the shanty is out on the ice in the desired location, and now has to be taken home.

Other shanties incorporate axles and wheels as part of the permanent assembly. To move them, you tip them onto the side with the wheels and then attach a hitch tongue to the car or truck. In effect, these shelters have a trailer built right into them and need the usual wiring and safety lights. Trailerable shelters should be designed with a low profile so they don't present any more "drag" than is necessary when on the highway. Some trailerable shanties feature retractable wheels.

Most shanties are built of ¼-inch plywood, with ½- to ¾-inch plywood floors. Because plywood is sold in 4 x 8 panels, shanties are typically designed to make the most efficient use of that size panel. The usual framing material is 2 x 4 lumber, though 2 x 2 framing can be used on the ceilings and side walls because they don't receive much stress. The floor frame takes almost all the heavy abuse, so it needs to be strong. Floors are built with openings for fishing, but remember that if a hole is too close to a wall, opening it up each time with a power auger can be difficult. Most shanties have removable plywood panels that fit over the holes. If a particular hole isn't being used, the panel makes that spot usable as floor space.

Plywood shanties need to be insulated unless they are very small. The most popular insulation is polystyrene beadboard. Poly panels can be fitted between frame members and glued to the walls. Insulation is especially important on the ceiling and beneath the floor.

To brighten up the interior, some shanty roofs are made with translucent fiberglass roofing material. Windows let in light and are even legally required in some states.

Quite a few home-built shanties incorporate lightweight products built for use in motor homes and campers. Many shanties use windows designed for campers or pickup toppers, for example. Camper doors are ideal for shanties. Other camper or topper products popular with shanty builders are ventilation grills, skylights, lights and other 12-volt electrical accessories. Another example: Camper accessory catalogs carry hardware that allows a dining room table to be mounted in a recessed floor fitting or removed when not needed.

Boats also require lightweight and simple fixtures and use 12-volt electrical systems. Boats, like campers and ice shelters, need to make the best use of limited space, so marine accessory catalogs are almost as useful as camper accessory catalogs for the shanty builder looking for practical lights, windows, vents and other products.

Every shelter that will be heated with some kind of stove or heater needs to be vented. A stove burning in an air-tight shelter will consume the available oxygen, which is dangerous. A number of anglers who failed to ventilate their shanties have died of asphyxiation. Ventilation can take many forms. Many shanties have a small aluminum vent near the top of the house, perhaps with another small one positioned near the floor. Windows and doors can be used for venting, too.

Another safety concern is fires. If you use a stove with a chimney, the chimney must pass through the wall or ceiling in a way that won't create a fire hazard.

BLOCKING A SHANTY

Once a plywood shanty is brought to its fishing location, it needs to be blocked. That is, it should be lifted by hand or with crowbars so a number of small blocks (usually short 2 x 4 sections) can be slipped between the frame and the ice.

An unblocked shanty will gather solar heat, melt the ice near the frame and often become frozen into the ice. A frozen-in shanty sometimes cannot be freed from the ice without it being destroyed. Often the shanty gets torn off the floor frame which is locked in the ice. In spring, these frames float about where they can damage boats. Don't let this be the fate of your shanty.

When you remove yours, try to retrieve the blocks so they, too, don't litter the lake.

BUYING A PORTABLE SHELTER

The most common type of portable shelter is the pop-up tent. Pop-ups are variations of the tents used by summer campers and are often made by companies that produce summer tents. Some feature canvas fabric, while others use nylon or other materials. Some have floors and some do not; those that don't might blow away unless you take the trouble of anchoring them to the ice. Special stakes called ice anchors are commercially made expressly for portable ice fishing shelters.

The major issue is whether or not the portable shelter you are looking at will be big enough. How many anglers will use it? If you jig, will there be room to manipulate your jig rod? Will there be room for a sonar unit, if you use one? Where will you put a lantern or propane heater, if you need one?

Don't buy a portable shelter without spending some time inside one that has been set up. Place a few chairs or ice buckets around to get a good idea of how many people could fish in comfort. Think about the gear you ordinarily fish with, and consider whether or not there will be room for it in the shelter. Remember that you might be able to keep some gear just outside the portable shelter within easy reach.

Think about lighting, too. Are there enough windows? Some portable shelters have inadequate windows or even none at all. Traditionally, portable shelters have been made of black fabric for warmth, but a few now feature panels of lighter fabric that make the interior brighter. Are the windows placed where you can monitor a tip-up outside the shelter while you are fishing inside?

How convenient is the door? Some doors can be fastened in an open or semi-open position; two-way zippers offer more flexibility in this regard. With a door open or partially open, you can let fresh air and light in. In some cases, you can leave gear outside the shelter but still reach it through an open door. But some portable shelter doors are designed so they almost have to be zipped shut when in use.

Ask the sales person to demonstrate how easily the portable shelter can be erected. Are there any small parts that could get lost? How well will the knocked-down shelter fit in your vehicle? Does it form a compact package that can be dragged on the ice like a sled?

There are several indications of quality workmanship that you should check for. How substantial is the fabric? Are the main points

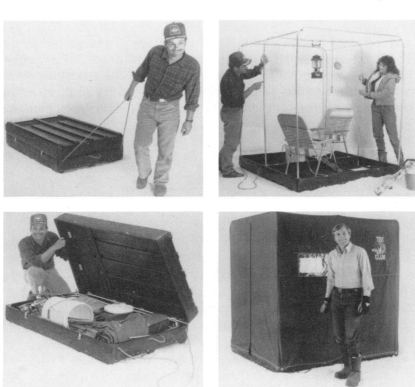

The Clam, a popular portable shelter: (1) Drag it out like a sled, (2) open the box, (3) pop up the frame, (4) secure the fabric and you're ready to fish.

of wear reinforced? Does the shelter include a floor, or is that something you'll need to provide? How sturdy and well designed is it? Some of the better portable shelters now have heat vents, or windows that can be opened to vent heat.

Ask about the warranty the maker offers. Try to buy from a manufacturer who has been in business several years and who has a record of standing behind its products.

Let's talk about three models of portable shelters to suggest the range of products available.

Canvas Plus offers a line of fabric shelters in several sizes. Quality touches include air vents fitted with Velcro fasteners near the peak of the tent, a two-way zipper, and a generous number of windows. An unusual feature is the availability of different fabric colors, including yellow. A yellow shelter is bright inside even without a lantern. If you fish at night, a yellow shelter glows to make your shelter visible to any snowmobilers zooming around in the dark.

A distinctive and popular portable shelter is The Clam. Disassembled, The Clam looks like a big flat polyethylene suitcase. This rugged outer case can be dragged along the ice without hurting the tent, which is protected inside. You can even store fishing gear inside. The "suitcase" opens to form the floor of the shelter. The fabric shelter, permanently attached to the floor, erects quickly. The Clam comes in sizes appropriate for a single angler or as many as four.

The Fish Trap is an unusual shelter that offers ice anglers the mobility of summer anglers. It is basically a sled that can be dragged by hand or with a snowmobile to the fishing location. Compartments hold ice fishing gear, and the sled is high enough to form a comfortable seat. In warm weather, you fish in the open. If you need protection, a tent-like shelter flips up out of the Fish Trap and drops around you. The ultimate system for serious anglers might include a Fish Trap behind a snowmobile, a sonar unit and a Loran-C unit for finding specific fish-holding structure. Both The Clam and The Fish Trap are now distributed by U.S.L. Products, Inc. (see Appendix).

SHELTER REGULATIONS

Since shelter regulations vary from state to state and province to province, you should study your own municipality's regulations. If you're in a hurry, call a conservation officer or the enforcement office of your DNR to learn what the current regulations are.

Some examples:

1. In most states, or provinces, the name of the owner must be prominently displayed on the shelter.
2. Some states or provinces require shelters left on the ice to display a special license.
3. Some states or provinces have regulations as to how late into the season an ice shelter may be left out.
4. Because conservation officers need access to shelters to check fishing licenses and so forth, it is usually illegal to lock a shelter door from the inside.
5. Shelters that have axles and wheels built in must meet safety standards for trailers.
6. Some states or provinces have regulations requiring shelters to have windows (so they cannot be used as spearing dark houses).

EQUIPPING A SHELTER

Every angler has a personal list of items that "must" be included to make a shelter complete. There's no need to record all the possibilities here; you know whether or not a shelter would seem barren without a deck of cards. But there are some general issues that we can talk about usefully. Most of these tips relate to plywood shanties, though a few apply equally to portable shelters.

You will need a source of illumination in any sort of shelter except spearing dark houses (which are legal in relatively few places). The least expensive illumination is daylight. Windows, translucent fiberglass panels, and skylights are all low-cost ways to brighten up a shelter interior.

Or you might want to use a lantern. Since battery-powered lanterns quickly fail in cold weather and are expensive to use, many anglers prefer the white gas lanterns so popular with summer campers. They can be hard to pump up when they are cold, but these lanterns cast a cheery light and are the only source of heat needed in small or well-insulated shelters. They are effective as a source of both heat and light in portable shelters.

A more deluxe light source is a fixed electric light. These are often found in plywood shanties. Most popular are 12-volt lights designed

Customizing your shanty is the fun part. This shipshape fish house has 8 holes for jigging, a small kerosene heater, and plenty of storage space.

for use in campers or boats. If you mean to run a television and other electrical accessories, you might want to put a portable generator on the ice (usually outside the shelter, to minimize noise). These generate a regular household current, but they are hardly necessary. Many inexpensive television sets run off 12-volt systems.

All in all, the most popular power source for electrical accessories is a 12-volt wet cell battery. Some anglers bring a 12-volt battery out each day and connect it to power leads in their shanties. Others park their vehicles close to the shelter and run power leads inside to drive electrical accessories. For simplicity's sake, it makes sense to use a single, well-designed system. A 12-volt system can power lights, fans (good for distributing the heat in a shelter), electric augers, television sets, Loran-C units, bait bucket aerators and sonar equipment.

Most shelters need a heat source. The favorite with ice anglers is the propane heater. Many shelters use the portable type which has a heating element mounted directly on top of a disposable or refillable propane tank. Larger, more deluxe shelters often have large, refillable propane tanks mounted outside, connected with hoses to propane lights, heating units, and cook stoves inside.

In general, you should maximize precious internal space when equipping a shanty. Build dining tables and bunks so they fold up into the walls when not needed. Consider building tackle lockers up high where they don't take up floor space. A propane tank or 12-volt battery mounted on an outside wall can work for you without hogging space.

SHANTY FANTASIES

People build shanties, we've noted, primarily for comfort and greater fishing efficiency. But for some anglers, shanties aren't just a fishing aid but a sort of playhouse or club house for grown-ups.

Designing, building and decorating shanties is an American folk art. Many people delight in creating shanties that are uniquely theirs and which represent their ingenuity. A person of modest means who could never afford a dream home with a lake view can, in winter, enjoy a luxurious ice shelter on the best lake in the area. For many anglers, shelters are a home away from home where they can escape the nagging cares of the world.

Anglers in regions with long ice seasons often get carried away in their quest to build the ultimate shanty. The more elegant models feature carpeted floors, walls finished with wood panelling, curtains on the windows, full electric power, complete kitchens, Porta-Potties, bunk beds, a color television, plus a premium quality sound system.

So far, nobody I know has equipped a shelter with a hot tub or cable television. But almost surely, somebody is trying to figure out how. In one luxurious shelter, if you put your hand in a certain place a cold beer automatically rolls down into it. You have to open the beer yourself.

CHAPTER 8

Using Your Head to Stay Warm

YOU'VE JUST ABOUT finished the last lap. If you counted right, it's the 16th time around the oval at your old high school track, and that means you've racked up four miles today.

As you come off the cinders you're breathing hard, but it feels good, and you reach for a towel draped over the railing in front of the bleachers.

One of your old buddies from school comes along, walking the dog and with a midriff protrusion that makes it pretty clear he couldn't do 16 laps around the track.

"Getting in shape for deer season?" he asks. He's a hunter, too.
"No — ice fishing," you reply.

His dog doesn't break stride and while he is a little curious he shuffles along on his way. He never bothers to ask just what in God's name running around a track is going to do for an ice fisherman.

There is no doubt that strenuous exercise is good for everyone who doesn't already have some severe affliction that prevents exercise. There is no doubt, either, that you can only be a better fisherman and hunter by keeping yourself in shape. But what, specifically, will vigorous aerobic exercise do for the serious ice fisherman?

Early morning routines and long days under brutal conditions will turn almost anyone into chopped meat, but you'll be much better able to take it if you exercise. Why? Foremost, your body will be "tuned up" and will process the food you give it correctly. Two end results of combustion (metabolism) are energy and heat. People who exercise regularly will, in general, stay warmer on the ice than people who don't.

Another benefit of regular exercise is that it helps you to do with less sleep. With your cardiovascular system better developed, you will simply be tired less of the time. You'll be able to fish harder and still have energy to spare at the end of the day.

Vigorous exercise will help you to sleep better. If you're already the relaxed sort — and sleep is nothing but effective relaxation — exercise will only help. If aspects of your life are making you tense, disturbing your sleep patterns and making getting up for those ice fishing trips all the harder, regular exercise could help enormously.

THE FOOD YOU EAT

I think every outdoors person could learn a few lessons from the serious backpacker. Because of the combination of extremely strenuous exercise and extreme limitations in what can be brought along, these people tend to become experts on eating for energy. They know more about carbohydrates, fats and proteins than many clinicians, and the better ones know just what to eat at what stage of the day. You, the ice fisherman, can stay warmer by eating the right foods. More importantly, you can stay healthy, and that will make your outdoor excursions all the more fun.

Most people know that carbohydrates (sugars and starches) yield quick bursts of energy over a short period of time while protein and fats yield energy over a more protracted period of time. But I'm not one of those who thinks that it's a great idea to nibble on highly processed snack foods all day long. I believe that a high percentage of the food in one's diet should be raw fruits, raw vegetables and even raw, uncooked grains (which can be soaked to soften them). An ice fisherman can get that quick-energy sugar very effectively from fruit. High sugar fruits like figs, dried apricots and especially dates will give you both sugar and starch in a natural, unprocessed state. Dried fruits like apples, pears, bananas and oranges are also excellent to munch on most of the day.

Because not all foods combine well, the ideal thing is to progress from simpler foods to more complex foods during the day. Fruit is best when eaten by itself, and preferably in the morning. You'll digest it in an hour or so and then your stomach will be ready to accept more complicated foods. About noontime I like a peanut butter sandwich, on dark bread and slathered with cream-style honey. I reason that the honey will help give me a shot of energy, in unprocessed form, that will help to warm me for the afternoon. The peanut butter will provide some protein as well as fat and this kind of sandwich will not get soggy as will cold cut sandwiches.

On long days, especially when it's very windy and cold, we increase our food intake. On those brutal days you will be hungrier and you should plan on that. We like to bring some venison sausage and crackers on some days.

What about the traditional cook-out on the ice? We do it a few times a year, and some thoughts on that topic may be found in Chapter 17.

The importance of hot drinks cannot be stressed enough. A cup of homemade chicken or turkey broth can provide some immediate warming, and that can be especially important when you've taken on a chill. A hot drink can "bring you back" the way even "rush foods" like sugared products cannot.

COVERING UP THE EXTREMITIES

Perhaps the most important piece of stay-warm equipment is the hat. Some say that at least 50% of all heat loss is through the head, so doesn't it make sense to give the head the most attention in winter?

I'm amazed at how few people use a ski mask when it's really cold. If you doubt how well it works, put one on and wear it for an hour, then take it off. It will be like someone turned on the air conditioning. Granted, a ski mask, which has openings only for the eyes and mouth, will blot out your senses to a fair degree. This will seldom be a problem in ice fishing, though. A balaclava, which is a cross between a hat and a ski mask, exposes more of your face, but would be an excellent choice for someone who feels just too confined inside a ski mask.

I might use the ski mask only every three trips, and even then I'll likely wear it only part of the day — the coldest or windiest part. But it will always be in my coat's back pocket, or in the truck.

Being a long-time outdoor writer, I have of course often appeared in photos accompanying my articles and books. I've had people look

Use your head to stay warm. A ski mask is all you need.

at these photos and say, "You still have on that same hat you had on 15 years ago!" They're referring to a red, white and blue watch cap that I put on in October and pretty much leave in place until about May first. On an Adirondack ice fishing trip, one buddy was pretty impressed that I never took the hat off once in three days, not even in the bunk at night.

I like the watch cap since it can be rolled up or down slightly to make you a little warmer or a little cooler. I like having this kind of thermostatic control, and few other hats give it to you. It's the same reason why I like zippered as opposed to buttoned outer or middle garments. So much more adjustment is possible. I have about six or seven of these watch caps, which some people refer to as stocking caps. Mine are not the real bulky ones that rise up off your head in a pyramid. The ones I like sit right on your head all around and really match the old sailors' watch caps. When the ski mask comes off, it's certain that my watch cap will go on.

Sportsmen seem to take better care of their feet, because feet tend to "get cold" whereas the head, except for the ears, doesn't really get cold but does invisibly squander away all that precious heat to make your whole body cold.

The way I see it, there are four categories of boots that an ice fisherman might choose from. I have a pair of boots from each of three of those categories.

On very wet days, as when it's raining or the snow on the ice is melting, I like all rubber boots ten inches high. The brand name I use is Red Ball. The ones I like are insulated, but these are still not especially warm boots. Yet it stands to reason that if it is wet on the ice, it can't be very cold. I find that the warmer boots I'll describe, even if rubber bottomed, will slowly let in moisture when you're wading through puddles all day long. The rubber boots, in these conditions, are superb.

The second kind of boot is the boot I recommend when it's moderately warm — 25 degrees F (-4°C) and up — and the ice is dry: the rubber-bottomed, leather-topped "pac." My choice in this category is the L.L. Bean Maine Hunting Shoe, in the insulated model (no felt liners). This edition of that venerable boot is both stronger and warmer than the standard Maine Hunting Shoe, and I use it for bird hunting as well as for medium temperature ice fishing. It has a chain tread that grips the ice surprisingly well, even though it was not specifically designed for this purpose. I treat the uppers on these boots with a product called Sno Proofing. So treated, the leathers are water resistant but they will of course let in some moisture on a very wet day.

In the third category should fall the boot for most ice fishermen under most conditions. This is the felt-lined boot, such as the Sorel company has helped to make popular. In essence, you have a pac with rubber bottoms and leather tops, but inside that shell goes a set of thick felt liners that can come out for drying. Get an extra set of liners when you buy the boots. If you fish two days in a row, the felts may not dry out completely overnight. In fact, if they get real wet they could take a few days to dry out. Then, too, on a long day trip, you might be wise to tote the extra liners in case conditions are really sloppy that day.

My approach to clothing for the outdoors parallels my overall approach to fishing and hunting gear: I like to carry, or wear, as little as I can get away with at any given time. I will always wear the much lighter boots when I can, but the felt-lined boots work extremely well and I use them in temperatures ranging from zero F (-18°C) to about 25 or 30 degrees F (-4° to -1°C).

I do not care to fish when it's below zero F mainly because we almost always fish in the open. The holes freeze up so fast and the mechanics of the sport become so difficult that I have to ask myself if it's really worthwhile.

Fishing out of a shelter is another matter. When I travel to a region where I'm either fishing from a heated shanty or have immediate access to one, below zero temperatures do not scare me. An important thing to remember, though, is that even if you fish from a shelter, you still may spend part of the time out in the open — either out of choice, as you try to find the fish, or out of necessity, as when you are coming and going, or setting up a portable shelter. That leads us to the last type of boot, the one you should consider if you routinely fish when it's below zero and even if you might somehow be employing a shelter.

These extremely warm and extremely heavy boots are typified by the "Mickey Mouse" boots of army issue. In this realm of super warm boots you may see felt liners, or some thicker kind of liners, and they may be augmented by collars of fleece or fur that line the top of the boot and help keep cold air from getting down next to the feet. In many cases, these boots are a few inches higher than standard cold weather boots. For example, in the Maine Hunting Shoe mentioned above, I like the 10-inch model. Ditto for the felt-lined boot. But were I ever to purchase one of these super-warm boots, I would opt for one that was at least 12 inches high.

Some of these very warm boots you even pump air into for greater insulation.

Always bring an extra pair of laces for your boots. Leave them in the glove compartment or the console, but have them along.

Gloves are at least as personal as any other item of clothing. Since I've never seen anyone set a tip-up with their feet, I operate on the basis that hands are even more important than feet in the keeping-warm category. Thus, whatever choice or choices you make here, they should be well considered.

Just as I keep a ski mask in the back pocket of my coat, so too do I keep a pair of mittens. I have a light pair for easy days and a much warmer pair for tough days.

The light pair was designed for cross country skiers. In fact, I use them for skiing. It has a nylon back and leather palms. It has some kind of not too warm shaggy lining. Because of the good gripping palms, these mittens are excellent for early morning hole cutting and for dragging gear on and off the ice.

The heavier pair cost around $40 and are down insulated. They have finger slits, which are very convenient. Needless to say, these mittens are extremely warm.

By the time I've cut the holes, I'm about ready to take the mittens off. They go into the back pocket of the coat and at that point I put on the very ordinary gloves that I wear for the rest of the day. These cost a big $5 a pair and I buy them three or four pair at a time. They're made of a combination of cotton and synthetic, and they're very soft to the feel. They absorb water like a sponge, but since I always have a few extra pair in the truck and usually an extra pair on the ice, I don't worry about them getting wet. I'm simply comfortable with these camouflage color gloves and wear them for deer hunting, small game hunting at times, ice fishing, snow shoveling and you name it. They're not practical but I like them, and your choice in gloves might similarly be steered by such irrational thought.

On a good crisp day, I'll sometimes go back to the mittens if there's a lot of standing around and little tip-up action. Because of the palm slits, I can operate a jig pole with the down mittens, although if I hook a big fish I quickly get those mittens off. This points up the importance of having lots of pockets in the outer garments, something touched on below. You can put things on and off at will, as circumstances dictate.

An interesting question is this: For what operations do you take the gloves off? I can jig and play a fish on the jig rod with my

Some ice anglers prefer gloves without fingertips, so they can perform the fine tasks the sport often demands.

somewhat clunky gloves, but handlining a fish that's taken a tip-up bait is out of the question. I always remove my gloves when tending a flag. The polypropylene gloves that have gained such favor in recent years are much more sensitive and many more operations could be done with these gloves on.

BODY GARMENTS

While the extremities are of paramount importance, body garments are only slightly less important. First, what will you place immediately next to your skin?

Here, again, synthetics have made strong inroads on the cotton and wool garments of yesteryear. Multiple-layer fabric like Gore-Tex is designed to wick moisture away from the skin, and thus allow the evaporation (and cooling) to take place one layer removed from the skin. The inner layer is usually polypropylene, which will not itself absorb moisture but which will transfer body perspiration to an outer cotton layer. This type of underwear has become extremely popular among people who do strenuous forms of outdoor exercise in winter. Hunters, cross country skiers and yes ice fishermen, have solidly embraced this technology.

There are two possible drawbacks, however. One, this generation of longjohns is much more expensive. And two, not everyone likes the feel of polypropylene next to the skin. As for me, I don't like anything clinging tightly to any part of my carcass, so I had a built in negative bias when this material came along. I used to wear the old, pure cotton "waffle" longjohns, but I never liked them and I still don't. On warmer days, I avoid long underwear bottoms and I never wear long underwear tops. But on colder days, I do use longjohn bottoms and the brand I like is Duofold.

If I frequently ice fished in very cold climes, I would use quilted thermal underwear both top and bottom. Some of these incorporate Gore-Tex and/or Thinsulate but all have some kind of filling for greatly increased warmth. A few decades ago, such underwear was typically filled with down. Now, many people argue for the synthetic filling, and that is mostly what you will have to choose from in quilted long underwear.

On the "loose is better" theory on which I always operate, a combination I have found that I like goes like this:

Cotton t-shirt
Flannel shirt
Down-filled vest
Cotton, zippered sweatshirt with hood

This is a layer system at its best, and is ideal in moderate weather. The sweatshirt easily comes off. So does the vest (with the sweatshirt often going back on).

Now, what about coats? A coat is, indeed, what I use, as opposed to a one or two piece snowmobile suit, and the coat is what goes over the other, lighter layers on very cold days. As I've said, I'm averse to tight fitting clothing and those jump suits fall into that category for me. Nonetheless, in a very cold region I would wear a two-piece jump suit consisting of bib 'n' overalls and a coat.

I rely on two types of coats. One is my wool deer hunting coat. The main reason I like this is that it has lots of pockets, including a large back pocket where I store my mittens and ski mask. It also has handwarmer slash pockets, four flap pockets in front and another pocket inside. Those pockets really come in handy in ice fishing. I wear this coat over the other things I've mentioned when it's very cold, say below 15°F (-9°C).

My lighter coat has a nylon shell, a pure wool lining, a hood, and just as many pockets as the deer hunting coat. Like the deer coat, if it's used in conjunction with the other body garments it's good down to zero F and below. The nylon shell of this Woolrich coat is very wind resistant, unlike the deer coat. The hood is also nice but I prefer to use the hood on the sweatshirt since it wraps around my head more neatly and more comfortably.

Warm pants are nice to have even if you do go the jump suit route. I use only wool and have two different weights. I like the green "Johnson Guide Pants" on most days. They're pure wool but not too heavy. They cost around $35 at present. The other pair is also pure wool and these are sometimes called "Malone Pants." They're substantially heavier and cost more like $50. I only use them when it's really cold.

In either case, a brisk wind will go through these pants. Longjohn underwear is essential on such days, especially when you're not wearing a jump suit over the whole thing.

You can see that dressing is part science and part art, but I'd say it's more of the latter. I'm totally sold on the layer approach, and rare indeed is the day when I'm not taking garments off and putting them back on again. Those plastic buckets described in other chapters are most useful in keeping your garments high and dry and away from the often sloppy carpet of the ice.

CHAPTER 9

How a Lake Changes in Winter

IF ICE IS MAGICAL IN A POETIC SENSE, it is also one of the wonders of science. Here you have a compound, H_2O, that contracts as it gets colder, but then — magically enough — begins to expand again when it reaches about 39 degrees F (4°C). But what if the Great Ice Fisherman had not designed it this way? If water kept contracting as it got colder, the rule for most substances, ice (if it would still be called that) would sink and the lake would quickly freeze from the bottom up, killing most life and certainly all fish life as we know it.

In the Gaea of the planet, the molecule that covers 75% of our planet is most cooperative. It makes books such as this one possible.

THE CURTAIN FALLS
The most obvious change in a lake, then, is the appearance of the ice itself, a dramatic curtain that ends one act in the life of the lake but begins another one of equal fascination. It's all governed by temperatures, of course.

In autumn, the distinct temperature zones that formed in late spring or summer are subject to the "fall turn-over." Usually from about June onward, those zones existed because their varying densities kept them from "mixing." Now, though, cool autumn weather chills the top layer so that its temperature and thus density is not much different from the zone below it. (In a classical scenario, before turn-over there will be a top, warm water layer or epilimnion; a middle transition layer or thermocline, where the temperature drops rapidly; and a bottom cold water layer or hypolimnion. In reality, there is enormous variation in how lakes stratify.)

With the temperatures and thus densities of a lake's layers now more equalized, much more mixing is possible. Eventually, after the turn-over, a lake's temperature may vary little from top to bottom. (Again, depending greatly on the lake.) For example, much of the lake's water may be around 41 – 45 degrees F (5° – 7°C).

The surface water will continue to cool, and when the uppermost layer reaches about 39 degrees F (4°C) — the densest water can be — the molecules in that layer will sink through the warmer, less dense molecules below. Through convection, those warmer molecules will then rise up. This is why, in so many lakes in winter, the very bottom layer of water will be 39° F. This could remain the case for several months. In very cold or unusually deep lakes, it could remain this way year-round.

It is not until the entire water column is chilled to a sufficient depth that the surface water can begin its march downward from 39 to 32 degrees, below which it must freeze. It should be noted that 32°F or 0°C is often called the "point of equilibrium." Above that, ice melts, below it, water freezes. However, the freezing point for salt water of average salinity is 28°F or -2°C. (Shipwreck victims take note: Salt water ice that's been out of contact with the sea for a while is virtually salt-free!)

When ice first forms on a lake, almost always on a still, cold night, the water undergoes a rapid crystalization process and expands by about 10%. It will now easily float on the substantially denser liquid water below it.

As you proceed downward in the water column, the temperature at this time will rise slowly, often from 32° – 39°F. However, the bottom or other levels of the water column could still be in the low forties, typically 40° or 41°F (5°C). It's significant to note that even a one or two degree difference, say from 39° – 40°F (4°C) can be enough to create a layer effect. Herein lies a great uncharted area in ice fishing: Will fish relate to these very subtle temperature breaks in winter the way they relate to the much more pronounced temperature breaks in summer? For example, let's say in a 60-foot-deep lake the water in winter is 34°F (1°C) from 30 feet all the way down to 60 feet where there is a comparatively large break to 36°F (2°C). Might they relate to this zone of change as some species would to a thermocline in summer?

When ice does form, it can thicken amazingly fast in extreme weather. One day you can have an open lake and, with sub-zero temperatures that night, you can have a solid covering of black ice the next day. It's unlikely but possible to be fishing a sandbar from a boat one day then through the ice the next.

All North American ice fishing species can easily tolerate water ranging from 32°F to 42°F (0° – 5°C). Thus, temperature in winter should not be a problem to them. Some species, smallmouth bass for example, seem to curtail greatly their activities, especially in a deep winter. Others, like largemouth bass, seem to become more lethargic. Still others like pike, yellow perch and lake trout seem to remain nearly as active as in summer. Cold blooded, all these species adapt in varying degrees to the colder water.

If anything, winter unchains fish. They can more freely roam into areas or lake levels where they could not even exist in summer. You can almost hear the fish saying, "Whew! That's one less thing we have to worry about for a few months."

THE OXYGEN FACTOR

Oxygen is another matter. Fish need stable amounts of it. It can be a Waterloo for some fish in some lakes in winter.

There are three primary ways that a lake is replenished with the oxygen that is consumed by fish and any other animals (or bacteria) within the lake that utilize oxygen: from tributary streams, from contact with the air, and from the photosynthesis of plants. The formation of ice shuts the second of these down completely, and the third substantially. Early in the season when the ice is clear, photosynthesis, especially in the shallows, may continue almost normally. But as soon as the ice becomes cloudy or snow covered, the photosynthesis is greatly and quickly curtailed. Nonetheless, it's been my experience that aquatic vegetation can survive some very opaque or deeply snow-covered ice. The good "green weed" that we prefer to see to the dead "brown weed" seems to persist very late into winter, especially in the shallows. As an example, we fished two Adirondack lakes on successive days this past season. The dates were March 10-

11. Each lake was snow-covered and each had about two feet of ice. Yet we found many areas of clean-looking weed in each lake. In a shallow (4 to 8 foot) bay of one of the lakes, the bottom was covered with thick, still alive weed. In that bay, I took a 3-pound largemouth on a jig pole. We also took several other largemouths of one to two and a half pounds. Later in the day, we caught more than two dozen crappies, plus some sunfish, in the deepest part of the lake (30 feet), where oxygen depletion is supposed to be most likely to occur.

Had winter killed this very tightly sealed-off lake? Hardly.

I know of some relatively shallow ponds in the Finger Lakes region of New York where documented winter fish kills have occurred. But there's a world of difference between a 15-acre, five-foot-deep lake and one that's a hundred acres or more and 25 or 35 feet deep. I believe that the winter kills you hear about are relatively uncommon. And that when this phenomenon does strike, it's almost always in a relatively small, shallow pond.

A large lake is well buffered from oxygen deficit in winter. First, as we stated, when the ice is clear as it usually is early in the season, photosynthesis continues. In water less than 20 feet deep, it may continue to some extent right through the winter. If the lake is fed by streams, that will also bring in much oxygen. Another source of oxygen is that which is stored in the lake and its sediments before the onset of winter. Cold water is capable of storing greatly more oxygen than is warm water, so in a large lake, tremendous amounts of oxygen will already have been stored up before the ice forms.

Of course, both early and late in the season, there may be open areas and this will allow oxygenation by contact with the air. Since about 10% of ice floats above the water level, any water lying on top of the ice will rush into whatever holes or fissures exist. These may be natural holes or those created by fishermen themselves. Particularly late in the season, there may be rotten or open areas, and this will promote re-oxygenation.

All this helps explain a great truth of ice fishing: First ice and last ice are best. Shortage of oxygen may be a problem to some degree in some winter lakes, but it is surely least a problem during early and late ice.

LIGHT PENETRATION

My partners and I have found that the times of day that fish feed do not change much, if at all, in winter. First, understand that in the

The more you know about a winter lake, the more fish will be piled up in front of you.

daytime it may not be that dark down there. A lot of light gets through ice until it gets very thick and snow covered, perhaps keeping fish on or close to their normal routine.

All my life I've been a stormy weather fisherman. I hole up like a woodchuck in summer until a heavy rain washes my favorite stream clean of its July torpor. Then I don my waders and head on down to some of the best trout fishing of the entire year.

Lakes are no different. Push a cold front through, with huge, billowing dark clouds, add a light-refracting surface chop, and you have the fixings for another type of good day. That time just before the front comes (about eight hours, I think) as well as during the stormy passing of the front, is often the best time to fish. Conversely, the first few days of that big, blue, high pressure system with it's sunny skies has usually meant the worst fishing for me.

I don't find ice fishing to be much different. I like that gloomy, still period before a storm has arrived. I like to fish during a drizzle or during light snow, or sometimes snow squalls. Almost without exception, gloomy skies portend better ice fishing on my lakes.

An important aspect of gloomy weather is that it seems to extend the feeding periods of crepuscular (dawn – dusk) fish later into the morning and earlier into the afternoon. As an example, the white perch almost always hit best in very late afternoon on the winter lakes in my area. But on a gloomy day, not necessarily precipitating, we sometimes start hitting the whites as early as about 2:30 p.m.

As you know, an approaching cold front is not always accompanied by heavy winds. It depends on the speed of the front and the air mass that it is encountering, among other things. I like the quieter fronts, with little wind. I just ache to get out there when it's 28 degrees (-2°C), cloudy, and deathly still, and the person on The Weather Channel is telling me that an Alberta Clipper is heading to my area. On the other hand, very intense storms with heavy snow or rain often prove to be very slow days, although we certainly have fished through them.

WATER CLARITY

When that first film of ice forms on a lake, any particles suspended in the water immediately begin to settle out. And, with wave action reduced to zero, and ambient run-off from the land also reduced to zero or near zero, little in the way of suspended sediments is introduced to a winter lake. This means that a clear lake will become clearer and a normally turbid lake may become startlingly more clear. Naturally, if a lake has a strong tributary entering it, that can be a source of some turbidity. But remember that most streams also run clearer in winter. If snow pack melts early, when a lake still has good ice, tributaries can help to make the lake very milky and off-color. Generally, though, clear water is the rule in winter.

I believe this is one of the reasons why aquatic vegetation persists surprisingly well in some lakes. The sun has to penetrate the ice and any snow that's on top of it, but once that solar energy hits the water, conductivity must be excellent.

Certainly, with greater water clarity comes greater vulnerability to any creature (baitfish or otherwise) that looks like a chocolate covered donut to some other creature.

In summer, gamefish or baitfish may feel comfortable in the often wind-disturbed surface zone. But in the clear, always calm water of winter, the surface zone would seem to have little to recommend it. That's one of the big reasons why I spend most of my time fishing on bottom in winter.

CURRENTS

Currents caused by tributary streams should not drastically change in winter, unless the rate of flow of a particular tributary is greatly altered at this time. Thus, if this type of current is significant in your lake in summer, it's at least reasonable to assume that it might also be in winter. As I've stated elsewhere, I've had surprisingly little luck while ice fishing at tributary entrance points. Why? Let's analyze it a bit.

What does that seemingly appealing current really have to offer the fish? Unless it's a hot-water discharge from a power plant (a very interesting prospect for an ice fisherman), it isn't going to bring in any wellspring of warm water. Most streams in the north country are in the thirties in winter. Tributaries will supply oxygen, but here we get back to my earlier premise that in most lakes, oxygen is not a problem for the fish.

But might not the stream bring in food? What food, I ask? There are few bugs to wash off trees or shrubs. Aquatic insects are relatively inactive. Earthworms are locked up in the frozen ground. Minnows from the stream, if any are washed down, are probably far less significant to the gamefish than is the natural forage in the lake.

Why, then, would a tributary mouth be a good place for a fish to be in winter? A fish will not waste precious energy fighting a current unless there is some real payoff. I fail to see what that payoff might be during the hard-water period.

In a very small pond, or a seriously eutrophicated (weed choked) small lake, winter oxygen deficit can be very real. Here, fish may mill just under the ice, or they may move to a stream or spring entrance point where oxygen is available. However, they very well may not be feeding much, since stressed fish are known to reduce their intake of food as well as their level of activity. Nonetheless, there is some rationale for seeking out the oxygen-rich current of an incoming stream in a small stillwater where you suspect that oxygen supplies could be tight.

It's true that late in the ice season, some early spring spawners like rainbow trout and walleyes may be drawn to tributary mouths. But other than this, the currents borne of tributary flowage seem to offer little. I can't remember one winter bonanza I've found around the mouth of a tributary, and I must have tried dozens. In many cases, the action near tributaries has been noteworthy for its slowness.

In very large lakes, such as the Great Lakes, immense, powerful currents are set up by prevailing wind patterns and various hydrological features. If such a large lake is totally ice covered, such currents may cease completely. It's logical to me that if, in a large lake, currents are important in summer, the elimination of currents in winter could also be important. For example, certain species that may have moved in schools in or along major currents may be more scattered as they search for food in a large winter lake. A very large lake is almost always a challenging proposition, one that requires as much pre-trip study as possible.

CHAPTER 10

To Understand Fish, Think Like a Human

LET'S SAY THAT YOU'RE AT a picnic on a perfect, summer Sunday afternoon. At 2 p.m., all the food has been prepared and is put out on several tables towards the middle of the park. Two picnic tables pushed together are the focus, and on these two tables go all the meat, salads, and so on. But a couple of tables just off to the side of the main table are also used for food. There's one table for watermelon and another set up with fresh steamed corn.

By 2:15, at least half the people attending the picnic are gathered around the main table. Some are loading up their plates and even taking seconds, while others are grabbing just a fast hot dog. Meanwhile, off at the fringes, a few people are digging into the watermelon and buttered corn.

Yet not all the people at the picnic are located in this "core" area. Some are lingering on the edges, beyond the food tables, and sidling in only often enough to glom a few potato chips. Other people are playing frisbee or strumming guitars and won't even be grabbing a bite until much later in the day. Finally, a few people are elderly or not feeling well and aren't interested in food.

Does this typical day in suburbia have anything to do with ice fishing? Let's use it as an entry point to my personal, #1 rule in fishing.

THINK LIKE A HUMAN

It's clear that no human being has ever really been able to think like a fish, or ever will be able to. But a human can think like a human, and thereby make predictions about what fish are going to do. Fish and people are metabolizing, reproducing organisms with similar (in many ways identical) needs and wants. With this in mind, let's look at that Sunday picnic from a slightly different viewpoint.

It's a thick, lush bed of cabomba weed, located in the middle of a big bay. The bed is about 100 feet square, and outside it, the bay is essentially bare save for a few smaller patches of weeds and a few scattered rocks. The cabomba patch is alive with shrimp, copepods, *Daphnia*, other types of plankton and minnows of every description. Most of the fish in the bay are in or around the weed bed, filling their plate and even taking seconds. A few, though, stay on the fringes, in the minor weed patches, and only sidle up to the "main table" now and again. Others are still further out and won't be eating until much later in the day. Finally....

I think you get the picture.

You can't think like a fish, but you can think, and when you do, you come to see that we really aren't that terribly different from our evolutionary relatives. A fish needs oxygen, food, and a temperature range in which it can survive. So do you. A fish wants safety, comfort, companionship at times, and a member of the opposite sex at times. So do you. You can't put yourself into the head of your quarry, but you can ask yourself how you would act in a given situation. By so doing, you will be going a long way towards fulfilling the great maxim from that ancient book, *The Art of War:* Know your enemy.

SAFETY

Like humans, after oxygen and survivable temperature fish are most concerned with safety — staying out of harm's way to the degree possible. Since like young children fish have not learned to doubt their inner signals, they don't swim around worrying about hurting themselves physically or emotionally. Thus, safety for a fish essentially means safety from predators.

To a wintertime panfish, a predator might be an otter, a mink, a human or, most typically, a large fish. To a wintertime gamefish a predator might be an otter, a mink, a human or, not too infrequently, an even larger gamefish.

Winter or summer there are four primary ways for a fish to avoid becoming a meal: (1) by remaining motionless, and depending on good camouflage; (2) by hiding in or around some physical object; (3) by moving away faster than a predator can or is willing to go; and (4) by moving to an area or depth where the predator, for one reason or another, can't or is not willing to go.

With temperature less of a factor in winter, a fish would appear to have more options in seeking out safety. Yet in many ways, winter also takes away safety options. Weeds die back. Water becomes clearer, negating to a large degree option #1. Wave action is reduced to zero, so a fish cannot possibly hide in a disturbed surface zone.

You might call it a wash, but I'd say there are fewer safety options in winter, based on the above. If there's a conclusion from this for the angler, I think it's that location is even more important in winter than in summer. And that physical objects like rocks, timber, and remaining weed patches loom as even more important to the fish and the fisherman in winter.

THE RULE OF RISKS

A big bass comes up to the surface that it normally shuns to take a juicy frog that has lost its way. A person jumps out of a plane with a parachute on. Risk? Of course. Reward? In the first case, frog lunch. In the second case, thrill. What I'm saying is that fish, like people, will very often risk their safety or comfort to obtain certain rewards. The bottom line here is that fishermen should expect fish to make many, many exceptions to their normal behavior patterns (and make no mistake, those patterns very much exist).

Let's go back to the picnic. There's a cooler full of vanilla ice cream bars but it's being kept well off to the side of the main table so people don't crash into it until later in the afternoon. But an enterprising 12-year-old boy is onto it, and has discovered that there are only about two-thirds as many ice cream bars as there are people. He really wants to make sure he gets his ice cream bar. Risk? Sure. His father is the stern type. Reward? Ice cream bar. So he sneaks away from the crowd, does the dirty deed and then almost certainly hies off to some even farther recess of the park to enjoy the spoils.

In a certain lake, all the fish are always concentrated on two prominent, sunken bars, and that's where all the fishermen always are, too. But one big walleye has discovered that a few nice-sized perch seem to gather in a small, spring-fed bay and he travels the long way down the ice to see if they're there today. Risk? Wasted time and energy, no small consideration in the wilds. Reward? A much bigger meal than the small minnows that the crew on the bar is dining on.

I'm sure you figured it out. One of the fishermen was willing to walk the long ways to the inconspicuous looking bay to set a few tip-ups. The walleye's gamble has backfired. The angler's has paid off in spades.

Fish will take risks. So will good fishermen. This is as true in winter as it is in summer. I don't know how many times I've gone to some strange part of a winter lake and found a glorious concentration of fish. The risk was not catching anything at all, since I had shunned the predictable action on the known hotspot. But the potential reward, even if it only came once in four trips, was always worth it.

When we talk about risk-taking behavior in fish, we aren't just talking about the risking of safety. Anytime a fish leaves an area that it prefers to be, it is taking some kind of risk, even if the loss is only a temporary loss of comfort. But they do it all the time.

That's why "evening feeders" can be and are taken in the day.

Ice fishing is an excellent family pastime.

That's why a trout will be found way out of its preferred temperature zone in summer.

That's why a species that "rarely goes deeper than 40 feet in winter" (quote whatever magazine article you like) is routinely taken at 70 feet in one particular lake.

That's why fish that are supposed to always school may not.

And that's why fishermen should take lots of risks out on that frozen lake.

SPAWNING URGES

If you can't recite when and where your favorite fish spawns, you haven't done your homework. It's true that for some species, the immediate time of the spawn can see fish off their feed. But it's just as true that the pre-spawn and post-spawn periods can be very productive. Pre-spawn fish activity is very much something for the ice angler to consider. Here are some examples:*

Chain pickerel	Spawn in early spring, when water temperature is 47-52°F (8-11°C). Usually 3-10 feet of water.
Northern pike	Spawn immediately after ice-out in shallows, when water temperature is 40-52°F (4-11°C); often in bays, inlet areas, shallow areas, heavily vegetated areas.
Yellow perch	Spawn in very early spring when water temperature is 44-54°F (7-12°C); often near rooted vegetation, submerged brush, fallen trees.
White perch	Spawn primarily in spring when water temperature is 52-59°F (11-15°C); little preference shown as to bottom type.

The single best thing about the pre/post spawn periods is that you can entertain the hope of finding fish more concentrated than usual. These are rarely the candlelit, private affairs of human ritual. More often, privacy is thrown to the wind, and fish sidle up (in some cases) almost fin to fin to perform the ancient rites.

*Spawning data from *Freshwater Fishes of Canada* (Bulletin 184), W. B. Scott and E. J. Crossman (Ottawa, Fisheries Research Board of Canada, 1973)

I used to think that the post-spawn period would be a good time to take brown trout under the ice. Since they most commonly spawn in late October and early November, might they not be near the feeder streams which they ascend for procreation? It seemed like a good theory. Here it is only mid December, in some years, and at least some of the brown trout ought to be close to the creeks. Unfortunately, the theory never panned out for me. At first ice, I used to concentrate at the mouths of key feeder streams on the reservoirs I fish, but while I did pick up a few straggler browns it was never a motherlode.

In spite of this failure, if a fish in your area spawns in late autumn, you should at least consider what implications that might have to your early season ice fishing.

Late ice is entirely another matter. It's often said that late ice is the next best thing to first ice, and I'll back that one up 100%. Some writers have observed that during late ice, many warm days in a row melt the snow and can clear up the ice, to allow photosynthesis to get cranking again. Also, cracks and openings in the ice will appear, and this presumably allows some re-oxygenation of a lake. Water on top of the ice (caused by warmer days) running into open holes or cracks in the ice must help too.

This may be true, but the fact that late ice is a pre-spawning time for so many fish may partially explain the upbeat catches often enjoyed in March (April in the coldest areas).

When the actual time for spawning has arrived, many fish eat less or stop feeding altogether. But during pre-spawn, fish are usually displaying very healthy appetites, perhaps even storing precious calories for the rigor of procreation.

The most dramatic example of excellent pre-spawn ice fishing I know of has been on chain pickerel and yellow perch. If you can find one of the shallow water areas they move into in late winter, you can score in a very big way on both species. Make sure that pickerel are still open, though. In my state, pickerel and pike season closes March 15, specifically to protect spawning fish.

There is minimal opportunity for rainbow trout in winter in my region, but if it were more available, I'd dedicate some time to ice fishing around the mouths of feeder creeks where rainbows go to spawn or attempt to spawn. The wandering rainbow has a habit of ascending tributary streams any time between mid autumn and mid spring. It would seem like a good reason to place some tip-ups near a creek mouth, with the idea that rainbows must pass by the spot to get up into the river. I have not tested this theory, however.

Walleyes often prove mystifying in late winter. If the lake lacks a good tributary, the walleye will spawn in the lake proper, but usually on a windswept shoreline. If there is a tributary, they will probably utilize it. It's useful to keep these facts in mind, but creel surveys usually show that walleye catches are best in early season and diminish towards late ice. I'd simply recommend that you talk to as many people as you can on a lake to find out where (and if) late-season walleyes are typically found by anglers.

In New York, walleye season also closes March 15. In some states it's February 15. Check your own state's or province's regulations before attempting to fish late in the season for this species.

Pike spawn in very early spring, and many writers cite examples of real upbeat catches in late winter.

FEEDING

We've already seen that a "core area" can be an important feature to look for. We've seen that the fringes of that core area can hold some fish, even if fewer than the core area itself. We've seen that at a given time, some fish will be very hungry, some will be a little hungry, and some won't be hungry at all. We've also seen that some fish will move off well away from the core area with the hope of making some big score on a cache of food that hasn't yet been discovered by the other fish. By examining human feeding behavior, we've learned some important principles about fish feeding behavior.

Let's now look at fish feeding patterns a little more closely.

Unless you're there with an underwater movie camera to actually see fish ingesting food, you can only speculate on when a fish in a frozen lake feeds. Yet I think it is reasonable to make the inference that when the fish are most active, which we witness as action on top of the ice, is when the fish are actively feeding.

Given that assumption, fish in winter seem to feed at pretty much the same times as they do in summer. Walleye like low-light periods, especially just after dark and just before dawn. Crappies often like the first two hours after darkness. Bluegills feed all day but often best in late afternoon. Trout are up and about in early morning and on gloomy days. Pike and pickerel feed best between about 7 a.m. and noon.

This is the way we've found it on our lakes, winter or summer, but exceptions (even dramatic ones) crop up all the time.

Do fish eat less in winter? I'd say it's certain, though more true with some species than others. Their metabolism lowered, their activities curtailed, they need less food. I believe that they eat less and less frequently, and so do a whole host of other people who study fish and ice fishing. Try smaller baits. It's a simple piece of advice that often works in winter. Work your lures more gingerly. It's another piece of advice that can pay off for the jigger. These are simple principles, easy for anyone to apply.

If fish eat less and less often in winter, doesn't it stand to reason that they will be choosier, more selective in what they do eat?

Let's go back to the picnic. What will the people who are just a little bit hungry select for a nibble? I'd say a tidbit of their favorite food. Maybe they really like cold slaw. So they take a small sidedish of that. Or maybe they truly love coffee and cake. They don't eat the main fare but they do dig in at coffee time.

Maybe these choosier winter fish have a more exact idea of what they really want. For example, it's widely known that largemouth bass love golden shiners. Maybe these would work especially well in winter, on the "favorite food/choosiness" platform. Bass aren't legal game in my area, so I haven't tried it.

It's also known that smallmouth bass have a strong preference for crawfish. Maybe they eat just a few crawdads from time to time throughout the winter, and take very little of the other stuff they normally eat. I don't know where you'd obtain crawfish in winter, although it might be possible.

Take a trout lake. Let's say sawbellies are the top forage. They key in on the 'bellies all summer long, that's for sure, but they also take in other food. But maybe in winter, when they ostensibly eat less, when they do eat they just want a few sawbellies and nothing else.

It's fun to speculate on these things, since every once in a while you come up with a theory that actually produces. I realize that this "favorite food/choosiness" idea has to be tempered with the reality that some of the prime foodforms just might not be available in winter. Then, another great reality takes over, and we're back at the picnic.

A few people had to work and arrive at the park late. The food was delicious and was pretty much eliminated by the hungry crowd. But there is a half burnt hot dog here and a bit of potato salad there.

What do the late comers do? They eat what's left! People, and fish, are opportunists. Unlike certain organisms whose diet only consists of one or two types of food-—and this lack of adaptability has led to the extinction or endangerment of many of these critters — fish, like people, have evolved to utilize a range of foodforms (notwithstanding certain fish species that eat only this or that particular organism). Clearly, this means that people who pursue fish ought to try to be as creative as the fish are adaptable.

Finally, we come to the last aspect of winter fish feeding behavior: How vigorously do they feed? We've all seen movies where the hero (or sometimes the villain) has walked across the desert or other forbidding area and has come upon a place where there is food, and water. He may try to ravenously fill his belly with food and drink, and his new found custodians of course have to step in and tell him to go more slowly. A less starved but still hungry person, perhaps one at our own picnic, may dig into his vittles with a real gusto, leaving the plate shiny clean. Finally, the person who is just not hungry will probably eat slowly, just picking really, and leave food on the plate.

Although I do feel that there are certain times when a great many fish are feeding all at the same time, I believe that at any given time, you'll find fish in all modes. I don't think that at 9 a.m. (or any time) all the fish are all feeding with the same motivation. I believe this is another aspect in which they are much like people. The primary conclusion is that one should not necessarily give up on a slow day. It only takes one hungry ten-pounder to make your trip. Also, anglers should experiment with bait size (as well as type) and lure size, and also with the way lures are worked. If the often productive slow approach fails, don't be afraid to work the lure really vigorously. At the same time, if the tip-ups aren't producing, keep going around and tugging at the baits to get them moving. Maybe the fish in your neighborhood, or at least a few of them, are in a motivated feeding mood. This is also a good rationale for physically moving. Most of the best ice fishermen are roamers, and hole cutters.

On some beautiful new black ice last season, I greeted the dawn with spud bar and jig rod. I gingerly cut a small hole, skimmed it and began bobbing my metal lure. After only about five minutes, something rocked the lure but didn't take it. I had a strong feeling that it was a trout. I kept teasing with the lure, and the fish bumped it again but still no connection.

Whenever I get a hit, even a light one, and don't hook the fish, my inclination is to right away check the hook points for sharpness. I started reeling the jig lure up to the hole, and I saw a trout swimming up right behind it. The jig lure was now right at the hole and I bobbed it a couple of times to try to entice the trout, which was swirling around the lure very excitedly. Sure enough, he hit, but he was so close to the hole, and there was so little line out, that I couldn't throw him slack quickly enough. He broke the line on me, and swam away.

Eventually I put down some baits on tip-ups and walked back to shore to have some soup. In less than an hour the hole where I'd jigged up the trout produced a flag. I set the hook into the fish and I knew it was a decent trout. When I got the fish to the hole, I noticed something shiny in his mouth. I didn't gaff it, but rather just coaxed it up through the thin ice. It was my fish! I extracted the Swedish Pimple from its mouth and placed the fish on my stringer. Then I thought to myself that this was one of the more motivated fish I'd ever caught. Fish sluggish in winter? Not always.

The truth is, at any given time some fish are bound to be very hungry and some less so. Don't become a slave to routine. Think like a human, and introduce the kind of variety to your fishing that you see in normal, human affairs. Fish are more like us than you think.

CHAPTER 11

Profiles of the Top Winter Targets

IN THIS CHAPTER, I'LL DISCUSS the winter species in their approximate order of importance in my area. The highly available and delicious yellow perch is indeed a good place to start.

YELLOW PERCH *(Perca flavescens)*

It would be hard indeed for me to imagine ice fishing without yellow perch. When it's too cold to head to the Adirondacks for pike, when the trout down my way just aren't biting, when the crappies aren't coming into the cove at night like they're supposed to, when even the bluegills have vanished-—when all this has befallen us, we're still confident that we can go out and drum up a few yellow perch for the dinner table. Happily, with the possible exception of smelt, there isn't a better tasting iceover fish.

My guiding light on yellow perch is this: They are one of the most far-roaming species. From shallow, weedy flats to deep water flats, the yellow can be found in any one of a whole host of different niches in a lake, or frozen river for that matter. More so than any other species I can think of, the yellow can readily be taken on broad flats near shore or offshore, where there is a real minimum of distinct features. On such broad, weedless flats, or on gently sloping points, the

A mixed take of yellow perch (smaller fish) and brown trout.

perch may roam widely, singly or in pairs or small groups. Virtually any tip-up may take a perch, though you'll often find that a particular tip-up will be consistently taking the larger specimens.

In areas of greater food concentration, perch are more apt to be found in schools. Yellows very often school by size. If you're into a group of throwbacks, consider moving. Conversely, when you hit the big humpbacks, milk the opportunity for all it's worth.

In the larger lakes and reservoirs we've fished, we've usually found small to medium size perch in shallow water of eight feet or less. When those bigger yellows have brightened the day, it's usually deeper water where we've found them. We've taken them as deep as 40 feet, but some ice anglers report encounters with yellows as deep as 70 feet.

Yellow perch can be consistently active throughout the winter. Astounding catches are sometimes made during late ice by anglers who have found a shallow flat or bar where pre-spawn yellows have started to bunch up.

These tough-skinned, sharp-finned panfish seem to be exclusively daytime feeders. I've never taken one at night — not one. We've seen it where the first few hours of daylight were best, but perhaps year in and year out we catch the most yellows between about 11 a.m. and 2 p.m. As with so many species, there can be a late afternoon flurry; on a recent very bright day, the perch started biting like mad between 4:30 and 5:00 p.m. Even on these days, the action shuts down pronto when actual twilight sets in.

Tip-ups are excellent when the fish are scattered over broad areas. Small minnows 1½ inches in length are ideal, though in some places, perch sharpies recommend larger minnows. Try a #10 hook with the smaller baits, a #6 with the bigger ones. Some say the perch is not line shy but I have fairly conclusive proof that more fish can be taken with lighter line. I use 4 lb. test. I also use in-line attractors or "flickers" for yellows. Lure-making components such as blades and beads are what I'm talking about here. Place them 18 to 24 inches above the bait, just above a small ball bearing swivel. The swivel is necessary to prevent or at least lessen line twisting.

When the perch are concentrated, jigging is the way to go. Small dot jigs tipped with bait work well on the smaller perch, those under nine inches. Fish over nine inches will readily take mid-size jigs of all types, with or without bait. Even the little guys take good-sized jigs, sometimes. We always fish with a small teaser above a bigger jig. For example, we may use a #2 Swedish Pimple tipped with a perch eye. A foot above this will go a small pearl jig or a hot orange and yellow ice fly.

Try lake areas where anglers rarely go. If you can't find structure, try both weedy and weedless flats. In most (but not all) lakes, avoid very steep areas.

The size of a perch fillet seems to increase geometrically. Seven or eight inchers may be frustrating to fillet, but each inch over eight inches makes a big difference in meat yield. Personally, I don't care to keep perch less than nine inches long. Males are smaller and seem to yield less meat than females of even the same size. In our area, females outnumber males by about seven to one in the catch.

CHAIN PICKEREL *(Esox niger)*

The eastern chain pickerel (just pickerel for the rest of this section) is an important gamefish in some areas, especially from southern New England south through eastern portions of the mid-Atlantic states. Its range extends up through the Hudson Valley and Mohawk Valley and into Lake Ontario and Lake Erie, as well as through much of Pennsylvania and the upper Ohio valley. A pike in miniature, it's a part of the same genus, *Esox*. Actually, it's not necessarily that miniature.

True, the biggest fish on record are right around 9½ pounds, and in most places a 7-pounder is a wall hanging trophy. But in good habitat, 24- to 28-inch pickerel are not especially uncommon. Most anglers find that, as with pike, small (even if legal) pickerel aren't worth keeping. Twenty-two inches is about the size we start keeping them.

Occasionally taken at night, the pickerel is nonetheless primarily a day feeder. On many days, that period from about 7 a.m. to 11 a.m. has been choice. On some lakes, there is a flurry in late afternoon, but we've rarely found it to match the morning action. Still, you can catch pickerel all day long.

A sight feeder and a weed lover, the pickerel will most often be found around weeds in shallow water. Good action can be experienced in as little as 5 to 7 feet of water. On occasion, a nice pickerel will be dragged up from water 20 feet deep or deeper, but it doesn't seem to happen often. Sometimes, I've found nice pickerel in stream channels 10 to 20 feet deep.

Live minnows on tip-ups are the top choice for this long-snouted eating machine, and if you think you're in a good spot, don't be too anxious to move the tip-ups. I believe that while pickerel may lie in waiting for food, they also search out food. By leaving a set of tip-ups in a good area you could experience a pick of action all day long.

Pickerel appear to be warier than pike, so I don't go heavier with terminal tackle than I feel I have to. I often use a 6 or 8 foot leader testing at 8 pound test. Like pike, pickerel have sharp teeth and may cut you off. Where large pickerel are common, I more and more often use light steel leaders testing at 12 lbs.

Jig lures can work, but you have to cut a lot of holes to find the fish and in the shallow water you'll typically be fishing, this ongoing disturbance could hurt the overall day's effort. Set out all your tip-ups then take your auger a good ways away and try jigging. Let the tip-up area settle down, especially when the ice is still thin and clear. I'll bet you'll do better jigging in the slightly deeper pickerel water, say 8 to 16 feet.

Let it never be said that the pickerel eats like a bird. Last season I was fishing a small lake called White Pond at first ice and I took a nice pickerel of about 24 inches. When I went to remove the hook, a tail of a fish was there to greet me. I pulled on the tail, and attached to it was an all banged up but still alive largemouth bass of eight inches. I put the bass in my minnow bucket, and it started making some effort to swim, although it was clear it had no chance of surviving. I brought the bucket and the bass out onto another lake that evening where a regular group of acquaintances was gathered. The bass was still alive at about 9 p.m. when, after everyone had heard the story, I eased it into one of the holes.

I usually use a single, #4 or #2 hook with the relatively large baits I normally put down for pickerel. If you decide to use a treble hook, I wouldn't recommend a real large one. For minnows up to about 4 or 5 inches, some will use a single, #8 treble. Personally, though, I've moved away from treble hooks, since they make release of undersized fish extremely difficult.

Wintertime pickerel are exceptionally good eating. Their reputation for boniness prompts even some old-timers who should know better to routinely toss them back. On my lakes, I yell like hell at the new breed of anglers who come out on Sunday and throw back 25-inchers. Then I calm down and tell them that everything they've learned is wrong, that it's fine to keep a few fish to eat. Finally, I patiently describe to them three or four ways to prepare this fish so it's delectable. By the end of the day they're keeping everything and I have to tell them not to go hog wild with it.

WHITE PERCH *(Morone americana)*
Like the chain pickerel, this fish is found in only a limited corner of the ice fishing world, especially New England and New York. Where it is found, it can roam in large schools and provide fast and furious winter action. Where stunting occurs, very small fish may predominate and they may be extraordinarily abundant. Where a lake is in better balance, the perch can average nine inches with fish of 10 to 12 inches mixing in. As with the yellow perch — not a close relative since the white perch is actually a bass — whites in their larger sizes are called humpbacks. At any size, though, they're much broader top to bottom than a yellow perch. Their flattened size makes them feel like a crappie when they're being pulled up to a hole.

"Find any whites?" is something I hear often on my lakes. Everyone knows that when you hit one you can easily pick up two dozen, or sometimes four dozen. Still, you will pick up a straggler once in a while.

This silvery-gray fish is enigmatic. It seems to come and go even within the same lake. There are good years and bad years, or perhaps we are only able to find them in some years.

Without doubt, we've experienced the best action on whites in late afternoon. That twilight period of 30 minutes or so can be hectic and you have to capitalize on it. Medium-sized flashy jigs are the ticket at such times. Use one that's heavy enough to get back to the bottom quickly. By day, your tip-ups may pick up stragglers, and when you do get one on bait, by all means try jigging either in that hole or in the immediate area. Use small minnows on your tip-ups. Whites have small mouths, but will take baitfish along with the plankton and other small stuff they dine on.

This is the perfect species for the peripatetic jigger who gets nervous staying in one place for more than about five minutes. Take your 5-inch corkscrew auger and your jig poles and roam to your heart's content. Keep searching for that school, and try all depths down to about 40 feet or even more. Seek out stream channels, rocky points, drop-offs and other structures. Unlike the yellow perch, whites do not seem to habituate broad, relatively structureless areas of a lake.

If you do hit them in the deeper water, say below about 30 feet, you might find that the late afternoon feeding period is longer in duration. For example, in certain deep, steep-sided reservoirs near my home, we sometimes have good white perch action between about 2:30 p.m. and dark in depths of about 30 to 45 feet, especially on cloudy days.

Follow any lead whatsoever as to the possible whereabouts of white perch. A hot area often stays that way for days in a row. On a particularly good piece of structure, for example a sunken bar or island, daytime action may be surprisingly good. On such a prime spot, we've sometimes experienced good early morning action while actually trying for trout.

While that late afternoon feeding period can be intense, it normally shuts off with abruptness. We have not taken white perch at night.

If anything, white perch taste even better than yellows. They fillet easier, too.

BROWN TROUT *(Salmo trutta)*

A 13-inch yellow perch comes up through the ice and everybody says, "Hey, that's a nice perch." They can easily visualize two nice-sized, cornmeal-coated fillets begging to be dropped into that bubbling hot butter.

Then some crappies drift into your spot and start to accrete on top of the ice. Someone wanders over and says, "That's a nice mess of crappies." But there isn't any real passion in his voice.

A 29-inch pike comes up through the hole and writhes furiously as it seeks a way back to freedom. "That's a better than decent pike" someone allows. But only the kids come over for a look-see, and after a couple of minutes the ice is back to normal.

Then, in the middle of a snow squall, a flag pops up on an isolated tip-up over deeper water. The angler, who has stayed to himself most of the day, is intent over the hole, and a dozen jiggers look up with real interest. Only midway through the hand-over-hand battle a dozen people have gathered around the fisherman, whose moment has come. It takes ten minutes but then a magnificently beautiful brown of 24 inches lies shimmering in all its glory. It is black and red and silver and golden, and it is shaped like a salmon, the way a fish ought to be shaped. There are hearty congratulations and when the six-pounder is dropped into the live well, no one can leave it for five minutes. Nor resist coming back to look at it every half hour.

There is nothing like a trout.

I make clear, in other chapters, the humility I assume when I'm trying to offer helpful advice on where the fish are going to be. When you start to talk about a pelagic fish like brown trout in lakes, I'm even more cautious. The truth, as I know it, and as most of the good fishermen in my area know it, is that brown trout are not normally easy to locate in winter.

Imported from Europe in the 1880's, the brown has had a glorious century on this continent. Wary, well shaped and hued, challenging, able to adapt to many situations, the brown is the wintertime prize where I live. The average specimens we take are between about 12 and 22 inches, but fish of 10 pounds and occasionally larger come up through the ice. In some lakes, even larger browns may be taken. The world record for this fish is a 37 lb. 7 oz. fish taken in Sweden.

Browns require an inflowing stream for spawning, so unless your pond or small lake has one, the chances are that you will be fishing over stocked fish. In very small ponds, where deep water is absent, brown trout management may well be a strictly put-and-take affair. Those fish that do make it through the season in such a stillwater face winter die-offs when the ice gets especially thick and snow-covered.

In these smallish waters, the trout are apt to roam the shoreline or that level just below the ice. On the other hand, if there is a deep hole in the lake, that might be another place to look for them. Pond shiners caught in the lake itself would be a good choice for bait.

But that's not the kind of brown trout lake I normally fish. Give me a big two-story reservoir, a genuine forage base, a stream running in and plenty of deep water, and you've got the fixings of a prime winter challenge: brown trout in big water.

It probably won't be an easy nut to crack.

We've found first ice to be by far the best time for browns, but there seems to be some very good action at late ice as well. If you do find a spot that produces, perhaps an exceptionally good piece of structure, remember that spot and try to be the first one on it when the ice forms. Because lakes freeze at different rates, you may be able to leapfrog from one to another, hitting your top spots at first ice on each one. Don't expect the action to last too long. Shallow water (under 30 feet) trout get rattled very easily and usually do a quick disappearing act when people start beating up on the ice with spud bars.

In a large, two-story lake such as I'm discussing here, try as close to the dam or in the deepest water that you legally can. Browns may be found anywhere in the lake, but this is the area where I would most expect to find them suspended. I don't know why, that's just the way we've seen it. I would set tip-ups from just under the ice down to about 30 feet, unless I had knowledge that fish are routinely taken deeper at the locale. I would then stay off the ice as much as possible.

Farther uplake, I would look for sunken bars and islands, especially where some deep water was immediately available. I'd also seek out saddles between islands and the shoreline; and narrow cuts, as under a bridge where two lakes or parts of one lake join together. Early morning has been very fruitful, but heed this important piece of advice for all species: The better the spot, the better the chance that action could occur any time. I like to arrive before dawn when trout fishing. I'll expect the best action between dawn and about 8 a.m., with the second best time from 8 a.m. to 11 a.m. Cloudy, snowy days offer better opportunity for daytime action, by our experience.

A number of my friends have taken browns at night, especially during that late ice period in March. I have to say that while I've ice fished for two or three days straight, camped under a tipped-over rowboat, I've still experienced the best action right at dawn.

Jigging can work extremely well, but I often set baits, too. I recommend both medium size minnows — whatever minnow means in your particular neck of the woods — and medium size jig lures.

More than anything, learn a particular lake well — it's productive spots and its peculiarities. Then, be the first one out, fish early in the morning, and make as little noise and commotion as you can.

However the trout in your lake taste in summer, they will only taste better in winter. Maybe much better.

NORTHERN PIKE *(Esox lucius)*

So much of what we think of when we visualize a classic predator is embodied in the pike. It has writhing power, an evil eye, a gaping mouth, and teeth enough to turn anything it doesn't like the looks of into chow mein. The Serengeti has its lions, the Gulf Stream has its great whites, and the waters of the north country have *Esox lucius,* the great northern pike.

Considering its size, availability, distribution and strong level of activity through the winter, the circumpolar pike could well be seen as the top gamefish for the ice angler. They're relatively easy to both locate and catch, and even a beginner can go out for pike and hope to catch a few. While in many lakes the average size caught is only about 2 to 5 pounds, 10 to 20 pounders are not rare. In prime habitat and lesser-fished lakes, 20 to 30-pounders are possible. The North America record came from Great Sacandaga Lake, right here in my home state of New York. It weighed 46 lbs. 2 oz. and was taken in 1940. Unless you journey to some very remote Canadian lake, you should not expect monstrous pike of over 20 pounds to be everyday fare.

Like the pickerel, this fish will very commonly be taken among or at the edges of weed beds. While we've done best on chain pickerel between 6 and 12 feet of water, we seem to catch the most pike between about 7 and 16 feet. I believe that, as with some other gamefish, larger pike may be the first to be scared deeper by heavy on-ice activity. Pike can be taken deeper than 16 feet, but they will be generally harder to locate, and that's one big reason why the fraternity seems to stick to those easily found shoreline weed beds. In places where it's legal, some anglers have sunken brush piles (like Christmas trees) and such brush can help to hold pike all winter. See Chapter 16.

Jigging for pike is a real thrill. With a light jig rod, most any pike will provide a smile, but latch onto one over five pounds on a wispy

30-inch stick and an exciting battle will ensue. Medium to large-sized lures are best, and should be tipped with bait if possible. Bait by itself, for example whole dead smelt or dead suckers, can be jigged. Treble hooks would be recommended here.

Not only are pike democratic as to what baitfish they will take, they also don't seem to care much how it's presented. I believe that with almost any species, even pike, you will get more takes with lighter line. It's just that with pike, much less caution in regard to lines and rigs seems to be mandated.

Special large, bent pike hooks, such as those used in Sweden and Finland, are available for fishing large deadbaits. This odd-looking hook is used to suspend a lifeless bait in a horizontal manner, but if your rigging causes the deadbait to tip front or rear, the less than brilliant pike may engulf it anyway.

Pike are especially good eating in winter. The infamous "Y-bones" are very difficult to cut out without sacrificing a lot of meat, but you can still dine on that firm, white flesh without ever ensuffering one bone.

First, you can pickle the fish. The acidic pickling brine will dissolve all the small bones within a week, if it's at the right strength. This makes a superb appetizer. You can fillet the fish, cut out the rib cage bones, and then grind up the meat for fish cakes or loafs. This will chop the remaining Y-bones so fine that they will not be noticeable.

SUNFISH (Family *Centrarchidae*)

You can get excited about sunfish in winter! It's living proof that ice fishing is magical, and that the magic elevates normally mundane experiences to a higher level.

In this book, as in so many others, sunfish will be used as an umbrella for a closely related group of species in the sunfish family. Some of the most often used common names for these species are bluegill — the most widely distributed of the group-—pumpkinseed, longear sunfish, redbreast sunfish, and redear sunfish. Crappies, and smallmouth and largemouth bass are also members of the sunfish family, but here we are discussing only the little critters of this important fish family.

This scrappy, cooperative little fish may average only five inches in your pond. If conditions are especially favorable, six or seven inches might be closer to the norm. When you do hit a lake where those dinner plates of nine inches or better exist, it is usually the bluegill itself as opposed to one of the other species. Surely, if you caught a 12-inch bluegill you'd have yourself a trophy, though not necessarily a record. The current all tackle world record for bluegill is a 4 lb. 12 oz. fish taken from Ketona Lake, Alabama.

They feed on tiny things. Many people use the word plankton, but aren't really sure what it means. One definition of plankton is "animals that float and drift passively in the water of the seas, lakes and rivers as distinct from animals which are attached to, or crawling on the bottom." In other words, a planker (an individual planktonic form) is a lifeform, or a stage of a lifeform before the organism is doing much, if anything, to control its own whereabouts. Minute plants are called phytoplankton and minute animals are called zooplankton. Bluegills will feed on both, as well as on the "attached" and "crawling" creatures that aren't technically plankton. Much plankton is too small to be effectively imitated by the jig lures that are used to catch sunfish (tip-ups are seldom used). In fact, the truth is, the vast majority of sunfish caught through the ice are taken on things that don't even vaguely resemble a true planktonic organism. Yes, there are jig lures meant to look like *Daphnia*, a waterborne insect, and ice flies that could represent certain other insects. But in most cases, a sunfish jig is really too large to be imitative. You simulate food with a sunfish jig lure.

Members of the sunfish family are normally quite cooperative in winter. To take bluegills and the others of this clan requires a light touch and fishing in the right spot.

If you really want to catch them, you'll use a tiny bit of bait on that simulative little jig. Any small grub is apt to greatly increase the fish-catching qualities of a small jig lure. Mealworms broken in half are super. Also try the scent-impregnated "synthetic" baits discussed in other parts of the text.

Since bluegill is the type of sunfish I most frequently try for, I'll use that name for the rest of this section.

A bluegill's mouth is small, and there's a very definite limit to what it can handle. Even those small pinhead shiners used on perch will rarely take a bluegill. Minnows are not what you want for 'gills, though worms work great, whether fished on a tip-up or a jig pole. It's just that there are faster ways of aggregating a nice mess of bluegills.

Generally, bluegills seem to gravitate to the weediest, shallowest parts of a lake in winter. This is what we've experienced in large reservoirs where rooted aquatic vegetation has been largely cropped back by ice season. In a small pond that remains weedy in winter, the 'gills are liable to be anywhere, but I'd certainly try where I knew springs to exist. In any case, I would start my search for bluegills in less than 10 feet of water, around weeds. If no action developed, I wouldn't hesitate to seek them out on clean (live) weeds between 10 and 25 feet of water.

An important concept with bluegills is that they often tend to concentrate in out-of-the-way or semi-detached shallow areas of a lake or reservoir. A bay connected to the main lake by a narrow cut would be a good place to look. So would a shallow lagoon, or shallow shoal between some islands and shore. So would a shallow, weedy channel between two lakes or two segments of the same lake.

These are school fish. If you catch one, it's almost a sure bet that more are around. They can school by size sometimes, but I'd say that's less of a rule than with yellow perch. You might get several real babies, then start hitting those "huge" eight-inchers one after the other. Don't be too quick to leave a spot that you believe might click just because you take a few throwbacks at the start. Also — and this is very important — keep coming back to a good hole after resting it for a period of five or ten minutes. Sometimes, with a good hole, you can come back again and again through the day and keep catching bluegills. This ploy can work with other species, too.

Use tiny jigs, size #10 or 12 hooks. In ice fishing catalogs I have, #10 is far and away the most popular bluegill jig hook size. Many times, you'll find that the bluegills won't hit the jig at all if it's bare. Other days, they will hit a bare jig, but rarely well. Add that bit of natural bait, though, and you're in business. A plain hook with a small grub can work well. Many use two jigs, or a jig on top and a baited hook on the bottom. In either case, separate the two offerings by a foot or 18 inches. You can get doubleheaders on occasion in this manner. Try tiny jigs or ice flies in hot colors like hot orange, blue or yellow. Try small ice flies with feathers. Try very small jigs with propellers on them.

Use the smallest amount of split shot you can get away with. Use the smallest, lightest bobbers you can get away with. Today, there are ultra sensitive bobbers or floats that are designed after ones used in Europe. One example is the Thill line of balsa wood bobbers, available from such mail order companies as Cabela's. They can help you detect even the most minuscule hit. That's important because very often a bluegill barely makes the line move when it engulfs your offering.

LAKE TROUT *(Salvelinus namaycush)*

Among the North American ice fishing species, the laker has a purity and an aura that is matched only by the brook trout. No vagabond from the Eurasian continent, the laker has been here for millions of years. Even though it is stocked in places, in many other waters the fish you catch are purely wild. The Great Lakes once had a fantastic population of lake trout, a population that supported extensive commercial fishing. That population is a shadow of what it was, but the Great Lakes basin, the upper midwest, northern New England and New York, and much of Canada still play host to this beautiful, cold water loving gamefish. It's a char, not a trout. It often grows with ponderous slowness, but where fishing pressure is not heavy, the average fish caught is large, over five pounds. Where stocking supports the fishery, fish of two to four pounds are more like the norm. Even in the more marginal waters, where fishing pressure is considerable and the laker population is small, very large fish are possible. Twenty-pounders are still taken from certain northeastern United States lakes that are located only a scant hour from a major city. Up in Canada, fish of thirty, forty, and even fifty pounds are caught, although not on any regular basis.

In the Great Lakes region and the northeast, summertime lakers seem most often to gather at depths where the bottom and 48 degrees F (9°C) coincide. It loves that cold water. Just as the walleye was once perceived to be strictly a bottom fish, so too was the laker. Now, the modern angler is well aware that this fish will come up...probably even more often in winter. While depths of 50 to 80 feet may be where the lakers are in summer, in many temperate-zone lakes you can frequently find them in 20 to 50 feet of water in winter. Some lakes I know of have a habit of giving up lakers caught on baits set right under the ice. In the dozens of articles I've read about ice fishing for lakers, there is a wide range of depths named as being most productive.

An ice-time trout is always a prize. Lakers like this one usually inhabit deep, clean, clear and cold lakes, in the United States and Canada.

Patience was the virtue that primarily defined the lake trout jiggers of yesteryear. I knew one named Herman Wilbur who would cut a hole over about 45 feet of water, a depth he said he liked in winter, and then jig in it all day. One day, I stood and talked to him for at least a couple of hours. At about noon, his jig rod doubled up and I got all excited. Attached to the business end of his large Swedish Pimple jig was a fine 17-inch brown trout. He didn't know what it was right away! Browns had only been put into that lake recently, and I presumed that this "new fish" was some kind of trash fish in the eyes of this great lake trout specialist. His lake corrupt, he nonetheless kept fishing, and I noticed that he tucked the brown into the back pocket of his brown hunting coat, where it wriggled strenuously for a good 45 minutes. Herman and his ancient red pick-up truck disappeared the next year, never to be seen by me again.

Patience is by no means out the window with this fish, but while I'm waiting patiently on those tip-up baits, I'm out roaming with my auger. I stay away from the tip-up area, to let that area settle down. Even in fairly deep water, I'm very leery of making a lot of noise on top of the ice when I'm after trout.

Certainly, the better cutting tools of today have made laker searching a lot less difficult. A power auger or a good sharp hand auger can give you the mobility that is so important when you're seeking a predatory fish that is normally deep, not usually in schools, and not overly abundant.

As for baits, try chubs or suckers in the six or seven inch class. These are very tough, energetic baits that should help to draw action in the deeps where visibility is limited. Exactly how big a bait you use will be determined by the size of the lakers found in your particular body of water.

Herman told me a lot of things. One was that he liked to paint the tip or the treble hook on his jig lure a phosphorescent color, usually orange. He swore by this, and did it to all his lures. He did not add bait to the end, but some lake trout fishermen know that a scaled and boned small minnow can sweeten the hook of a jig lure and increase one's odds of connecting.

Cold water lake trout are normally superb eating.

CRAPPIES (Genus *Pomoxis)*

This is one of those fish that makes me think of days long ago. I can visualize Huck Finn and his cronies dapping for crappies in some Mississippi oxbow with only a cane pole and a homemade bobber. To my knowledge, neither Huck nor any of his buddies ever competed in the Crappie Master Classic (or is it the Crappie Classic Master?) or

Big black crappies, some over two pounds.

did endorsements for the sporting catalogs. Word has it, though, that they knew how to have a good time when they went fishin'.

You can have fun too, even without satellite-based Loran or Liquid Crystal Display units that tell you everything but the name of the fish that's swimming underneath your hole.

There are two species, the black crappie and the white crappie. In the north country, the black is the more common. There are several ways to distinguish between the two, but the easiest sure way is to count the dorsal spines. The black crappie has five or six while the white has seven or eight. (Rare exceptions to this have been reported.) Also, the white crappie has 7 to 9 fairly distinct black vertical bars, while the barring on the black crappie is usually more scattered. The white is known to tolerate greater turbidity than the black, which seems to favor cooler, cleaner waters. One more thing: The white is known for periodic population explosions. This occurs less frequently with the black.

Almost all my wintertime experience has been with black crappies. The following comments should be looked at in that light.

We've almost always done best from just after the fall of darkness to 9 or 10 p.m. On the two or three lakes where we've enjoyed this good night action, we have never been able to locate the fish during daylight. Also, we've never taken too many between about 10 p.m. and dawn, although there has been a flurry around dawn at times.

So that means you have to fish at night, right? No. I know of lakes where there can be fine daytime action. Are these resting fish that, nonetheless, are motivated enough to take a bait or lure? Or on these lakes, do the fish feed by day instead of night? Or maybe day and night, depending on various circumstances? Fishing is complicated and I don't have these answers. On the large reservoirs we concentrate on, we do hit pockets of crappies in the daytime. This usually amounts to a few fish, maybe four or five in a pocket. Stragglers also visit our tip-ups every so often during the day.

In spite of all this, there is wide agreement that the first several hours after darkness can be a prime time for crappies, even if it isn't the only time on all lakes.

Crappies are one of the wintertime species that are most apt to suspend, which means to remain off the bottom. Research has shown that they will commonly rest, suspended out over deep water, and then penetrate shallow bays at night to feed. Perhaps "resting" doesn't necessarily mean "non-feeding," since, as I've said, good daytime scores are made on crappies.

When they do penetrate a shallow water area to feed, they may remain somewhat off bottom. Try from right under the ice, especially in shallow water, down to the tops of the weeds. Friends of mine who do use depth finders have reported them "coming in" about four to six feet off the bottom.

It is axiomatic that the crappie "feeds up" (look at how its eyes are positioned) and so it may pay to be above rather than below them. I have, I should mention, seen one report that shows that crappies do feed down at times.

I like a medium size minnow and a Partridge #6 Quick-strike double hook for this species. This hook has two hook points essentially riding on one shank. The larger point is impaled in the bait, while the smaller one remains outside the bait. Made in England, this hook seems to be increasingly hard to find. Now an American manufacturer, Tackle Marketing, is making a similar two-point hook that they call a "Fast-strike" hook. Unlike the Partridge hook, the smaller point is at a 90-degree angle to the larger one. I have not tried it yet.

If you're on the fish, jigs will get them. I like small lead-head jigs with various action-producing tails. One example would be a small auger tail in chartreuse. A small jigging Rapala has worked well, but I think at the right time and place most any jig would catch some fish. When you do jig, by all means try different depths, especially the first six feet or so above where you know good bottom structure (including weeds) to exist.

This is the fish of a zillion common names. Papermouth is one, but my favorite is strawberry bass.

Crappies fillet nicely and taste good, though a bit stronger than perch.

WALLEYES *(Stizostedion vitreum)*

Old glasseye is easily the most popular target in many areas. In Minnesota, perhaps America's most important ice fishing state, the walleye is the most avidly sought gamefish. It is not far behind in some other upper midwest states.

A true predator, a challenging and wary gamefish, a peerless table fish: The walleye is religion in the heart of the ice fishing world.

In the extensive literature on the walleye, a fish whose life cycle and habits have been studied at least as well as those of the largemouth and smallmouth bass, two traits are named more than any other: a propensity to feed during low light periods, and a desire to stay right on the bottom much of the time.

The walleye is probably somewhat less wary than a brown trout, although telemetric studies have literally watched walleyes being scared deeper by on-ice activity. But while a brown usually takes a bait or lure very energetically, the strike of a walleye can often be quite gentle. Before today's carefully engineered tip-ups came along, many sportsmen would make tip-ups expressly for walleye fishing. These would feature delicate settings that would let a flag pop up with even a light bite. Light line is also recommended for this careful gamefish, with six pound test usually being about right. In deeper water where light penetrates less well, many anglers will go to eight or ten pound test.

There is widespread agreement that the best times for walleyes are dawn and dusk. To be more specific, that period from about a half hour before darkness to a few hours after dark is usually considered choice. From just before dawn to just after dawn is usually cited as the sec-

The walleye holds sway in many parts of the ice fishing world. Note the nicely appointed shanty. (Steve Grooms photo)

ond best time, with a third choice being the hours of darkness between these two periods. On overcast days, action may continue later in the morning. This is true of some other species as well.

A general pattern for walleyes sees them moving shallower in the evening to feed, and then easing deeper in the daytime to rest. Some experts say that they often go less deep in the daytime in winter. Although the bottom is always a good place to start one's search, it's no secret any more that walleyes will suspend off bottom, often over or around structure like rocks or bars. Any submerged bar in a good walleye lake would be a feature worth exploring.

As with virtually every other wintertime gamefish, jigging can be very effective. On a given walleye lake, a particular lure may gain favor but any minnow-imitating jig lure can draw action. A small live minnow on the end of a small lead-head jig can be a deadly combination, and this combo is fished by slowly raising then lowering it back to the bottom.

You'd have to put the walleye up there with the yellow perch and the smelt in eating quality, and there's no doubt that many would place the walleye at the pinnacle of North American fresh water table fish. It is very versatile in the kitchen, and most cooking methods will work. A thick steak or fillet bakes up beautifully, but you can also deep fry it or make an interesting sauce to adorn it. That most pleasant of interludes, the shore lunch, often includes walleye, along with potatoes, onions and satiny smooth cast iron skillets. In winter, the entire lake is the shore, so turn to Chapter 17 and discover a few ways to honor the provender that the gods of winter have blessed you with.

OTHER SPECIES

I've fished for all of the above species, though walleyes least of all. Collectively, these nine species or groups of species account for the lion's share of angler effort expended in winter in North America.

But you could travel across the ice fishing belt and hear, "What, you don't fish smelt out there? They're right now up 12 feet over 45 feet in the boat channel."

Or, "Give me a big lawyer at the end of my line. That's what I want, a nice two-foot lawyer. My wife loves the liver."

Or, "I don't fool around with those small fish under a hundred pounds. Sturgeon's my game — and spears, mister, spears."

Or yet, "We took six big tullibees before noon, and then got down to business and did some musky fishing."

Or even, "I want three or four of them kokes (kokanee salmon). Man, that red flesh. Nothing eats like a koke."

I doubt there is anyone in North America who even knows all the different species that are fished for through the ice, let alone how they're fished for. There are no ice fishing experts, as I've said elsewhere.

Here are brief looks, then, at some of the "secondary" ice fishing targets that, nonetheless, are important to many anglers in some regions:

OTHER TROUT. Rainbow trout, including steelhead, (both *Oncorhynchus mykiss*), and brook trout *(Salvelinus fontinalis)* are taken through the ice. In western North America, there is wintertime activity for cutthroat trout *(Salmo clarki)*. I have heard reports that there is also some ice fishing out west for golden trout *(Salmo*

Largemouth bass like this near-six-pounder are more available in winter than is commonly believed.

aquabonita) and dolly varden trout *(Salvelinus malma)*. I've caught a few each of rainbows and brookies through the ice, but their availability is extremely limited (in winter) in my area. Expect difficulties finding the often far-roaming, pelagic rainbows in big water. Prior research and discussion with local people in the know is essential.

LARGEMOUTH AND SMALLMOUTH BASS *(Micropterus salmoides* and *Micropterus dolomieui)*. I figured out that largemouth and smallmouth bass will become increasingly important in hard-water circles. It's a three-part formula that goes like this: great interest in bass + greatly increased ice fishing activity + more liberal seasons on bass equals what I just said. Some of the biggest winter thrills we've

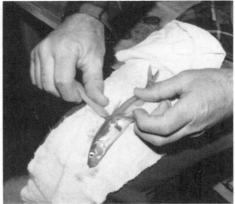

The deep-water smelt can be taken by the hundreds on a good day.
A strip off the side of the smelt makes the best bait.

had have involved tape-stretching bucketmouths up to about seven pounds. We've also thrilled to smallmouths up to four pounds. I essentially agree with the two primary theories on winter bass: First ice and last ice are easily the best times, and the largemouth is more active than the smallmouth. The deeper the winter and the thicker the ice, the poorer the bass fishing, by our experience. Make sure bass can legally be taken in your water.

MUSKELLUNGE *(Esox masquinongy)*. A magnificent trophy, of course, but not widely available or legal in winter, and never abundant where it can be taken. Big bait would be indicated but again, prior research on any body of water would be considered essential. Make sure gaffing is legal if you normally carry a gaff and plan to keep a musky.

SMELT *(Osmerus mordax)*. I may not agree with what you say, but I'll defend to the death your right to eat a fish that tastes better than a smelt, if you think you can find one. A deep-water combination baitfish-predator, common in New England and in parts of the Great Lakes region and Canada, this five to ten inch long silvery fish is religion where the ice is thick and the shanties are smoking warm. All manner of cunning devices are used to take smelt, some of them special reels that are mounted on shanty walls. But perhaps the most common method is handlines. Strips from the side of the smelt itself usually make the best bait, though jig poles with small lures can be used. Hold onto your hat when you're smelt fishing, because every once in a while a big old laker or landlock will come along, and suddenly the fish on the end of your line isn't five inches long anymore. Depth can be critically important with smelt. By all means compare notes with anglers around you, if someone's connecting and you're not.

BURBOT *(Lota lota)*. Here you have one heck of an interesting fish! Burbot is the only fresh water member of the cod family in North America, and is even called ling, not to mention cusk and lawyer (I'm researching where that moniker "lawyer" came from). With its elongate, almost eel-like body, small whiskers, and big paunch, the burbot almost looks like a caricature of some political figure, or perhaps a late-middle-age British magistrate. There are a couple of races, including a large one found in Alaska, but the Great Lakes race averages only 18 inches while reaching a maximum length of about 30 inches. It's a cold water species and has been taken at least as deep as 700 feet. I might be one of the few anglers on the continent to stand a chance with such creatures of the abyss, since I have 1,200 feet of line on every spool (you don't think they would run more than 500 feet, do you?)

TIGER MUSKELLUNGE *(Esox masquinongy* x *Esox lucius)*. The fisheries crew started out by calling this hybrid critter a norlunge, but I guess that wasn't Madison Avenue enough and now it's mostly called tiger musky. It's a cross between a northern pike and a muskellunge, and it's sterile, or non-reproducing. Thus, if 500 are put into your weedy, local lake, you will not catch one after 500 have died or are caught. It seems sensible to check carefully on stocking numbers and locations when pursuing this fish. My friends and I have tried for tigers in two or three local waters, but haven't connected yet. We use eight-inch steel leaders and six-inch suckers, and sometimes, treble hooks. Every year we hear a few harrowing stories of this or that tiger musky that was lost at the hole. It is a fast-growing fish, and starts to eat as soon as it leaves the hatchery truck. It can get to be 20 to 25 pounds and more.

WHITEFISH (Genus *Coregonus)*. The whitefish is neither a trout nor a salmon, but is very closely related to both. It is, in fact, part of the same family, *Salmonidae*. It's a popular winter fish in very particular areas or bodies of water. There are three principal species: lake whitefish, mountain whitefish and round whitefish. Lake whitefish is the most commonly taken by anglers at any time of year, according to two different sources.

SAUGER *(Stizostedion canadense)*. This fish is so similar to a walleye that you'd have to know what to look for to be able to make a positive identification. Also, the range of the sauger very closely coincides with that of the walleye. These two species are taken side by side in many lakes, but the sauger averages substantially smaller, about one to two pounds. The sauger is said to tolerate somewhat higher turbidity than the walleye. Feeding habits, though, are very similar to those of the walleye, and the very same baits and lures will often work. Saugers are reported to like deeper water than the walleye.

CHAPTER 12

Sensible Tip-up Placement

IN HOLLYWOOD, THERE ARE very definite character types. There's the blonde bombshell, the debonair leading man, the hapless sidekick.

It's the same way with ice fishermen.

First you have the fellow who sets his tip-ups in a straight line out from shore. The first one is usually 50 feet from shore and the last one is 250 feet. They are perfectly spaced and if you line them up with your eye it looks like he used surveying equipment, they're so straight. This type of linear personality is neat, organized, and likes to line up the heels of his shoes in the bedroom closet.

Then you have the person who sets his tip-ups in a circle around the hole he will eventually jig through. These are usually friendly, well-rounded individuals who like to talk and share a Thermos with you.

Not to be forgotten is the fisherman who sets his tip-ups so close together that he can almost tend them from the 5-gallon bucket he is sitting on. The minnows on these tip-ups never get lonely all day because they are only inches away from each other. My theory is that this personality might have had a very protected childhood.

There is, however, at least one more type of ice fisherman. This is the type who catches fish. It's quite possible that you won't

The strong current in this reservoir revealed itself clearly by this swath of thin, weak ice. The author placed a tip-up at the right-hand edge of it.

encounter him at all because he likes to go out on weekdays, fish during snowstorms, and stay off the ice and in the woods over a little fire when he's after wary gamefish. If you do run into him, his tip-ups may well be set in some pattern that's undecipherable to you. They will be set neither far apart nor close together, but in the best possible pattern to produce. Almost certainly, this angler will have ice fished for many years and will have spent one hour reading, planning, and tackle tinkering for every two hours spent on the ice.

On a given body of water, a given fish is liable to be anywhere on a given day and at a given time. Species of fish certainly do have patterns, as well as biological limits regarding certain environmental factors. But it's still folly to try and tell someone with any real certainty where he's liable to find the fish.

Accordingly, this chapter will discuss how to think about placing your tip-ups, rather than where to exactly place them. What I would do for perch (or any other species) on my lake could be radically different from what you would have to do on yours. The underlying thought processes, though, might be very similar.

In my home state of New York, you are allowed five tip-ups on most waters. The following discussion is geared around that reality. If your state or province allows you fewer, you'll have to be even more thoughtful about placement.

STRATEGIES FOR A STRANGE LAKE

The worst of all possible scenarios is to walk out onto a frozen lake about which you have no specific knowledge. By all means, do as much

This reservoir was down about 10 feet. Notice the old rock walls revealed. Sometimes these continue out under the ice and provide good winter cover for various species of fish.

prior research on a target lake as you can. Talk to other anglers, to tackle shop owners, to conservation department officials. These days, there aren't many lakes about which no body of knowledge exists. But with no contour map, no open water experience and no advice from someone in the know, where do you start to look for fish?

If it's a relatively small pond, a couple of anglers may be able to cover the water with jig rods and quickly get a bead on what's happening. Small ponds are infinitely easier to ice fish than large lakes and reservoirs. On these latter, concentrated groups of fishermen will often belie a spot that is hot, or at least that is sometimes hot. But if there are few people out, or the people over the well-known honeyhole just aren't scoring, where do you place your tip-ups?

Lacking a contour map on a strange lake, my inclination would be to space my tip-ups extremely far apart, perhaps a hundred or more yards apart. (Check on laws which state how far you may be from your sets.) By so doing, I'm hoping on blind luck to find something down there that is holding fish. I almost certainly would put at least two close to shore. One of these I might put extremely close to shore. Binoculars are useful, by the way, for checking far-away tip-ups.

In flat country the dilemma is greatest. Here, the lay of the land won't even tell you where there might be sunken bars or islands, rock rubble, old stream channels, and other such features. In hilly terrain, the topography adjacent to the lake will sometimes help, though not as often as you might imagine. One thing I will look for is a steeply sloping shore. Here, you may find water dropping off to 10 or 15 feet or more just a few yards out from shore. Brown trout will cruise along such shorelines in winter. So will crappies, chain pickerel, bass and other fish from time to time. Many times I have set tip-ups so close to shore as to prompt jokes from other fishermen. They drink their beer, laugh a lot, and make innuendos about my activities. Then I slap a 20-inch trout in a well with their 6-inch perch and they quiet down for a while.

Another thing I'll look for is an old stone wall on shore that may continue out under the ice. In certain impoundments, these stone walls are very common.

The shoreline is a dynamic zone that fishermen concentrate on in summer but mysteriously shun in winter. On a lake where you just don't know the patterns yet, the shore is always worth a few tip-ups.

Similarly, on a strange lake in hilly country I have often set tip-ups around points of land. It's a natural inclination — everyone does it. Points do produce at times in winter, but for me it's rarely been in dramatic fashion. You need more to go on. If you have a map, as we'll discuss, you might be able to find a combination of factors that includes a point and that spells good fishing. Combination structures can be superb — for example a good weed bed around a rubble-strewn point.

On a very cold, windy morning, setting out the five or more tip-ups permitted in some areas can be arduous. On such mornings, you won't be much inclined to move your spread of tip-ups around. Thus on a strange lake or a new area of a known lake, I won't automatically set out all five at once. Rather, I'll put out a couple, then warm up with some tea while I wait to see if any action develops, either with tip-ups or with the jig poles. If it does, then naturally I'll put at least one of the remaining tip-ups in the hot area.

This past winter I did a lot of exploring on new lakes, and new sections of some lakes I'd fished before. I had only very crude sub-surface contour maps. Two of the exceptionally hot spots I found were quite opposite in nature. Both reaffirmed some theories I'd been developing about tip-up placement.

The first spot is a several-hundred-yard-wide section of a twisting reservoir. Contours are gradual, and depths range up to about 25 feet. Taking my own advice, I spread my tip-ups widely the first day I fished the spot. One flag popped almost immediately. I moved another one close by. Both of them went up! As the other three weren't producing, I quickly moved them into the hot area. It didn't take me long to figure out that I was over a productive, still-alive weed bed, in 14-18 feet of water, near the edge of (but not in) a vague submerged stream channel. That day I caught 20 big yellow perch, a few white perch, several bass, a chain pickerel and a bluegill, all in about 2½ hours of fishing. (On the next trip, I took a 5-lb. bass and broke off two even bigger fish.) But the tip-ups had to be right over the weeds. The hot area was about 70 yards in diameter, but a "core" area only about 25 yards across produced most of the fish. I noticed that this core area seemed to have the thickest weeds, as judging by what came up on the jig lures. Jigging, in fact, produced very well, as I'd expect it would in an area of fish concentration.

The second spot also produced a marvelous day of tip-up fishing for jumbo yellow perch and a few white perch. This was a very steep-sided, bowl-shaped arm of another reservoir. Depths ranged up to about 40 feet. There were no weeds at all, and no detectable bottom structure. (There probably were some old stone walls that I could not pinpoint.) At this spot, I also spaced my tip-ups widely, at depths of about 10 to 35 feet. Yet here, no one tip-up outproduced the others. Every single one yielded some action. Jigging did not produce at all. Clearly, the fish in this spot were roaming and were not schooling as perch often do.

My conclusions? First, it pays to spread your tip-ups out when you haven't fished a spot before, and to quickly group them together when something clicks. Second, when food is concentrated (as in a weed bed), fish may also be very concentrated; when food is more scattered, so might the fish be. Finally, depth as an isolated factor just isn't enough to go on in winter. No panfish or gamefish reads magazine articles to find out what depth it should be at. With water temperature variations fairly minimal under the ice, fish can and will relate to a wide range of depths. This is especially true in deep, clean, clear lakes where oxygen depletion rarely occurs. In small lakes or ponds, heavy snow cover and thick ice can deplete the oxygen enough so that fish are forced up into that stratum immediately below the ice. More often, this does not happen.

In the first of the two spots I described, weeds (Eurasian milfoil) were quite thick. I'm sure there had been a die-off of weeds since summer, but that thick milfoil was still growing up several feet from the bottom. Since weeds can hold a lot of food of all types, a weed bed is often an excellent place to set tip-ups. In fact, with the amount of weeds far less than in summer, fish can often be concentrated where weed beds persist in winter. At times, pieces of some types of weeds will break off and float up to lie under the ice. You may be able to locate some productive salad in just this way.

Just as the shoreline is strangely ignored by many ice anglers, so too is shallow water. In the shallows, which of course do not have to be near shore, the machinery of photosynthesis may continue deep into winter, especially if there is little snow cover. I'm not sure if this means more oxygen in the shallows, but I know it means more weeds. And more weeds often mean more fish.

Fish the shore. Fish the shallows. Fish the weeds. You do it all the time in summer, don't stop doing it in winter. You may be surprised to find that even normally deep water species often move shallower in winter.

ON MORE FAMILIAR GROUND

Thus far, we've mainly been discussing those times when you find yourself on a strange lake and without a good map, an all too common dilemma. Let's now move into situations where you do have some knowledge of the lake you find yourself standing on.

The best way to fish for white and yellow perch, crappies and some other panfish is with a group of several people. Some theorize that several baits in the water at once seem to help attract panfish schools and keep them around. Whether that's true or not, it's certainly easy to locate and relocate panfish schools with a larger group of anglers.

Let's say, then, that your group finds itself on some body of water known to harbor nice perch. Drill four holes roughly 15 feet apart in a circle. Set small minnow baits in three of them. Now move 50 or so yards away and auger four more holes close together. Again, use three of the holes for tip-ups. Repeat this process until you've gotten in all the tip-ups permitted by law in your area. Now, spread your buddies out so that each one is jigging in the hole in each grouping that doesn't have a tip-up. When a school does reach one of your four-hole groupings, the several baits (plus the flashing jig lures) may help to keep them around. When the school moves, they may run into another one of your groupings. At day's end, your jig poles may account for a high percentage of the perch you land, but I theorize that the groups of live baits will attract the perch and help hold them for you.

Try to make your tip-up locations as species-specific as possible.

Instead of trying all depths — the straight line out from shore approach — don't be afraid to put all your tip-ups at the same depth or location if that's where you've had luck on a given lake before. Where big trout are possible, I do spread out my tip-ups regardless. I just don't want a tangle to louse up a big-trout opportunity.

Let's take a relatively shallow, weedy lake. You're mainly after pike or chain pickerel, yet you know the lake also harbors some nice panfish. Because live bait is the best choice for members of the *Esox* genus, I'd dedicate all five tip-ups to them that day. I'd set all five close or reasonably close to shore and in or at the edge of weeds. Don't be afraid to set your tip-ups in less than 10 feet of water. For chain pickerel, you should even set some in 4 to 8 feet of water. Pike will probably be a little deeper. When plotting a spread of tip-ups for these species, don't be scared away by weeds. As I discussed above, rooted, aquatic vegetation has figured heavily in a great many of the most successful ice fishing trips we've taken. As you set your tip-ups, be looking through the holes as much as possible to see what's down there. If bottom-rooted vegetation rose up to only four feet from the ice, I wouldn't hesitate to set the baits only one or two feet below the spool of the tip-up. In a cove of one lake I fish, where the depth averages six to eight feet, there is only about four feet between the tops of the weeds and the tip-up spool. We sometimes fish here with only 12 inches of line out, and we kid each other that it's a good thing pickerel have teeth so they can pluck the bait off the spool. We also take large crappies in this manner.

Now that you have all your baits down, take your jig pole and go exploring for panfish. By temporarily vacating the tip-up area, you will be letting that area "settle down." In shallow water or with fairly thin ice, minimizing commotion where your baits are set can make all the difference.

MORE PLACEMENT IDEAS

A sunken sandbar or submerged island can be one of the deadliest of all places to ice fish. I believe such a spot will be most fruitful for gamefish when deep water braces at least one side of the structure, or at least is somewhere close by. Panfish species may be attracted to most any bar, but the need for a proximity to deep water seems to be pronounced with gamefish, especially trout.

I have virtual proof that trout can easily be chased off a shallow water location. I discuss this in Chapter 16. But if trout or any other species is being scared out of one area of a lake, can you intercept them at another area?

Let's say you're fishing a pond or small lake and all the activity, for one reason or another, is at one end of that pond. Perhaps that's where the parking area is, or the bait shop, or maybe there's an ice fishing derby going on. It's quite possible that the fish would be chased deeper, but if there is no deep water, the larger, warier gamefish might simply move down to the other end of the pond. In this scenario, the ideal thing would be to arrive before the place started to buzz. Go to the far end of the pond and put your tip-ups in beforehand.

I've heard it proposed that fish can be "corralled" into some corner of an ice-covered lake by persons on top of the ice intentionally making noise. For example, several people could start at the mouth of a narrow bay and pound their way towards the innermost part of the bay, presumably herding the fish into that corner where they would then be easy prey. That's very interesting, but I'd have to think that the fish would be too frightened to bite. Nonetheless, it isn't such a crazy idea. On some frozen rivers, suckers are herded up or downstream by "beaters" who pound on the ice as they walk in the direction of the "hookers." The hookers wield hook-like spears which they jab through holes pre-cut in the ice. Of course, this method does not depend on any appeal to a fish's hunger. It's simply a matter of intercepting groups of fish that have been driven your way.

Getting back to gamefish for a moment, if I'm really serious about a trout dinner, I'll go cut my holes in the afternoon and then come back the next morning (often before dawn) and set the tip-ups in. In my area, there's likely to be only a light skin of ice and I can very quietly open the holes up and get my baits down. Then I get off the ice completely, stay on shore, and hope that no one else shows up.

If you're in what you know already to be a good spot, cut fewer holes and try to capitalize on the ones you do cut. Use a sharp manual auger or a power auger.

Let's say that you've cleverly used your contour map to find a nice sunken bar or island, and that you're able to set up with a minimum of banging. Just where do you set the tip-ups? My experience is that the fish, and not just trout, are apt to be anywhere around the bar. But, on any given bar, there may well be a particular spot that produces best, so don't be afraid to move your tip-ups to pursue that action. We've all heard of the "hot hole" and that's a phenomenon I'm sold on. If you visit a lake frequently, it can even pay to mark a particular hole, by brush, or a mark in the ice or whatever. Please don't use any human trash for this purpose, though.

There are all kinds of sunken bars. As I said, for gamefish I like a bar that offers immediate access to deep water. But, this is not to say that the gamefish will restrict themselves to the deep water side of the structure; they could be on the crest of the bar or off to any side of it. It's just that I think the bar will be more productive if deep water is nearby.

Sunken islands can be dynamite. Curiously, you may find no-nonsense predators in large sizes and panfish of all sizes on a sunken island. You'd think that the panfish would be spooked away by the presence of the big gamefish, but there seems to be a lot of commingling. For example, let's say the prime forage for gamefish is emerald shiners in your lake. The gamefish may so heavily skew to emerald shiners that small panfish are all but ignored as food. Thus you may find good-sized gamefish and keeping size panfish together on the same bar or other structure.

When you do find a good bar, try to find that hot core area (which may be only one hole!) but at the same time spread your tip-ups out and explore the fringes of the bar. If you find a really exceptional hole, it might not pay to cut a lot of holes around it. You might scare off the fish you've been so lucky to find. Just keep working that honey hole, resting it for short periods every so often.

As far as placing tip-ups over weeds, the same truth seems to exist: There may well be a hot core area but at least some action might be found anywhere on the bed. I think the perch, for example, will often be right in the middle of the bed. But the pike and the pickerel may like to hang out at the edges of the weed bed. So might the large-mouth bass. The edge of a bed is a dynamic zone that is usually easy to locate in summer but not so easy in winter. Visual observation through the hole can help. But maybe the easiest way is to cut a bunch of holes and go around jigging them. A treble hook will almost unfailingly pick up weeds, where they exist. With a little effort you may be able to detect the perimeter of the weed bed.

Shame on you if you ever forget a spot where a big gamefish was taken, by you or anyone else. Lightning does strike twice, even in winter.

Many times we've found fish right next to shrubs or bent trees that hang over the water and are frozen into the ice. One friend of mine has a theory that fish "remember" that these areas provided food in summer and continue to visit them in winter, even though there are no longer any juicy bugs dropping off them. Whether or not this theory has validity I can't say, but the brush certainly does provide concealment (if part of the brush is frozen in below the water line). We've most often found crappies, sunfish and small largemouth bass in such places.

With or without a map, you can easily tell where a stream enters a frozen lake. It's gotta be a great spot, right? I wish you better luck in such locations than I've had. The ice can always be extremely tricky in such locales, but when we have gotten on, we've rarely experienced any noteworthy action. My thoughts on tributary mouths appear in Chapter 9.

EXPERIMENT

Maybe the single most important consideration in tip-up placement is not to be a slave to routine. I don't know how many times I've placed a tip-up or two in some offbeat corner of a lake and wound up with a honeyhole that hardly anyone else knows about. Water temperature is much less of a limiting factor in winter, since there is no lethally high stratum of water, and very little variation overall. Even if it is generally true that fish in winter are more concentrated — which I believe — many individual fish or groups of fish will roam into areas of a lake where you would not expect to find them in summer. I'll still look for bottom structure, but I'll be very democratic as to where I'll look for it.

Discussions with anglers coming off the ice can be tremendously useful, since at least half of them will like to talk. Try to remember everything they tell you. I often add tidbits of information gleaned from other anglers into my log book that evening, lest I forget the location of a spot that produced for someone.

Yet while it pays to follow the crowd at times, it also pays to follow a whim or just a feeling to an overlooked piece of ice where there are no holes, and never were.

It's on those kinds of days that memories are usually made.

CHAPTER 13

Jigging: The Deadly Alternative

IT'S ONE OF MY FAVORITE fishing stories of all time.

7:00 a.m., January 13th. Late for first ice in my region. I pulled into the parking space and saw that Jimmy had beaten me to the spot. Only by a few minutes, I figured by the sign in the snow, which turned out to be correct.

I poked my way out carefully with my ice spud. Thin, magical black ice, a window to the mysterious world sealed off below. First ice, best ice. I learned it early on and never forgot it. This spot was funny, though. Not only did it produce only at first ice, but you literally had to be the first ones out there. The browns gather on and around a submerged sand bar, but it takes only a day's worth of fishing to chase them off — and they never come back the whole season. Usually, on the second day you'll pick up a few stragglers but we make every effort to be out the first conceivable morning. The action even slows down the afternoon of the first day. To me, all this is proof positive that commotion and chopping on the ice can quickly scare away wary gamefish. It's a point to keep in mind the entire ice fishing season.

"I just got here — nothing yet," he said.

After ten years of fishing it, I knew the bar in detail. I chopped a hole very gingerly. The ice was just thick enough.

"What will you give me if I catch a trout on the first jig?"

He hardly had mouthed his snide retort when my little two-foot jig pole took a nosedive towards the hole. What would soon be a tarragon-broiled brown trout flopped on the ice and to this day, I swear to Jimmy that it was on the very first jig of the lure.

But that was only the beginning. Before eleven a.m., we had taken 23 browns between 13 and 18 inches, and had kept a few less than the legal limit of five apiece. Also flopping on the ice were about 18 big white perch and a half dozen yellow perch of more humble size. At 1:00 p.m. an acquaintance from my home town just happened to spot my truck and though he did not really know about the spot, he walked out to see what was up. He arrived just in time to see me land the best fish of the day, a brown of 20½ inches. At about 5:30 p.m., after everyone else had gone home (and taken the only gaff we'd had), I lost the biggest trout I've ever hooked through the ice: a magnificent brown of 8 or 10 pounds. All the fish were taken on an unbaited 4N silver Swedish Pimple.

Although tip-ups are the method most commonly associated with ice fishing, jigging is the more dynamic and productive method. Over the years, my jig poles have produced probably twice as many fish as my tip-ups, and remember, I often set out five tip-ups while I'm using only one jig pole. Many days we never set tip-ups, but you'll never catch me out there without a jig pole. This is also true of all the other serious ice fishermen I know. Many of these fellows never use tip-ups the entire season. Then too, some anglers refuse to fish with any kind of bait. In winter, these people jig exclusively.

Why is jigging so often more productive? The mobility of the jigger seems like the logical answer, but I think the fact that the lure is constantly moving and flashing owns a share of the credit. Another factor is the hand-held nature of the jig pole: You're in direct contact with your lure and if you're skillful, you can take the necessary steps to confound light biters. By contrast, a tip-up is left to itself on the ice and you have to hope that the take is a good one.

For those totally new to the sport, we'll start with a few rudiments of jigging.

SOME JIGGING BASICS

To jig, you cut a hole in the ice, lower a jig lure (with or without bait attached) usually close to the bottom, and then continually move the lure in a variety of ways by raising, lowering, and otherwise moving your rod. Most popular jig lures are specifically designed to work correctly in this vertical manner. No doubt some of your "horizontal" open water lures will work at times, but your ice fishing lure box will mainly be filled with lures made primarily for hard water fishing.

In my region, there is no popular ice fishing quarry that cannot be caught by jigging. It is nonetheless true that some species respond much better to bait than lures. We always set baited tip-ups for chain pickerel and pike, though I've taken each of those species on jig lures.

At the other end of the spectrum, some species are fished for almost exclusively with jig poles. The sunfish family comes first to mind. I've never caught one or seen one caught with a tip-up. Sunfish, even the bigger bluegills, have small mouths and cannot usually handle even the smaller minnows that fishermen normally bait tip-ups with. Also, their diet does not skew to minnows. A very small jig lure tipped with some little piece of natural bait is the deadliest weapon for the sunfish and all its kin.

Every year I see fishermen out there using six and even seven foot rods for ice jigging. I wonder what these people will do when they hook a large gamefish. How will they play the fish with the rod hand and attempt to get it up through the hole with the other? It's true to a point that you can back the rod up in your hand, moving your rod hand closer to the tip. However, when you do this, you inevitably lose a measure of control of the rod and thus the fish. And this loss of control comes at the worst possible moment, when the fish is floundering at the hole.

All my jig poles are between 24 and 42 inches in length, though I will be testing out a 48-inch model this winter. I use both bait casting (conventional) jig rods — those with an offset real seat — and spinning rods with straight handles. I use strictly graphite spinning rods but I have some bait casting rods in fiberglass. I have some very particular ideas on jig rods and reels and will outline some of them here.

For panfish, I always use spinning equipment. For one thing, the spinning rods made for ice jigging are almost always lighter than the bait casting models. You need a very, very light-tipped jig rod to consistently take panfish. Another reason is that with spinning gear, you can let the lure free-spool back to the bottom (or to the fish zone) whereas with a bait casting outfit you will probably have to strip line

There is a group of devotees who prefer unusually long jig rods. This one is close to five feet in length.

off manually. When you hit a fast moving school of panfish, you want to get back in business as quickly as possible after taking a fish. I am also more comfortable with a spinning rod when I am using a bobber, which I often do use when after small panfish.

Conversely, I usually use a bait casting set-up when fishing for larger panfish and all gamefish. The somewhat more rigid pole is a plus with large gamefish but the bigger reason has to do with the mechanics of bait casting versus spinning.

With a spinning reel, the drag automatically plays the fish. This may sometimes be an advantage in open water fishing, but I like the sensitivity of a well educated thumb on the spool. I can give line at will, or check the fish a bit, and this all can matter a great deal when the fish is at the hole and makes one last lunge for freedom. Many spinning reel drags are not smooth, and in winter they are even less smooth. I trust my thumb more.

Perhaps the biggest reason I prefer bait casting in winter is that it gives me the chance to use a wonderful coterie of old bait casting reels bequeathed to me from relatives and old-timers who have now passed on. Many of these are beautifully crafted and engineered, and all have a fantastic patina and spirit no modern reel could ever possess. None of these have drags, horrendous plastic parts or onboard computers. A smile never fails to come to my face when I pull down the jig poles with these old reels and place them in the 5-gallon bucket at the start of each winter.

As with most types of fishing, there is more to ice jigging than meets the eye. Trying to be on the fish is overwhelmingly the primary concern, but equipment does matter. Getting set up with the right rods and reels lays the foundation. Next comes line.

WHAT LINE IS RIGHT?

How important is light line? Will you get enough additional strikes with very light line to compensate for the fish that you will break off? Are some species more line shy than others? Does line color matter?

I don't think the answers to these questions are black and white, although today's high-tech angler might have you believe that they are. To the first question, I would say yes, light line can be important. To each of the other questions, I would offer a qualified "yes."

We were standing on six inches of black ice. It was a super spot I'd found only the day before. An inch of new ice had grown in the holes since the afternoon previous, so my pal John and I opened them with our spud bars. It was just after 7:00 a.m., and I'd made him big promises.

The day before, big yellows plus a few white perch and crappies had taken the small baits and jig lures with abandon. Largemouth bass and pickerel were also present. We were 10–15 feet over weeds, with a deadly creek channel and an even deadlier creek channel point in the vicinity.

But Johnny couldn't quite click. He took a few of those big yellow beauties but my tip-ups drew three times as much action. He had excellent tip-ups, but, unlike mine, the spools weren't interchangeable. He was going after these panfish with eight to ten pound test line, very short leaders of only a few feet, and number six hooks. It was the set-up he used when fishing for large crappies at night, and pickerel by day, on a lake near his home. It was quite different from the set-up I was using.

I was using long, 12-foot leaders of 4 and 6 pound test. My running line was black, unlike his very bright, nearly pure white dacron. I was using #8 and #10 hooks, and, in addition, I had little "flickers" (attracting devices) in-line. My jig poles (which took a lot of fish that day) also had lighter line on them.

What made the difference that day? I'm convinced the lighter line and longer leaders made the big difference, although the smaller hooks I believe accounted for a higher hooking percentage on my part.

I use four and six pound test line for panfish, the heavier one only when large gamefish are possible. I have experimented with two pound test line but don't like it. Class Tackle makes a line rated at 3.2 pound test, and this is the lightest I go in winter.

I use four and six pound test for trout, mostly six. For pike I use 12 to 14 pound test, and while jigging has never helped me ice a large number of pike I've taken enough to prompt me to allocate one comparatively heavy jig pole for just pike. I use a steel leader just as I do with my tip-ups.

The line color I prefer is clear. I have not done any controlled experiments on the ice pitting fluorescent or other colored lines against clear lines; furthermore, I cannot say with certainty, and I'm not sure anyone else can, which line fish see least under various light conditions. My instinct is simply to use clear on the theory that it is probably the least visible under the ice.

Whatever line you use on your jig poles, don't be shy about putting some backing on first. The fuller the spool the less cranking to get the fish up. This can pay dividends when you're onto a school of fast-moving panfish. It can also help when you're trying to pull a big gamefish quickly away from the bottom when you suspect that there are bottom snags or heavy weeds in the vicinity. Cheap mono line is fine for backing, but a dark colored braided dacron or nylon of about 12 or 15 pound test is even better. With this you'll be better able to see when your working line is getting short and you need to add some more. I add little stick-on labels to the sides of my jig reels. I write, in indelible ink, the dates that both backing and working mono line were put onto the reel. I also note type and pound test.

Homer Circle, one of the deans of American fishing writers, once said that the single biggest mistake experienced fishermen make is not cutting off a few feet of line before starting a new day of fishing. It's those first few feet that take the most abuse. It's less true in ice fishing, but take Homer's advice and cut off at least a few feet each time. Actually, the most abuse to the line may come at the distance from the lure where the line is touching the rim of the hole. Let's say you're consistently jigging at 20 to 30 feet. If that's the case the line on your jig reel may become most frayed that distance from the end. A good practice is to simply strip thirty or so feet off the reel before starting a new day

A simple jig rod with a horizontally mounted reel. Fifteen feet beneath the bobber is a small minnow, set for perch.

of fishing. If you tie on a hundred yards or so of working mono line, you should be able to fish five or six days before adding more of it.

JIG LURES FOR ALL OCCASIONS

After line comes lures, or baits, since sometimes bait alone is used on jig poles.

There are all kinds of jig lures. Although it's an oversimplification, there are two main types: the jigs used for gamefish and the smaller ones used for panfish. In the former category there are many designs, a few very realistic but most simulative. The clever tinkerers of the fishing lure industry have devised some jig lures that

When a jig rod is set down over a bucket, very tiny bites can be seen.
Note the Strike Guard on the handle of the reel. (see p. 179)

swim in a little circle if you raise and lower your rod tip at the right tempo. The popular Jigging Rapala is one. There are also the "Airplane Jigs" which have little wings. Between straight up and down lures and the true swimming jigs, you have a range of lures that flutter in various ways as they're maneuvered by the fisherman. Some have propellers, some now even have sound chambers. The popular Russian Hook is a very productive single-hook jig that has an especially unusual fluttering motion.

When you're specifically after panfish, a small jig lure may be desirable or in some cases absolutely essential. Still, there are plenty of days each year when both nice-sized panfish and very nice-sized gamefish fall to a 4N Swedish Pimple, one of my favorite all around ice jigs. If I'm after trout, I'll often step up to a 6N Pimple, although I seem to take a lot of trout with the 4N as well. For deep water jigging for lake trout, I'll tie on a 7N Pimple or some even larger lure. For smaller perch, whites or yellows, or smaller crappies, I'll usually use a 3N or 4N Pimple, if I'm electing to use a Pimple in the first place. When you step down this small, you'll even occasionally pick up a nice-sized sunfish.

Nonetheless, if you're really after sunfish you need small sunfish jigs. Of course other panfish and even gamefish will hit these colorful little miniature jigs, but the reverse is not true: Most sunfish just don't have a big enough mouth to go after the bigger jigs with any consistency.

What are sunfish jigs? They're sometimes generically called "dot jigs" or "teardrop jigs" but really, these are particular types of panfish jigs. Almost all of these small panfish jigs (and keep remembering, they're good for the larger panfish too) have a single hook. Many have little blades. They come in a kaleidoscope of colors. Many have little rubber skirts. Some have pearl finishes. Many have fluorescent finishes. Some are, in fact, little replicas of the standard lead-head jigs so effective in many other types of fishing. Some of the best ones are adorned with wisps of feathers.

Day in and day out, you'll take more fish just off bottom than in any other zone in the water. So looking at it simplistically, just let your lure settle to the bottom, pull it up a foot or 18 inches, and start jigging in the manner needed to make the lure work in the way it is designed to. If you don't know what that is, talk to some experts, or just experiment by jiggling the lure a few inches under the ice.

Sometimes you'll hit weeds and then you'll have to pull your jig up farther. If it's not too deep, you might be able to count the turns of the reel handle it takes to get down to just above the weeds. Then, instead of lowering it to the bottom and pulling up, you simply lower to the right depth (right number of handle turns) in the first place. Now you know your lure is not fouled.

I imagine just about any wintertime species can be found suspended on occasion, but a few are almost completely bottom dwellers and several others are mostly found on the bottom. If you decide to start jigging at some zone other than the bottom, you should have some very real reason for doing so. Perhaps others nearby are hitting the smelt at 25 feet over very deep water. If there are other anglers out who are scoring and willing to share their formula, try to pry it out of them. I don't use any electronics in fishing, but finding suspended fish would certainly be one of the top applications for a fish finder in winter. Some members of our local ice fishing clique scored well on crappies last year by using a fish finder. They discovered that at dusk, the fish were moving into a cove to begin feeding — a common inclination for this species — but they could not hit these fish until the fish finder told them that the crappies were several feet off the bottom.

The next chapter goes into much greater detail on fishing through the ice with a jig rod.

CHAPTER 14

Deeper into Jigging

SOMEWHERE IN THE DARK netherworld below, a savage blue-fish was swimming into my consciousness. In the building sea, the head boat swayed nauseatingly, and I tried to mentally block out what the scopolamine had not. For all I was worth, I concentrated, until there was nothing but me, the jig lure and the fish. By my side was a master of the art.

"It's not a hit — it's a sensation. That's where you have to get 'im."

His sack was thumping and it was easy for him to say.

But the presence of the big bluefish was palpable. I was about to make a mistake and do it right.

I sensed the fish, and then immediately worked the jig. The 16-pounder crashed into the lure and I, for a brief shining moment, stepped into the world of the master angler.

Then I snapped back to reality. It had been a kind of déja vu, a daydream. The fish below me was only 13 inches, the water was hard and the only thing making me sick was the iceboaters who every so often lost control and tried to kill me.

The art was the same, though.

The perch were in their finickiest of moods, not crashing, or hit-ting, or even nudging the lure most times. You had to entice them to bite, but you had to feel them there before you offered that enticement.

The man on the head boat was right: It can only be described as a sensation, a slight pressure of moving water against the lure, water rushing in to fill the vacuum left by a fish that is swirling around the lure but not yet taking it. It is how the bluefish masters on the east coast party boat circuit earn their reputations. And I'd just found out that it could be applied to ice fishing.

I'd like to be able to say that I can tell you exactly how to manipulate your jig lure for each species, in each of its three feeding modes, in each of the three ice fishing periods, and so on and so forth. Some authors profess to be able to do this. Jiggle the lure for five seconds, hold for two, bounce four times, study the fish finder, glance at the oxygen meter, raise the lure six inches, repeat three times...good God!

I can't do that but I can tell you four things with some assurance:

1 How you manipulate the lure can sometimes be very important.
2. The size of the lure can be very important at times.
3. The color of the lure seems to matter sometimes.
4. The weight (thickness) of the line you use can matter at times.

Let's start with the first of those.

WORKING THE LURE

Generally, ice anglers overjig for panfish. They work the jig too hard, too fast, and sometimes too hard and too fast. It's true that some panfish like perch and crappies eat a lot of minnows, but most scientists believe that most fish feed less often in winter and eat less when they do feed. As a consequence of this, it's logical to me that they will also expend less energy in chasing a meal. If the larger jigs aren't producing, definitely try smaller ones and work them a little more lightly. "Tease" would be an appropriate description for the way to entice panfish a high percentage of the time. Sometimes the slightest motions imaginable will prove to be most effective. The classic two-foot-lift-and-then-fall will work on plenty of days, but when it doesn't just gently lift or jiggle the lure an inch or two. The action level can be brought down even another notch. Just use a hand to tap the wrist of the arm that's holding the pole. On at least several occasions, I can remember fish hitting jigs that were held absolutely still, with the jig rod resting on a bucket. This has not just happened to me with very realistic lures like the Jigging Rapala. A number of times I've had both trout and panfish hit motionless "tins" like a Swedish Pimple or Jig-A-Whopper. These weren't even tipped with bait in some instances.

Strict concentration is helpful when jigging. So are a few little tricks.

When the panfish are really picky, drop the lure to the bottom, reel up to the desired depth, close the bail if it's a spinning outfit, and then hold the line a few feet below the tip-top of the rod. Then it's one on one, you and the fish. A hand on the line is many times more sensitive than any rod, yet it's surprising how few jiggers are onto this trick. With this hand-hold approach, not only can you manipulate the lure in very tiny increments, but you can feel even a minuscule hit. (Admittedly, it's best not to wear a glove on the hand holding the line.) Set the hook with your hand, then use the reel to bring the fish in.

The other way to foil light biters is by using a spring bobber, which is pictured in this chapter. This ploy is especially useful when you're sitting on a bucket, you're cold or tired, and you don't want to concentrate every second on what you're doing. With the spring bobber on the rod tip, you can even set the rod down on the bucket or the sled and get up and stretch, or have a hot drink, or go skim the holes. Out of the corner of your eye you can watch the spring bobber for its telltale twitch, or ask someone else to.

Bluegills will not usually hesitate to hit a motionless small jig that's tipped with a grub; they'll be much less apt to hit it without the bait on the end of the hook. I guess the point of all this is that you don't always have to hold the jig rod if you have some means of detecting a strike. A spring bobber is certainly one way, and with bigger fish, a bouncing of the rod tip will telegraph the appropriate message.

Getting back to the bluefish analogy, sometimes you can even tell how big a fish is by the sensation, the pressure or suction against your lure. When ice fishing, I have several times felt a big fish near my jig, and predicted what I was about to catch. Sometimes, it was a combination of a sensation and a preliminary hit on the lure by the fish. Of course the habitat and depth told me whether I had a largemouth, a pike, a trout or whatever swirling around the lure.

Let's say you have or are able to cultivate this skill. When you feel that sensation, exactly what do you do? That whole process is very hard to describe. When I feel the presence of a fish by my lure, some little voice tells me when to jig the lure and when not to. You just have to experience this. But make no mistake — you can feel it.

There is a correlation in all this to setting the hook, and this too can very much apply to light biting fish. Here, the sensation you feel is not the swirling of a fish around the lure or a bumping into the lure but the odd slack in the line caused by a lure that was moving and no longer is. Or that had weight to it and no longer does. The lure has, of course, been engulfed by a fish. This sensation, too, can often be extremely subtle. More often than not, a fish will hit a lure in its fallback phase. Thus, when the time comes that you should be feeling that thump of the lure reaching its lowest point, and that thump doesn't come, it's usually best to set the hook to make sure. When the fish are biting very lightly, one may grab it after it's reached the bottom of its fall and then you won't feel him until you jig again. If you're lucky, the fish won't yet have rejected the lure. But the trick is to sense them on the line as soon as possible.

Ice fishing can be very popular on Lake Erie, and I've spent some time reading about hard water angling on that Great Lake. I read about one gent who would constantly jiggle the jig lure for at least two or three minutes non-stop. I tried it this year and found that it works quite well at times. The movements you make are small but you are keeping the lure moving almost non-stop. This jigging pattern worked dramatically well a few times when other people using more conventional motions weren't doing a thing. This tactic might possibly fall into the realm of exciter fishing: You repeatedly do something with your bait or lure to either excite or aggravate your quarry into biting.

It pays, then, to experiment with jigging motions, but I wouldn't encourage you to make generalizations, or to take too seriously those made by other people. Keep trying new things. The willingness to do so is one of the traits of almost all the top fishermen.

In deeper water, as for trout or lake trout, I will experiment by making higher and more vigorous lifts. I have a theory that the more baitfish-oriented a particular fish is, the more active a lure it will strike. Take a bluegill or other small panfish, either of which probably feeds heavily on plankton or other very small forms of food. Even if they take a minnow once in a while, they will not frequently strike a large, minnow-imitating jig lure. Bigger jig lures, moved quickly, may even scare them off. Now take some of the bigger panfish. They might eat a mix of small stuff along with a fair number of minnows. You can use larger lures and work them more energetically with this group of fish. Finally you have the large gamefish that feed mostly on minnows. This is their bread and butter and they will be more apt to strike a larger lure, and one that's being jigged quite vigorously.

At least, this is the way I've found it to be.

It's pretty basic to have to say, but know how your lure is supposed to work. Some lures, for example airplane jigs, are designed to swim in circles. But these swimming lures must be worked at the right pace. See what that pace is by working the lure at the hole first. Do it over and over until that rhythm has been indelibly pressed into your muscle memory. Sometimes, being just a hair off with your motion can cause the lure to work totally wrong.

Spend some time thinking about what you're trying to imitate when you jig. You may have observed that an injured minnow will struggle upward for several seconds before inevitably being drawn back towards the bottom. When you try different jigging motions, try to duplicate as much as possible what you've observed in nature. It's quite true that most jig lures are impressionistic—they don't so much imitate as simulate a form of food. But there is quite a bit of room for creativity when you're doing that simulating.

Let's move on to the next item on the list.

LURE SIZE

As discussed in the preceding chapter, very small jigs are what to use when you are in fact using lures and are after sunfish. The smaller perch and crappies, not to mention rock bass, small largemouth bass and smelt will take these sunfish jigs, sometimes quite well. But for bragging size panfish, I usually go to a somewhat larger jig, like a 2N Pimple, a Russian Hook, or any other lure in this class.

I have a theory that the deeper you go, for any species, the bigger the lure you should try. It stands to reason that there is less light the deeper you proceed in the water column, and that a large lure is more apt to be seen or felt, and to draw results. This theory I temper somewhat with the sure knowledge that on some days, certain species or individual fish simply do not want to eat a big mouthful.

For deep water jigging for fish like lake trout, big pike, large

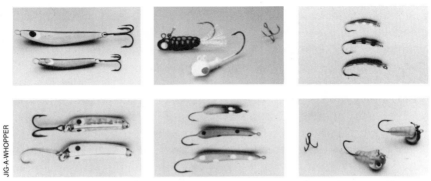

Jig-A-Whopper (see Appendix) offers one of the largest selections of ice jigging lures. Top row, l. to r.: Rocker Minnow, Competition Jig, Flutter Bug Glow. Bottom row, l. to r.: Knocker Minnow, Walleye Hawger, Competition Brite Eye.

brown trout or even bass, don't be afraid to experiment with really large jig lures. I'm talking about jigs or spoons made for open water trolling, casting or jigging — lures in the three to six inch long category. It seems clear that attracting fish to your lure or bait is one of the big tasks when you're fishing in the dark deeps. The size, flash, and sound (vibration) of a large lure may be just what you need to attract some mean-eyed gamefish in the depths. One lure I've used is the Mooselook Wobbler, popular for both trolling and jigging during the open water period in northern New England.

THE VOODOO WORLD OF LURE COLOR

When it comes to lure color in ice jigs, even the pundits of the angling world seem to lighten up a bit. I have no idea what the best color is, but I can tell you that among the best ice fishermen in the area where I live and fish, there is wide consensus that orange is a top color. The most productive small lures I've used have been orange, or part orange. For example, for sunfish, I like a small, orange colored single hook lure with a propeller-type blade that swings on the hook. That's the one that has done best for me on sunfish (but with bait attached, always). I've also had reports from some really good ice fishermen that they've scored in big ways with an orange Jigging Rapala.

In on-the-ice discussions, the other color that comes up very frequently is chartreuse. When I was in college, this was an offbeat drink that you ordered when you wanted to impress everyone by not ordering beer. In the past decade or so, this odd, light, greenish-yellow color has gotten a lot of print in the area of fishing lures. I have to say, it has a lifelike quality, in its own way, that orange certainly doesn't have.

I like a little bit of red on my lures. That's because red looks like blood. I realize that's a simple explanation for today's glamorous world of high-tech fishing, but it's the best I can offer.

I guess I've already made it clear that I like the Swedish Pimple. It has worked well for me, and I think that's the bottom line. It comes in different sizes and colors, and they even give you a single hook to replace the treble when you want to hang a nice minnow on the end. It also has different colored tails that come in the package with the lure (take note — usually red and orange!) I have confidence in this lure and use it a high percentage of the time, when in fact I'm using a jig in this category. I've recently obtained a number of innovative jig lures through mail order catalogs, and some of these have features that are extremely interesting. I notice that a great many feature hot colors like hot blue, hot orange, hot chartreuse, hot green and so on. Many have oversize eyes painted on, a little touch that I approve of.

For the past two seasons, I have been experimenting with the 4N Pimple in hammered copper. I have always had a great fondness for stream trout lures in copper, and I was attracted to this winter jig lure when I saw it. It did seem to produce as well as or better than the silver or gold Pimple that I so often use.

I always wondered why lure companies didn't make more lures in white. Then one day, I saw a Pimple in pure white on the sport shop rack. I tried it for two seasons, and it seemed to work less well than the other three colors I just mentioned. I did give it a work-out on about six or seven different species.

I have read that the last color in the spectrum to fade out as light decreases is blue. Accordingly, I have a few Kastmasters in that popular blue and silver pattern. I use these fast-sinking lures when fishing deep, but I can't recall any really noteworthy action with blue-colored lures.

These are my first-hand observations on color for jig lures. I still think that being on the fish is the single biggest factor, but it is fun to experiment with colors. Such experimentation makes for great theories, but conclusions, for me, are hard to draw since virtually every color I've used has worked at one time or another.

Hot orange or hot red or hot any color is not necessarily the same thing as a phosphorescent color. A lure with a phosphorescent finish actually absorbs light and doles it back out slowly so that the lure glows in the dark. I always have a hard time with the idea of vision and fish, since no human, in spite of valiant scientific research, can ever know how a fish really sees. But a phosphorescent lure sure appears to glow to the human eye, and I have done well with phosphorescent orange during those twilight periods when fish like trout, white perch, walleyes and many other crepuscular creatures seem to bite best. Such a lure would also seem to be a good thing to try during darkness. I recommend that you try these lures — anytime, but especially after dark, in dingy water, or in deep water. By the way, phosphorescent lures should be brought up from time to time to recharge them. In total darkness, you could recharge the lure by exposing it to the intense, focused light of a camera flash.

LINE WEIGHT: THE CHOICES

Almost all monofilament or copolymer line has gotten thinner in the past decade. For the same breaking strength, you get a thinner line. This may be an argument for not going to the extremely low pound test lines that many ice fishermen advocate. I stated my preferences in the preceding chapter and have but little to add here.

I have gone down as light as two pound test line, but this line is very difficult to work with in winter. Our experience is that when the bluegills are biting, 4 lb. test works just fine. Some angling authors like to talk about going down to two and even one or three-fourths pound test. Have you ever tried to ice fish with line this thin? Forget about the fact that you virtually cannot lift any weight with it. The technical difficulties associated with fishing a line that thin and light in winter are immense. Nowadays, the lightest panfish line I use is 3.2 pound test. This line gives me a fighting chance of doing battle with a large panfish, or a gamefish if one comes along.

SWEETENING THE JIG LURE

Should you enhance your jig lure with some kind of natural or synthetic bait that gives off scent and eye appeal? When we fish for sunfish, we rarely get many hits when the jig lure's hook is bare. Without a grub or something on the end, your take of bluegills and other sunfish will be greatly diminished. As for the larger panfish, I've seen

Most jiggers add natural bait to their jig lures. In these two containers are meal worms (left) and mousie grubs. They are both insect larva — the most popular kind of jig lure enhancer.

two situations prevail: you had to tip the lure to do well, or it didn't seem to matter much. But since the first scenario is possible, you should bring bait.

Here we get into one of those areas where there is tremendous variation from region to region. In my area, mousie grubs and spikes are the sweeteners most commonly seen in sport shops. Right behind them are mealworms, which are much larger. Increasingly popular are the Eurolarvae, which come in different colors. In any case, all these are larval stages of insects. Some energetic ice fishermen gather their own bait in winter, as in summer. You can, for example, pry grubs out of the galls (bulbous growths) on the dried stems of certain weeds. Goldenrod is one of them. You can also pry off the bark on a dead log and sometimes be rewarded with free bait.

Still talking about panfish, small bits of worm are very effective. So are small bits of shrimp. So are, sometimes, small pieces of fish. A perch eye from a fresh-killed yellow perch is an extremely effective and durable jig lure sweetener.

If it's bigger fish you're after, let's say big panfish or gamefish, you can tip your jig with a whole minnow, live or dead. If you do use dead minnows, here's a little trick. With the small blade of a pen knife, scale both sides of the minnow. Then split the minnow in half and pry out the little backbone. With the bones and scales removed, the half-minnow (its head can be removed) will be incredibly supple and lifelike in the water. When you wind up a day with some dead minnows, do this surgery on them that night and then freeze them in little plastic bags. You'll have an excellent sweetener waiting for you when your next trip rolls around.

It's best to use a single hook on a jig lure when tipping it with a minnow. If you use a treble, the minnow or half-minnow will look less lifelike and will flop up and get caught on another prong of the treble hook.

Some anglers use the head of a dead minnow, nothing else. Some like to use just the tail of the fish. With a swimming lure, it's smart to use only this small piece of minnow. If you were to put a whole one on, it could greatly throw off the action of the lure.

Synthetic baits like Berkley's line of Power Baits are drawing much attention in ice fishing circles.

Not to be overlooked are the new scent-impregnated synthetic baits. Synthetic is a funny word here. Because they have real essence of fish in them, and some are even digestible, they might be considered semi-synthetic. Two companies now making these baits are Berkley and Dr. Juice. In certain situations, my friends and I have had some spectacular results with these baits. Not only do they have scent — with some brands that scent is not detectable by humans, with others it is — but some even have real taste. I remember the first time I got some Berkley Power Wigglers. My father took them up to the pond to try and catch some crab bait. He said the bluegills were going crazy for them, swirling round and around and attacking the bait. In that same line of baits from Berkley the ice angler might also try Power Nuggets or Power Maggots.

For bluegills, here is a deadly combination. Take a small orange jig with a single hook and a little blade attached to the bend of the

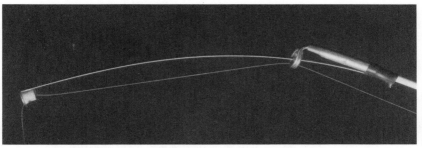

A spring bobber attaches to the end of a jig rod (the means of attachment are several). This extremely sensitive device will communicate the most minuscule tap from a panfish.

hook, my personal favorite design. Break a mealworm in half and place just half on the hook. Lower it down to the zone where the 'gills are located that day. The results should be excellent, as the mealworm broken in half leaves a distinct milky trail. Change the piece of mealworm frequently.

When the panfish other than bluegills are biting fast and well, I often skip the bait. Yellow perch, white perch, and crappies have, on many days, taken jig lures unadorned with bait without hesitation. Especially when you expect the action to be hurried, as with that late afternoon flurry with white perch, sweetening the hook can cost you precious moments and may not be worth it.

FINER POINTS OF WEIGHTS AND FLOATS

Bobbers or floats definitely do have their place in ice fishing, and in my view, that place is whenever or wherever you're in the happy process of reeling in some tasty, small panfish. A float here serves two distinct purposes: It lets you detect the bite of a small fish, and it lets you immediately go back to the same depth, i.e. simply drop the bait down until the floating bobber stops it.

Small panfish can bite incredibly lightly at times. They are used to feeding on small lifeforms that often have little or no means of escape. Zooplankton like *Daphnia* (sometimes called water fleas, a type of insect) and scud (fresh water shrimp) can be important foods for bluegills and other small panfish. But an aggressive chase and attack is seldom required. A bluegill will often just mouth the bait, engulf it, or gently nip at it. If you're not sharp enough to detect these often microscopic bites, you're not ready to deal with winter panfish.

Using a bobber (float) can help you. But if you do use a float, unless it's the right kind of slip float, you'll have to handline the fish in if the water is deeper than about four feet, since the bobber will prevent full reel-up. With bluegills in shallow water I often use a bobber, as will be discussed. But for all the other species in most situations, I prefer not to have the encumbrance of a bobber on my line. If a wayward big fish hits a small jig and there's a fixed bobber on the line, you'll curse a big curse. Caught with your pants all the way down, you can begin handlining the fish or you can furiously try to unsnap the bobber while the angry gamefish is tugging for all it's worth. In either case, it's usually a free lunch for the gamefish.

Believe it or not, even a small, light bobber may not always telegraph the necessary message. Clever ice fishermen in the midwest make their bobbers more sensitive by weighting them. Very tiny shot is placed on the line below the bobber, to the point where the bobber has almost neutral buoyancy. In other words, it's just barely floating, and it's extremely sensitive like that. You could even weight it so that it sinks extremely slowly, and thus offer your bait to the fish in an enticing and very slow free-fall towards the bottom. To accomplish this, you must have a variety of very tiny shot and you must experiment with it. Some authors who get into these fine points forget about practical considerations. Frankly, in very cold weather, trying to place precisely the right amount of small split shot on fine line is not much of a vacation. If you're fishing from a heated shelter, such delicate work may be easy, but if you're outside it's just this kind of precision operation that you want to avoid. If you're up for it, you'll have to avail yourself of the packets of shot made either for fly fishermen — for weighting small wet flies — or the ones made just for ice fishermen, by some specialty companies. In either case, you get a variety of shot ranging in size from tiny to really miniature. You then place enough on the line to bring that bobber ever so slowly right down into the water, or just below the water line as you wish.

A slip float, alluded to above, can be useful. This allows you to set your lure or bait at any desired depth. A slip float can slide freely along the line; it is not clinched on tight. You set the depth you want your bait or lure to be at by placing a "bobber stop" that many feet from the bait. When you hook a fish, the stop reels right in through the guides and onto the reel. Since the bobber is free-sliding, you can reel the fish all the way in. Slip floats (they usually come with the stop) are most often used in conjunction with spinning equipment. With some of the old bait casting reels I use for ice fishing, the stop will not easily glide through (or back out of) the level wind mechanism of the reel. This is one of the things that has stopped me from using the slip float more often in winter.

PLAIN BAIT ON A JIG POLE

I was heartened to see that some of the same fishing catalogs that now sell enough high-tech gear to communicate with alien life still sell the prosaic handline! I am fond of the thought that maybe, just maybe, there's a forgotten little county in some corner of the ice fishing world where everyone ice fishes with handlines, and where you can give your kid something to fish with without sending him off to the local community college to learn how to use it.

You could place a bait on a handline, like days of yore. Indeed, in some areas, many ice anglers use handlines. More commonly, bait through the ice is fished with a jig pole.

A SWish-Rod is a brand name of a device that is actually a cross between a tip-up and a jig rod. You can put the bait down to the desired depth, set the flag that attaches to the rod, then reel the fish in when the flag goes up. The odd, flat-mounted reel has a smooth drag, and there is a little tripod that supports the rod off the ice.

Using bait alone on a jig rod raises some interesting questions and challenges.

How will you know when you have a strike? Will you use spinning or bait casting? If you use spinning and the bail is closed, what will happen if you get a strong hit? If you use a bobber to help detect a bite — regardless of whether you hand-hold the rod or set it down — what size and type bobber should it be, and will the fish drop the bait if it feels the substantial resistance of a float?

On the cove of one productive lake, we begin fishing around 3 p.m. We normally find that the best bluegill action in this weedy, shallow cove is between then and 5 p.m. After dark, we set tip-ups and then rig the extra rod or two with bait. After dark in this particular spot we catch largemouth bass up to five pounds, black crappies up to 2½ to 3 pounds, bullheads, and occasionally chain pickerel. All these possibilities make rigging quite interesting. I prefer to work with a combination of a Strike Guard and a flashlight. The Strike Guard is a device that holds the line from an open-bailed spinning reel then releases it when a fish hits, allowing line to pay out freely. It attaches to the top of the rod's handle. When line is released, there is quite an audible little snap. But since I may not be next to the rod when the release occurs, I use a flashlight to keep an eye on the rod and the Strike Guard. Typically, at the spot I'm describing, we all set in five tip-ups and get most of our quality crappies on the minnows used on the tip-ups. But the baited jig rods account for a few of those big crappies, not to mention surprises in the form of the other species I named.

I'll set the rod down across the open top of a white bucket. I'll drop the bait down a few feet, which is the productive depth here, open the bail on the spinning reel, and place the line inside the "ball bearing" or tension unit of the Strike Guard. Then it's just a matter of listening for the snap of a release, and checking visually with a flashlight from time to time.

Clearly, with this approach spinning is best. I know that some modern bait casting reels have free-spooling, and extremely light drags, but I use old antique bait casting reels with no such features, and they simply would not pay out line freely enough when the Strike Guard released the line.

As is my practice in tip-up fishing, I use the lightest split shot I can get away with. The idea of "anchoring" a bait with a heavy sinker, an idea that some writers advocate, is not for me. Even a small split shot will eventually bring a bait down to at least the level of the shot (bigger bait require somewhat bigger shot, of course). But the bait will try to struggle against a light split shot, and will offer a tempting target for several seconds or even minutes in deeper water. I want this to occur. Then, when the bait gets down to the level of the split shot, I want it to be able to move around as much as possible.

Some anglers buy or rig little lights for their jig poles, for just this kind of night fishing. This can be expensive and complicated. Stay closer to your rod or rods at night and avoid these complications. Some others like to use a bobber, to suspend the bait at the desired level.

By day, the approach for fishing bait on a jig rod doesn't really change, except that you can see if the line has been pulled free from the Strike Guard. Day or night, though, you are faced with the question of how to mark the line, so you can quickly get back to the same depth if you score at that depth. It's a thorny problem. If it's not too deep, I just count the number of reel handle turns and then back off that many turns to return to the desired depth. In deeper water that's a little bit slow, and it can frustrate you when you know that those big humpback perch will be moseying on, or those fat, suspended crappies can wander off any minute. A very small shot placed on the line is one possibility, but it has to be small enough to go through the guides and onto the spool of the spinning reel. It should of course be a removable type split shot. I hate squeezing things onto my line that far from the hook, since it can only hurt and not help the line, although you can avail yourself of the "soft shot" that is available today and is said not to damage line. The bottom line, for me, is the count-the-reel-handle-turns approach most of the time. This can work two ways. If the fish are just off the bottom, you can merely reel up a few turns after dropping the bait to the bottom (you need a split shot, perhaps a good-sized one, to pull the line so that slack can then tell you when you have indeed reached bottom). If the fish are closer to the top than the bottom, you have to start your counting as you lower rather than retrieve the bait. If you use a depth finder, you should be able to see exactly where your bait is by looking at the screen of the unit.

I have no qualms at all about fishing a tiny piece of bait on a bare hook (as opposed to a hook on a jig lure). Pinch on a split shot, bait the hook, lower it down and you're in business. Any tiny piece of natural bait that you would use on the end of a tear drop or other small jig can catch fish by itself. As an example, I find that a big, juicy mealworm fished in this way is deadly on large bluegills, small yellow perch, or rock bass. Of course you can double up on these fun little fish by presenting both a jig and a plain hook with bait, as discussed a bit earlier. You then have the flash of the lure to attract the fish, and the bait to trigger it to bite. Best of all, with such a tandem rig you can see if the 'gills, or other fish, have a preference that day. With bluegills, you'll get more on the baited plain hook than on the unbaited jig lure, I'm pretty sure of that.

Hook size is a matter of common sense here. I'd recommend #10 straight sproat hooks for bluegills. If the fish are running small, #12 might be best. If the 'gills are slab sized and/or some other more hefty panfish are in the mix, step down to a size #8. I steer away from beaked (inward turned) hook points, the main reason being that they are difficult to keep sharpened. Perfect bend is all right, but I like the exaggerated gap of a sproat bend. I prefer straight as opposed to bent hook eyes for panfish.

You can fish a whole dead minnow or "deadbait" as it is called off a jig pole. Northern pike, for example, will readily take bait either suspended off bottom or even lying right on bottom. The bait, if suspended, does not even have to hang in a horizontal manner. Trout will sometimes take a dead sawbelly lying on the bottom, in lakes where this baitfish is found. This fact is pleasing, because sawbellies *(Alosa pseudoharengus)* or "alewives" as they are also commonly called are usually difficult or impossible to buy or obtain in winter.

In summer, you might actively fish a deadbait, for example a salted minnow, in streams for trout. By the same token, you can also actively work a deadbait that you're delivering with your jig rod. A good-sized sucker, chub, smelt or cisco can make a good deadbait for pike. I've heard reports of people using these fairly large deadbaits for lake trout as well, but I have no first-hand experience with that.

Although I rarely use treble hooks with bait these days, for reasons discussed in other chapters, with these big deadbaits consider using them. A set of tandem trebles, with the rear treble a sliding or adjustable one, makes a smart rigging. The front treble would be placed aft of the dorsal fin while the second sliding treble would be placed closer to the tail. With either of these set-ups, you would set the hook immediately upon a take. That's why they are sometimes called "quick-strike" rigs. (Quick-strike is the name used for several different commercially-made hooks or rigs. Anglers also use the term generically.) Any time you use trebles, there is a serious potential for damaging fish you wish to return. But when jigging a deadbait, the hooks will probably not go too deep.

What weight wire to use is always an interesting question when it comes to rigging for pike. First off, use the wire. Period. Otherwise, big fish comes along, cuts the mono, wags his tail, and everyone else on the ice has to hear your profanity. I would recommend 12 or 18 pound test single strand wire for pike in the small to medium class, meaning up to about twelve pounds. If you routinely fish for pike that can go to 20 pounds and better, try 27 pound test wire. Don't be cheap with wire pike rigs. If one gets a crimp in it, discard it. It just doesn't pay to mess around, since bent wire in inevitably weakened.

I use uncoated wire. Nylon-coated wire is available but has a somewhat larger diameter in any pound test. Sure the pike is not too choosy, but there's no sense in trying to offend the fish with overly clubby terminal tackle.

Success in jigging requires a good location plus paying attention to the fine points.

You can jig these big deadbaits just as you would a lure. All you're trying to do is get the attention of the fish. The jigging does not have to be strenuous. In fact, this is another application where a relatively gentle jigging motion can often draw the best results. You'll of course want to use a rod with some beef to it, especially if both the baits and the fish are oversize. I strongly favor conventional jig rods and reels for this work. An ideal jig rod would be about 32 inches long and would have some real backbone to it.

SOME MINOR TACTICS

I often add oversize trebles to my jig lures. Not that I like huge hooks. I don't. I think that very large hooks are oftentimes a disadvantage. But the ones I find on many of the lures I like are just a bit small, and I usually remove them and add a treble that's one hook size larger. You must have split ring pliers to accomplish this. Also, you should analyze whether or not a larger split ring is indicated when you increase the size of the treble. If you jig a minnow on the end of a lure, try a size #6 sproat hook.

I just discussed how trebles fished with bait can be very hard on fish to be put back. With lures it's far less of a problem, but if you release most or all of your fish, cut back the single treble found on most jig lures to two points.

When fishing for panfish, we almost always use a "cheater" or "teaser" a foot or 18 inches above the main lure. For example, with perch we might use a small metal jig lure tipped with a perch eye on bottom and a bright-colored small jig above it. For the top lure or cheater, I experiment with many kinds but I like a small feathered ice fly in a hot color best of all. Almost always, you'll get some fish on the cheater as well as on the bottom lure.

For bluegills, I'll fish two small lures, or one small lure or ice fly and one plain hook. I usually put grubs on both.

When fishing tandem like this, offer them not only a choice in colors but also sizes. Use one small lure and one a little larger. Just tie an improved clinch knot in the eye of the top lure, leaving a 15-inch tag end. Then tie on the bottom lure with the terminal knot of your choice.

I don't recommend using a cheater when fishing for gamefish. First, the line will sometimes pop at the top knot where the cheater is tied on; I haven't discovered a good knot for this purpose yet. Second, the cheater will catch on the rim of the hole one time in four, possibly causing the line to break at that point if there's an angry, thrashing gamefish only a foot below.

CHAPTER 15

Advanced Ice Fishing Mechanics

IT WAS A SPOT WHERE I KNEW a 10 pound trout could be taken.

Four hundred yards to the southwest was a causeway where moving water kept the reservoir open deep into winter. To the immediate right was a small point of land. Out before me was a long, wide, sunken point which I knew rose up about 10 feet above the surrounding subsurface topography.

It was 9:30 a.m. Two anglers already had their ten tip-ups in and, reading the sign in the snow, I figured out that this was the very first morning anyone had been out. First ice: exciting, even with the snow cover.

I stood on shore watching. I had no tip-ups, only a jig pole. The two young men either knew about the sunken point or else were very lucky. Their tip-ups were in good locations.

Too good. The spot I really wanted to be — at the tip of the sunken point — had a tip-up over it. I walked out carefully, kicking the snow aside and poking at the ice with my spud. It was good, but certainly very new ice. I started jigging in 15 feet of water, well inshore of all the tip-ups. It was extremely cold.

I started catching small yellow perch, all throwbacks. I stopped fishing, and watched the ice as I contemplated my next move.

Suddenly, the tip-up near the tip of the sunken point sprang up.

I just had that feeling. One of the two anglers ran to it and knelt down to the hole. I couldn't see much, other than that the fisherman looked intense.

A minute or so later he stood up and cursed one time, very loudly. Then he jumped up in the air, did some kind of somersault and landed in the snow. Then he rolled over in the snow a couple of times. Finally, he got up and started yelling and swearing. This continued for about ten minutes.

Eventually I worked my way out and queried him.

"Big brown," he moaned.

"How did you lose him?"

"The line broke."

"Where did it break?" This question stopped him for a second.

"Did it break at the knot?"

"Yeah, I think at the knot," he answered.

"Bad mechanics," I said to myself as I turned away, but I didn't say it to him. That's the new expression among me and my fishing pals. Bad mechanics. It's a catchy phrase. Whenever one of us loses a fish due to some kind of mechanical problem, we just turn to that person and say, "bad mechanics." It has a lot of truth to it, usually.

"Good mechanics" are terribly important in ice fishing. For one thing, you either have no rod (when using tip-ups) or only a very short one (when jigging) and so there is little to help compensate for your errors in hooking and playing the fish. Also, most fish feed less in winter and opportunities are sometimes very few. A chance at an eight pound trout might well be the chance of an ice fishing career. Bad mechanics can send you to bed very unhappy.

THE IMPORTANCE OF SPOOLS AND LINES

First, you need to start with the right spool. My recommendations are made in Chapter 5. I wind each spool with approximately 350 yards of cheap monofilament, in 12 pound test. Don't use anything heavier as it will be too difficult to wind onto that narrow arbor. This line costs me $1.99 for 400 yards, so the cost is reasonable even considering the many spools I wind.

Next, I add on 50 measured yards of 45-pound test braided dacron in black. This line is expensive, and that's why I fill the spool to about 80% full with the low-cost mono. By the time you add the dacron, the spool should be within about ⅛ inch of full.

The Berkley Co. makes both nylon and dacron braided lines in the heavy pound test the author favors.

At this point, I add an 18-inch section of 18 or 20 pound test mono. I use the Ande brand of line which I use for salt water fishing. This piece makes stepping down to a fine tippet much easier. Finally, I add a high quality mono leader in a size and weight to match my target species and the conditions I expect to encounter.

Attach the fully rigged and loaded spool to your tip-up with a wing nut, set the flag spring, and give the spool a very gentle twirl. You'll be amazed at how easily the flag mechanism is tripped. Now think back to the time when you used the tiny, aluminum spool loaded with, perhaps, 50 yards of 20-pound-test nylon (the usual rig for many) along with a short leader. How many fish did you lose because the flag never went up? You won't have that problem any more, or only very, very rarely.

My fully loaded spool weighs in at nearly 3½ ounces. A small aluminum spool partially full with line will weigh only about half that. The difference in the momentum developed is substantial. But it isn't just the heaviness of the spool that matters. The type of line is also important.

You could get into the mono backing and, in fact, I did so twice this past winter. These were very large bass or tiger muskies. I'll never know because one broke the line and the other pulled free, probably in heavy weeds. (I was not expecting heavy fish that day — I was using my all-around 6-pound leaders.) What's most important, then, is what I call the working line, the heavy dacron, as well as the leader attached to it.

You might find what they call "greendot" dacron in a heavy weight, which is a nearly white line with little green dots on it. But I prefer the harder to find black since I theorize that it may be less visible to the fish. I searched for a long time before I found the 45 pound dacron, which is available from the Berkley Company and comes in bulk spools of 600 yards. I like a line that heavy because it makes handlining a fish much easier. Also, a braided line that heavy is almost impossible to tangle on the ice. I use dacron instead of nylon because dacron has extremely low stretch. Some scientific tests show that it's around 10%, versus up to 30% for some nylon monofilament. I favor fairly long leaders, and I figure that my leader gives me the stretch I need to prevent break-offs. When I'm trying to set the hook on a big gamefish that's a hundred or more feet from the hole, excessive stretch in the working line is not what I want.

There is one exception, though. I rig up at least five spools with an equally heavy braided nylon. These are for shallow water fishing where I use very short leaders, usually for chain pickerel and pike. Here the leader is so short and the amount of line out typically so little, that there is not enough "buffer" (stretch) to prevent break-offs. The nylon working line in this situation provides that extra buffer. Heavy braided nylon is also available from the Berkley Company.

What weight and length leader you use is sometimes an important consideration. Luckily, with the interchangeable spool system, you can easily change line weights as you see fit.

I always have five spools rigged up with 12 feet of 4 lb. test monofilament. I use these when I'm fishing for panfish in places where I don't expect to get burned by a big gamefish. For yellow perch, white perch and black crappies, the 4 lb. is perfect and it does draw more strikes than heavier line. We have one spot where we fish for very large crappies at night. Here, I use short, 8 lb. test leaders. When we're fishing for panfish in a place where gamefish are none too uncommon, I'll usually use my all around leader, 6 lb. test.

I keep another five spools rigged up with six or eight feet of 8-pound test monofilament. I use these spools for chain pickerel, a very important wintertime target where I fish. I also sometimes use these spools for deep water trout or lake trout, although I prefer 6 lb. test for trout when I feel I can get away with it.

If I'll be fishing in very heavy vegetation for pickerel, I'll change to a 10 lb. test line. Pickerel have teeth like pike, but due to their lesser size, they will break you off less frequently. Nonetheless, due to some recent unhappy experiences, I have begun to use light (12-lb. test) steel leaders for pickerel. The Sevenstrand Company makes a steel wire in "bronze camouflage" which I prefer to the bright stainless steel finish.

Finally, I keep five spools rigged up for pike. The Adirondack Mountain pike we fish for average on the small side so I don't use as heavy a line as I might if I fished where trophy pike were common. Usually, I use 14 lb. test abrasion-resistant mono, with an 18 lb. test steel leader on the end.

Pike frequently swallow the bait if you use single loose hooks; a five pounder will easily swallow a six or seven inch perch. I started measuring the distance in a pike's mouth from where the line of a swallowed bait ends at the gullet to the farthest projection of the fish's jaw. In the size pike I catch, it's about six inches. I thus determined that a six-inch steel leader is not quite enough. I make sure the hooks I buy have steel leaders at least eight inches long. Otherwise, I use steel wire in conjunction with loose hooks, and make up the rigs myself.

When 4:30 rolls around, the wind is howling and you look around at all the gear you have to collect, you know the toughest part of the day is at hand. You're cold and tired, and the tendency is to just haul the tip-ups in as quickly as possible. This sloppiness can help undermine your next trip, however.

Once you wind up your tip-up, what will you do with the hook? Some of the modern, well engineered tip-ups have a little space where the hook can be stored between trips. But with a standard wooden tip-up, there is no such provision. Will you just bury the point of the hook in the line? Don't do it! And don't let your invited friends do it to your equipment. I pay a lot of money for that heavy dacron, and I'm not about to chew it up with hook points. Lay the hook shank

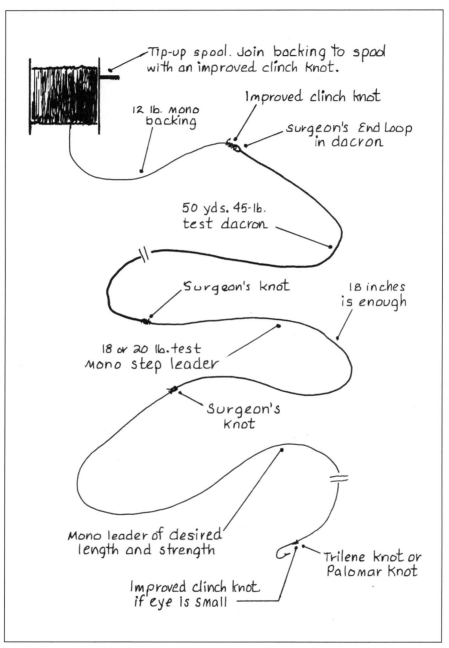

Fig. 15.1 Line and knot system for tip-ups

along the line but make sure the point of the hook is on the outside of the spool. Then use a rubber band to keep the hook in place and the line from unravelling.

KNOTS FOR THE ICE ANGLER

We should now look at the knots used to join the four different lines together. Attach the mono backing to the spool arbor with an improved clinch knot. In an entire ice fishing career you probably won't have a fish take out 400 yards of line (which is what I have on all my spools) but I still go on the assumption that it could happen. I make sure it's a good clinch knot. For that matter, whenever I tie a knot and I'm for any reason unhappy with the way it looks, I cut it and tie a new one. I do this even with knots that can take a half hour, like the nail knot or the albright knot.

Attaching the 12 lb. test mono backing to the dacron presents a challenge. After much experimentation, I settled on this. I tie a small surgeon's end loop in the dacron. Then I attach the mono with an improved clinch knot. In the course of a season, this knot might possibly be tested once or twice, so I make sure these knots are sound.

To join the short "step" leader to the dacron I use the surgeon's knot (not the same as a surgeon's end loop). This useful knot is very strong and is extremely easy to tie when you have three standing ends as opposed to only two.

I also use the surgeon's knot to join the mono end leader to the step leader. Since the step leader is usually eighteen pound test, I am comfortable adding any tippet down to and including 6 lb. test. The surgeon's knot is known as being viable even when the difference in the line weights is at least a factor of four. But on those spools where I am placing 4 lb. test leaders, I add an additional step leader of 10 pound test. This, too, is spliced in with the surgeon's knot.

I used to use the blood knot for joining the leader to the step leader. I don't care for this knot in the heavier line weights, though, so I would only typically use it where (a) the difference in the line weights is not great, and (b) neither line exceeds 8 lb. test.

For tying on a hook or a lure with a relatively large eye I use either the Trilene knot or the Palomar knot. I use the improved clinch knot when the eye is quite small.

Don't use swivels to join line on your tip-ups. When a big fish is running, the line still on the spool could snag on the swivel and cause

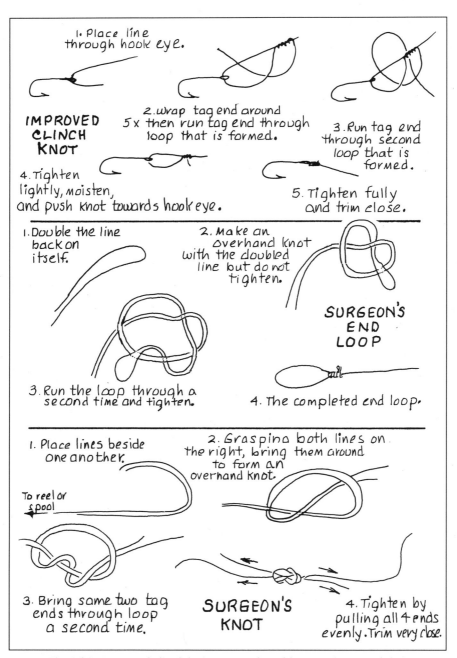

1. Place line through hook eye.

2. wrap tag end around 5x then run tag end through loop that is formed.

3. Run tag end through second loop that is formed.

IMPROVED CLINCH KNOT

4. Tighten lightly, moisten, and push knot towards hook eye.

5. Tighten fully and trim close.

1. Double the line back on itself.

2. Make an overhand knot with the doubled line but do not tighten.

SURGEON'S END LOOP

3. Run the loop through a second time and tighten.

4. The completed end loop.

1. Place lines beside one another.

2. Grasping both lines on the right, bring them around to form an overhand knot.

To reel or spool

3. Bring same two tag ends through loop a second time.

SURGEON'S KNOT

4. Tighten by pulling all 4 ends evenly. Trim very close.

Fig. 15.2 Improved clinch knot, surgeon's end loop, and surgeon's knot

the line to break. The swivel could also catch on the hole as you're trying to coax a big fish in.

But there is an instance where swivels are necessary: when using in-line flickers. These attractors, little beads and blades, will increase your success rate on panfish, but they will greatly increase line twist. A small ball bearing barrel swivel just below the attractor, and perhaps 18 inches from the bait, will minimize twisting. If you consistently fish in deep water, you may also find line twist to be a problem, and ball bearing swivels to be a solution.

I defined the typical set-up for ice fishing as being a small, shiny aluminum spool, 50 yards of 15 to 20 pound test braided nylon, and then a short mono leader of about four feet. I disapprove of all of this, but one other fault of this set-up is the fact that the spool is just not full. The closer your spool is to being full, the less the chance the line will catch on the edge of the spool when a large fish goes off at an extreme angle to the submerged arm of the tip-up. When he feels the extra tension, he may drop the bait, or indeed the line could even break. Keep your tip-up spools filled almost to the brim. A clearance of ⅛ inch is what I prefer, but go to ³⁄₁₆ inch if you'd prefer. This will, of course, be determined by how much backing and dacron you put on. Line running over the rim of the spool, you worry? Because my spool turns so smoothly, this almost never happens.

POST-TRIP DETAILS

When you get home from ice fishing, take just a few minutes to sort out your gear. You'll be tired and you won't feel like doing it, but not doing it will cause you problems later.

Bring the tip-ups inside to thaw out and dry out. Next morning, rewrap them tightly and examine your terminal rigs.

Most important of all, bring your lure boxes inside and see if water has gotten into them. It can take only one dunking and two or three days to rust the hooks on every single one of your lures. Don't let it happen! If the boxes look at all wet inside, lay some newspaper down on your workbench and spread everything out on the paper to dry. If the contents of the boxes look dry, there still may be dampness that will cause slow oxidation. Open the boxes and place them inside the oven with the pilot light on or with the temperature on the lowest setting. Be very careful here — too hot an oven can ruin a good plastic box! Experiment with a piece of scrap plastic.

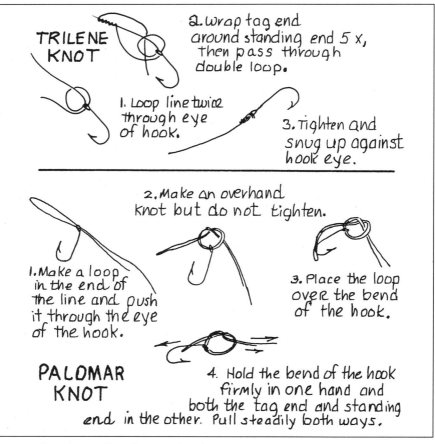

Fig. 15.3 Trilene knot and Palomar knot

Rinse out your fish bucket with a combination of liquid detergent and a bit of bleach or ammonia. It will smell clean next time you head out.

KEEP IT SHARP

How would you feel in society if you were 40 years old and walked around all day with your shoe laces untied because you didn't know how to tie them? As basic as that skill is to adulthood, keeping hooks sharp is fundamental to all successful fishermen. In tip-up fishing, its importance doubles, since you don't have that long, powerful rod to slam home the steel.

One day I was really on the fish and I performed a little experiment. I cleanly hooked about 7 or 8 trout and a few panfish in a row. Then I started hooking only about half that hit. Then, after about another hour and 20 or so fish total, I was only hooking about one in four that hit. I intentionally did not sharpen the points on my lure's treble hook during this period, and it was amazing how my success rate dropped off. When I finally quit around noontime, I checked the hook points. Surprisingly, they felt quite sharp to the touch. Yet the numerous fish I had caught undeniably had dulled the razor sharp points I had started the day with.

Don't just sharpen your hooks when you start out: Resharpen them after taking a few fish and always after getting hung up on bottom. It will make all the difference in the world. On the other hand, don't oversharpen! A few strokes should do it. When you start to wear the original point back, you quickly get into the thicker metal and then you must change the hook or the treble completely.

I prefer the slightly triangular sharpening stone with a groove on one side. The groove is especially useful with very small hooks.

MORE ON BAIT

You probably use small split shot with small shiners and larger split shot with larger shiners. That's very logical, but for any size bait, drop down to a smaller shot size and you might be surprised at the results. It will take longer for the bait to get to the bottom, but that's just what you want. Watch it as it flutters down, struggling against the light weight but not sucked immediately downward by it. It's the most dangerous time for the shiner.

Store bought shiners, such as the "Arkansas shiners" most prevalent in my area, are one of the baits you can use. By no means are they the only bait. Try pond shiners, small dace and small chubs that you can catch yourself in the local millpond or stream. Small suckers are also sometimes very catchable and make excellent bait for lake trout and pike. Chubs and suckers are bottom fish and they will continually struggle to try and get back to bottom. These active baits are much more apt to attract attention than regular shiners, which all too often sit like statues until you tug at them. If there are different kinds of natural bait frequently used in your region, try trapping them yourself. You'll save money and you may improve your fishing.

A stale piece of sweet cake will work well for many types of baitfish. A couple-day-old Danish would be perfect. When trapping bait in bodies of water that contain predatory fish, you must try to locate the traps where the predators are not apt to roam. If game-fish are around, the baitfish will not enter your trap. An ideal situation is to place your traps in a small pond or a small stream where no predatory fish are found.

Most monofilament lines are not engineered to perform at peak level in frigid temperatures. In fact, the lines I like to use in summer get very stiff and kinky in winter. Some lines might be marketed as being for cold weather, but industry analyists say that's mostly what it is: marketing.

My favorite ice fishing line was not designed specifically for winter, but it does perform very well in cold weather. It's called Silver Thread, made by Pradco, which also has a fine diameter for its strength.

I spoke with a company that specializes in testing fishing tackle. They state that cold weather almost universally lowers the strength of monofilament lines. They quickly added, though, that the breaking strength of most mono lines exceeds what the label says, at least under normal temperatures. For example, a line that's rated at 10 pound test might typically test at 12 or 13 pounds in summer. In frigid water, it might actually be "brought back" closer to the 10 pounds it's rated at.

Don't even think about using a cheapie brand of monofilament in winter. A brittle line will cost you many fish before the season's out.

AND YET MORE DETAILS

When you spud a hole, take the time to clear away all the ice chips for at least two feet all around. If it's trout I'm after, I'll make the cleared area as much as ten feet in diameter. Then use your foot or your skimmer and really smooth that area out. On a sub-freezing day I'll even scoop some water out of the hole and splash it around. When it freezes, it will form a very smooth, glazed surface. Conversely, if you leave all those chips lying around the hole, the line is liable to catch on them when you're playing a large fish. This is most critical when it's below freezing since the ice chips will freeze up and will not give at all if your line catches underneath one of them. A good, clean area all around the hole can save the day, or the season, when you're playing a give-and-take game with some monster gamefish that

Incorrect (left) and correct (right). If you don't clear the ice shavings away from the hole, your line could tangle in them when you're playing a fish.

just doesn't want to come in. But even if you've cleared around the hole, you still have to play the fish effectively. Unless your gloves are neoprene or some other very sensitive material, it's best to remove the gloves to play a good fish. You'll have no drag, no reverse spooling to lend you a hand. With handlining, it's all by feel, and there's nothing like a real hand on the line.

Round off the inside bottom of the hole with your spud. Or, purchase a dual skimmer/mini chisel and use the chisel end to "clean up" the hole. When a big fish grabs your bait, there can be great pressure where the line meets the hole. A ragged bit of ice can pop your line or at least fray it and set the stage for later problems.

In the early stages of playing a big fish, try to stand. This will let you walk around the hole to get opposite the direction the fish is pulling. (You're not really standing — you're crouching.) This will somewhat ease the pressure of the line against the bottom edge of the hole. As the prize fish gets nearer the hole, you'll probably have to kneel to be able to land it. If the ice is wet that day, your pants will get wet. My buddy has solved this problem by carrying a hot seat with him. He leaves it hooked on his belt directly over his fanny. He unhooks it anytime he has to kneel down to the hole.

Now you'll have to make a decision. Will you gaff it? Will you gill it? Will you grab it just behind the head? Will you try to grab it under the belly? Or will you ask your buddy to do one of these things? The important thing is that you know ahead of time what you're going to do. Personally, I don't like to impose on anyone to help me land a fish. I don't want them to agonize over a lost fish that may have gotten free no matter what they did. I try to do it myself, but will ask for help with a really large fish.

Any time you dead-lift a fish, expect the line to break. Therefore, don't do it if it's a fish you really care about. Naturally, experience will tell you how much weight you can lift with what pound test line, but it's still risky business.

Pike, chain pickerel, walleyes and saugers can effectively be grabbed behind the head. Bass, which will usually be quite lethargic in winter, can often be grabbed by the lower jaw which will naturally open as you pull the fish close to the hole. If you use this approach with bass, don't support the weight of the bass by holding the bottom jaw open like a hinge, for example if you're posing for the camera. This can injure the fish.

Even big pike can be pulled up then grabbed behind the head, but make sure you have gloves on. Ditto for tiger muskies and muskies. Where these long torpedoes can be both legally taken and legally gaffed, gaffing certainly is an option. Big trout, over 20 inches, I always try to gaff since there is really no way to get a hold of them. Gilling big trout is possible but risky.

If you use a gaff, here's the most important thing: Be decisive. Have the gaff at the water line, wait for the right moment, then make one quick, effective motion. Don't poke at the fish. If you're going to gaff him, gaff him. Use the gaffs made just for ice fishing. H. T. Enterprises sells a good one of just the right size and with just the right bend in the hook. The address for H. T. is in the Appendix.

Every ice angler knows that small panfish are hauled right on up using the rod only. With sunfish and small perch and crappies this is fine, but sooner or later this lazy person's approach will result in an indiscretion with a fish that's just a little bit too big for this treatment. The line will pop and your fish will plop back to his watery haven. But wait — you haven't lost him yet! When a fish breaks off and falls back into the hole, it will be disoriented for a few seconds as it tries to figure out which way is down. If you have good reflexes, you can reach down and scoop him up out of the hole before he finds his way.

One time I used a skimmer to do this. Another time a friend was amazed when I "retrieved" a 14½ inch yellow perch that he intrepidly tried to winch on up with his jig rod. I acted very fast, on instinct, but while I did save his prize yellow I got both of my gloves wet.

SOME DEEP WATER TACTICS

There are a few special considerations when fishing deeper water, which I'll define here as water deeper than 30 feet. I believe it's smart to use heavier line in deep water, for several reasons. For one thing, visibility will be less at that depth and I have to think that you can get away with a heavier line, even with trout. Second, line twist is a very real problem when you fish deep, and the heavier line will twist less easily. Finally, there is more strain on the line irrespective of the weight of the fish you might be fighting.

I said earlier that it is almost impossible to tangle my 45 lb. test braided dacron on top of the ice. Digest the word almost. Last year I was fishing deep for white perch in an angular reservoir and I had two or three really disgusting tangles. Two were so bad that I had to cut out a section of the dacron and splice it back together. That was the first time that happened in the five years I've used the heavy dacron.

Two things combined to cause the problem: deep water, and warm temperatures.

When you're fishing deep and it's a cold day, a reasonably heavy braided line will become stiff very quickly on contact with the air. In these conditions, tangles should not occur. But when it's in the mid-thirties or warmer, the line no matter how heavy will stay limp and then you better watch out. If you're fishing deep, any time you retrieve the line to pull in a fish or check or change bait, carefully lay the line in very large coils on top of the ice. Be extra careful not to kick into your coils with your foot. It can take only one careless body movement to coax those neat coils into chaos. Because of the extra twisting that will occur in deep water, you have to be especially aware of this problem when you're down past 30 feet or so. It's a smart idea to carry one pre-rigged spool in your bucket or satchel, with a tippet to match what you're doing that day. Snap the replacement spool on when bad things happen, and wrestle with the tangle when you get home.

A mobile ice fisherman is a successful ice fisherman. That's why I often bring only jig poles. But mobility of this sort doesn't come without its price. If your manual auger is dull, cutting will be such a chore that you'll be inclined to stay put where you've cut your first couple of holes. Most people send their manual auger blades back to the manufacturer to be sharpened, and that is not a bad idea. Unfortunately, though, you can only maintain that razor sharpness for one or two trips if you cut a lot of holes. I know some fishermen who actually have accumulated three or four sets of blades for their auger. They keep sending them in for sharpening, at five dollars a pop. Between the sharpening, the postage, and the cost of the spare blades, you could spend as much as you would on a new auger in a few seasons.

SHARPENING MANUAL AUGER BLADES

I'm willing to bet that most sportsmen have the same problem with knives. They just don't know how to sharpen them properly, or don't have the right equipment to do so. If you purchase the stones I will recommend, you can sharpen not only your auger blades but all your knives, chisels, plane irons and certain other tools.

You should get a two-sided India stone with a 90 (coarse) grit on one side and a 600 (fine) grit on the other. In addition, you should purchase a white hard Arkansas finishing stone with a very fine grit. With these two stones and some diligent practice, you can effectively keep your auger blades sharp enough to shave your arm. If you're more serious about sharpening your tools, you could additionally purchase a black hard Arkansas. This much more expensive stone is essentially a polishing stone and is definitely optional.

Don't whatever you do buy stones that are too small. Buy the large "bench stones." My India stone measures (in inches) 11½ x 2½ x 1 while my Arkansas (which comes mounted in a nice box) measures 8 x 2 x 1. I purchased both stones from Garrett Wade, of New York City, a company specializing in fine tools. At the present time, the India stone costs $35.95 while the white hard Arkansas costs $35.25 (prices tend to fluctuate according to availability of materials). But each stone should last a very long time, possibly your lifetime and beyond. The address for Garrett Wade is given in the Appendix.

The proper way to sharpen auger blades is by placing your stone in a vise. Be careful to grab enough of the bottom of the stone with the vise jaws so as not to chip the bottom of the stone. If the stone is mounted in wood, this will not be a concern. Use plenty of oil. The blade should be continually "pushing oil."

Lift the edge of the auger blade up so that the cutting edge is at a 20° angle to the stone. Using both hands, sweep the blade across the stone as if you were trying to cut a thin slice off the stone. Because the blade is curved, your sweeping motion will form somewhat of a curve. Understand very clearly that you will not master this right off. Auger blades are hard, and it might take you a lot of practice to get it right. An important thing to remember is that, as with a knife blade, you are attempting to put a bevel on a bevel. That's why you must lift the blade up about 20°. If you swept the auger blade across the stone on its existing bevel, without raising it up, you would not get the blade sharp.

Power auger blades will dull like any other sharp object, but I have found that they stay sharp enough for an entire season. If you do a great deal of ice fishing through consistently very thick ice, you might want to keep an extra set of blades. The manufacturer recommends that power auger blades not be sharpened by the user.

In winter, as in summer, the most important thing is being over the fish. But the second most important thing is avoiding mechanical errors. Details make the difference in fishing, and that is doubly or triply so when the hard breath of winter rides down on your favorite lake.

Nonetheless, somewhere, sometime, some place, in spite of your most valiant efforts, some little equipment failure is going to cost you a very big fish. Just curse once, tell yourself "bad mechanics," and — if it makes you feel any better — roll around in the snow for awhile until the hurt goes away.

CHAPTER 16

Eight Ice Fishing Situations

IN THIS BOOK, IT'S NOT SO much my aim to tell you how to ice fish as to tell you what I've experienced. There are hundreds of thousands of lakes in North America comprising millions of acres and hundreds upon hundreds of ecological combinations. Setting down absolutes about any species or technique is folly. No one fishes more than a tiny corner of the ice fishing world.

What follows are descriptions of eight ice fishing locations where we've done especially well. Each location falls into one of two categories: (1) We've scored consistently at this spot over a long period of time, or (2) we've scored at this spot a lesser number of times but the spot or scenario is interesting enough to bear scrutiny.

The value of keeping a log book cannot be overemphasized. I fill in the data on the first side in no more than ten minutes. Then, if it's warranted, I turn the page over and make a little map depicting the location. I use arrows or call-outs to describe exactly what happened and where. When writing this book, I had a large looseleaf worth of notes to turn back on. Eventually, you do start to learn things, though the insights are often gained with painful slowness.

#1: SUNKEN BAR

One of the deadliest of all ice fishing situations is a bar that rises up distinctly from the bottom. Possibly the best ice fishing I've ever had has been over such a bar on a reservoir just 30 minutes from my home.

As shown on the maps, the long bar runs parallel to shore and about 60 or 70 yards offshore. Its length is a few hundred yards but it has only produced at its west end where it curls towards shore and is more narrow. I discovered it during a severe drawdown years ago. It is comprised of sand; there is very little if any rock. We consistently take most of our fish in a core area (circle) approximately 35 yards in diameter.

Right on the bar is where we do best, but we do almost as well in the pocket between the bar and the shore. It's interesting that we take a few fish on the deep side of the bar but not many. And never deeper than 25 feet.

Like many reservoirs, the water level here fluctuates. In some years, the water is down about six to eight feet when first ice comes. When this is the case, there are usually no fish at all on the bar. We can only speculate that the bar in this instance just doesn't have enough water over it to attract gamefish, or the baitfish the bigger ones dine on. The maps depict the location with the reservoir at full pool.

When the lake is full, the bar produces something like three years in four. What happens in the off year? We haven't the slightest idea. Further, when there are fish, their number seems to vary dramatically.

The action here is amazingly short-lived. I try to be the very first one out at this spot. If the fish are there, action is usually fantastic the first morning. By afternoon it will have tapered off and by the second day you may only pick up a straggler. After two or three days, after which time at least several anglers will have been out there, you can pretty much forget the spot. The fish, especially the trout, do not seem to come back the whole season. We know because we've gone back to the locale intermittently later in the season. One time we did take a few nice largemouth bass here at last ice.

My friends and I have taken as many as about 25 browns here in one day, mostly between one and three pounds but several over twenty inches. That parallels the size you typically take in this lake in summer. We've also lost a couple of trout here between about 6 and 10 pounds. Most of the trout are crammed with sawbellies, the prin-

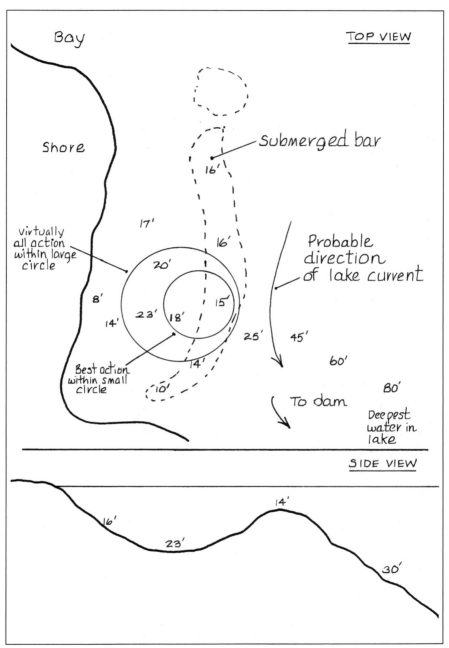

Fig. 16.1 Sunken bar

Two nice browns taken from a sunken bar at early ice.

cipal forage species in this lake, but we certainly cannot prove that the trout are finding the baitfish at this location. However, some of the trout literally spit bait out of their mouths when caught, so it's at least a reasonable assumption that some of that bait is coming off the bar. A couple of seasons we've done fantastically well on big white perch here. Most years we don't take any whites. This is consistent with our experience with this elusive species in a number of other lakes. There are always a few small yellow perch, and in a good year, we take quite

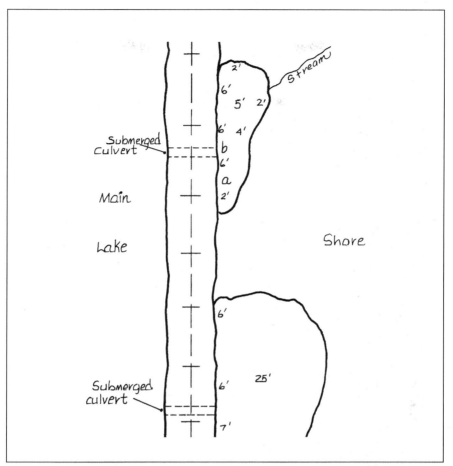

Fig. 16.2 Detached lake areas

a number of yellows including some keepers. But in a bad year, which we define as one when no trout are present, even the perch are all but absent.

The bar certainly offers more mysteries than answers.

Another significant feature of the bar is that the deep side drops off and just keeps on going down to the reservoir's greatest depth of about 70 or 80 feet. The proximity to this deep water is at least one reason why the trout like this spot, we speculate.

Because the bar is very near the dam, it may experience some effect of the strong current that an overflow normally creates. We think that the current sweeps by the bar as it curves around and makes its way to the dam's spillover.

I consider it incontrovertible that on-ice noise chases the fish off this bar each season. It's a good lesson, one we always keep in mind when we're pursuing trout. Perhaps in deep water, banging and other commotion on the ice does not disturb trout. I can't say for sure. But in a shallow water location, noise is a big factor. The really puzzling thing is why the trout do not return to what is obviously a desirable location later in the season, when few anglers are out and about. Do they "remember" having been chased away from the spot? Or maybe the baitfish are only here in early winter.

#2: DETACHED LAKE AREAS

I'd say the single biggest revelation I've had as an ice fisherman is the great potential of shallow water. In summer, you see people rowing around (in our lakes, where motors are forbidden) and almost always it's the shoreline they're casting towards. Why, then, do winter anglers spend so much time soaking baits in 30, 40 even 50 or more feet of water? I think they're so fascinated with the idea of standing on top of all that water that they forget some of the most basic lessons of the sport.

Next is a location that is indeed shallow, and that has opened our eyes to a special scenario to look for. What you have in situation #2 is two small "ponds" semi-detached from a large reservoir. They are actually connected to the reservoir by submerged conduits, and fish can freely roam in and out if they wish. But the ponds are separated by railroad tracks that are propped up on a bank about six to eight feet high and just wide enough to accommodate one set of tracks.

One is shallow and very small and the other is about five times as big and substantially deeper. So far, it's been the small pond that has produced. Here, black crappies, bluegills, and small largemouth bass are consistently to be found. None of the fish are bragging size but they are numerous and the pond is nice to have in the hip pocket since it freezes up very early and keeps ice very late.

We've only fished the large pond once or twice, and we connected with only a couple of yellows. I was troubled by the lack of weeds in that bigger pond, but I still intend to try it again.

To get back to the small pond, there is a nice little stream running in and that may help. There are also some weeds, though not a lot. There appears to be quite a bit of brush at the bottom.

The bluegills may sometimes be caught all day, but late afternoon is the best time. The crappies, which average about eight inches, only hit in late afternoon. The narrow neck of the pond (a) can produce some crappies, but consistently the best action is right along the embankment (b) which is the deepest spot in the pond.

Since we've found this little pond, I've gone out of my way to investigate similar pieces of lakes. Such places have proven to be deadly for bluegills and other sunfish, occasionally crappies and every once in a while, decent size gamefish. If you have maps of lakes in your region, they will inform you of the location of such offshoot pieces of water.

#3: BACKWATER LAGOON

One of our most consistently productive ice fishing locations is a backwater lagoon located on a 650 acre lake. This lake contains bluegills, largemouth bass, yellow perch, and very large black crappies. This is shallow water fishing once again, but this location is quite a bit different from location #2. First, it isn't by any means cut off from the lake. There is a narrow strait located at the north end, and vigorous winds out of the north keep the lagoon replenished with well oxygenated water (in summer, and winter when only the lagoon is frozen). The lagoon is also tied to the main lake by a narrow passageway on the inside.

Bluegills can be taken all day long, but this is another spot where the action on 'gills is best in the latter part of the afternoon. Large chain pickerel can also be caught all day, though early morning and late afternoon are best. Largemouth bass up to five pounds mix in but aren't terribly numerous. We catch them in late afternoon and at night, mostly. On cloudy days, anything but the crappies can be caught all day.

And that's the big attraction, jumbo black crappies, which average about two pounds and which have been caught up to almost three pounds — until just a year ago, only two ounces off the state record. Since more fishermen have discovered the spot in recent years, the number of crappies caught has gone down, but the size hasn't. Other bays in the lake also can produce these large crappies.

The crappie action is as predictable as any wintertime action we've experienced. Most of us work and can't get there until about 5 p.m. We set out five tip-ups each and then jig. You never know what

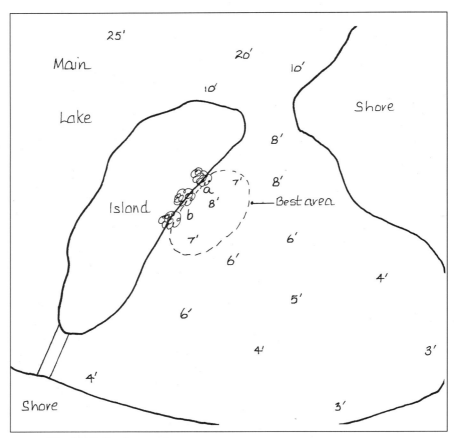

Fig. 16.3 Backwater lagoon

you'll get on a jig, but if you set out to catch bluegills you'll usually get them. By 5:30 the Coleman lanterns are humming and the action is about to get under way. Between about 5:30 and 9:30, the crappies hit the baits which are set only a few feet under the ice. The depth of the lagoon averages only about six or eight feet, and since the weeds grow up from the bottom quite high in places, it would not be possible to set the baits any deeper. In fact, we have to constantly check the baits to make sure there's no weed on the hook and bait. This spot produces the best crappie action in late February and early March. Earlier in the winter few crappies are taken.

This location helped to confirm two classic theories on crappies: They feed best of all just after dark, and they often penetrate shallow bays at night to feed. The theory makers even stipulate that crappies like bays connected by a fairly narrow opening to the main lake. This spot certainly fills that bill.

It's not surprising that pickerel and largemouth bass also find the conditions here favorable. It must be a prime spot in the lake for juvenile fish of all sorts. It's interesting that no yellows are taken here. Rather, they are taken deeper on some of the broad flats and points in other sections of the lake. This is exactly as I would expect it to be.

One more thing: We've explored all over this lagoon and the large crappies are consistently taken best in the area within the circle. (Interestingly, in the back part of the bay the crappies that are caught are usually little ones.) Within the circled part of the lagoon there is slightly deeper water, and there are also some overhanging willows, the tips of which may actually be frozen into the ice. Right around the willows (a and b) is the top spot.

#4: WEED BED – CREEK CHANNEL POINT

This is one of the hottest spots I've found. Enjoying success here the very first day was especially gratifying since I had studied a contour map of the lake the night before and had "sniffed" the spot out.

It's really two honeyholes in one. They're completely distinct, but close enough together that they can both be fished at the same time.

This is an arm of a long, narrow, many-fingered watershed reservoir. Down the middle of this arm, a very discernible current exists. Unfortunately, this current helps to keep this enjoyable spot open deep into winter, and sometimes all winter.

The first of these two adjacent spots is contained within the rough circle. It has a flat to gently sloping bottom and a rich growth of weeds on that bottom, mostly Eurasian milfoil. The weeds seem to be thickest in one particular area, but beyond the fingers of the weed bed the bottom appears to be almost completely bare. In the heart of the weed bed, fine yellow perch averaging a foot in length have set up shop, and respond extremely well to both small minnows and jig lures. As with trout fishing (see location #1), angler activity puts a definite squelch on the action, but never completely. There seem to always be a few big perch rooting around, but when the spot is being hit hard I go early in the morning and I get my five or six big ones before anyone else even gets there. It's as if the fish are driven off during the day but regroup to some extent between dusk and

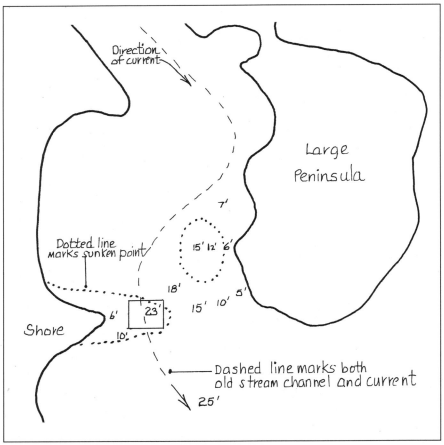

Fig. 16.4 Weed bed – creek channel point

dawn. This concept is one to be kept in mind for other species and other kinds of locations.

We've taken a few bluegills here and I suspect that if we tried harder for them we'd get more. Other types of fish have never showed up on the end of our line.

The other spot, within the square, is about seven to eight feet deeper and seems to have no weeds at all. There is an old creek channel here, and a point that runs out towards it. In the bass fishing literature, a "creek channel point" is cited as one of the best bass locations. Certainly, this second location, within the square, is the deepest part of this arm of the reservoir.

Virtually every trip we tangle with a nice largemouth bass. I landed a five pounder one day and that same day broke off two even larger fish. These could have been tiger muskellunge but were more likely very large bass. Interestingly, the spot also produces a few chain pickerel, and these have been small. Finally, a small brown trout has shown up from time to time.

On the perch weed bed, one or two holes consistently are the busiest. The spots with the thickest weeds seem to be best. Similarly, one very small section in the other area, within the square, also seems to provide the bulk of the action. I've gotten so I know almost exactly where to set the tip-ups, and I'm seldom disappointed.

Some writers have spoken of yellow perch as preferring clean bottom. It's another example of the futility of making generalizations. We definitely have found perch roaming clean, open flats, but they sure like the weeds here. It's interesting to note that on a different arm of this same reservoir, there is an extremely productive weed bed for perch. Here the depth is only half as much, about six or eight feet, and the perch are substantially smaller. This back-up spot is a jigger's mini-heaven.

#5: WATCHPOINT

I call this type of feature a watchpoint, but it might also be called an entranceway. As shown on the map, it is the "neck" leading into a small bay. Such a spot seems to only be viable when the neck itself is fairly narrow.

Anytime you take a seven pound bass it's worthwhile taking note of what you did. I took one nearly this big last winter, lost another large fish here (letter a), and also took a nice bass and lost a few larger ones at letter b, a similar spot. I've also seen this type of location pan out during open water.

Largemouth bass are thought to be extremely territorial, and I believe that such a "watchpoint" is where a big bass stands sentinel at the entrance to "his" bay.

Just off the small point at letter c, we've done very well with good-sized yellow perch. In spite of all the attraction of points to the average ice fisherman, this is one of the relatively few ones where I've had days to get excited about. The fact that both a weedy bay and a deep channel are very close could help explain the productiveness of this small point.

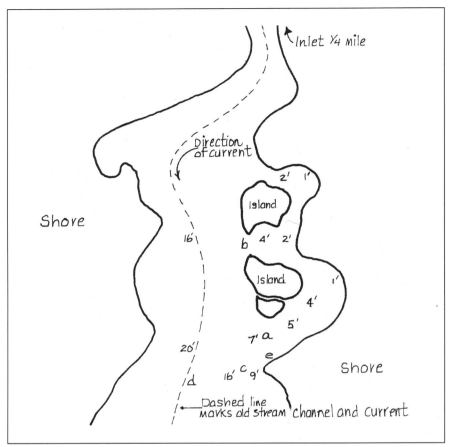

Fig. 16.5 Watchpoint

I took a better than decent smallmouth bass in the main channel at letter d. Amazingly, two 11-inch brook trout were taken by my partner up against the little sloping bank at e. These were without question strays from a good trout stream that feeds the reservoir. Nonetheless, brookies in this string of reservoirs are rare, and it was a thrill seeing them come up through the ice. They were both wild fish.

#6: LAKE SADDLE

A saddle is a part of a lake that joins an island or a barely submerged bar to the shoreline. As opposed to a simple shoal that

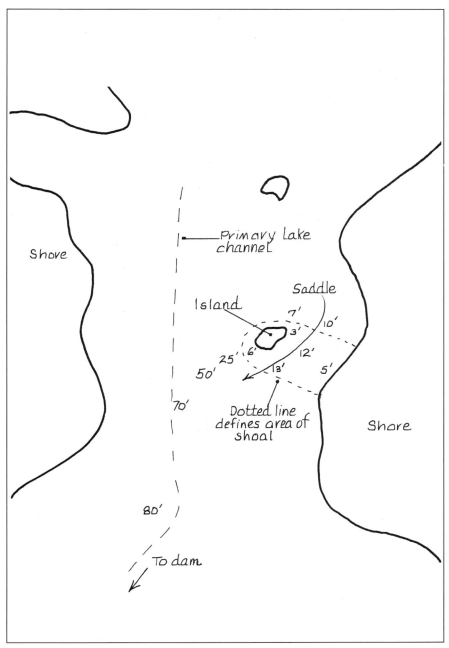

Fig. 16.6 Lake saddle

runs out from shore at a steady angle (perhaps to join an emergent island), a saddle has enough depth to make it an interesting, and potentially fish-holding area.

If you study enough lake contour maps, you come to see that saddles are relatively common features. Have you been trying them? My experience is that saddles that are in reasonable proximity to some deep water hold the most potential. Even if the bottom is relatively bare of weeds, rock, or other structure, a saddle by its nature can be fishy. I see it as a kind of funnel, a travel lane between shallow water and deep water, between two deep water areas, or between a feeding area and a resting area. The particular one depicted on the map has been a good spot for both brown trout and bass (largemouths and smallmouths). The ubiquitous yellow perch will also mix in here from time to time, but this saddle seems to be primarily a gamefish hang-out.

Exactly why the gamefish are here, or travel through here, we can only conjecture. For sure, they may spend a good deal of the day in the deep water out beyond the island and then move in here during darkness. We don't night fish this spot but early morning is always best. It's also possible that the substantial little channel that traverses this saddle is a travel lane for baitfish.

#7 ARTIFICIAL REEF

One enterprising guide whose lodge we stay at decided to make a particular section of his lake a bit more appealing to northern pike. Over a period of some years, he submerged Christmas trees (in a scattered fashion) in an area roughly 75 yards square. The spot is easy to find because the guide keeps his shanty right in the middle of it. Probably the most consistent pike fishing in this lake is around this artificial structure. Also to be found here are crappies — a species well known for haunting submerged brush — pumpkinseed sunfish, and largemouth bass. The bottom here appears to be paved with tiny yellow perch, mostly 4 to 7 inches long. These we can jig up at will, and they make for fine pike bait.

Our guide and host obviously knows a bit about pike. He placed the trees in an area that already had some things going for it.

First, he dropped the trees mostly in that 8 to 15-foot depth range that has accounted for such a high percentage of our winter pike take. Further, he located the trees just offshore and more or

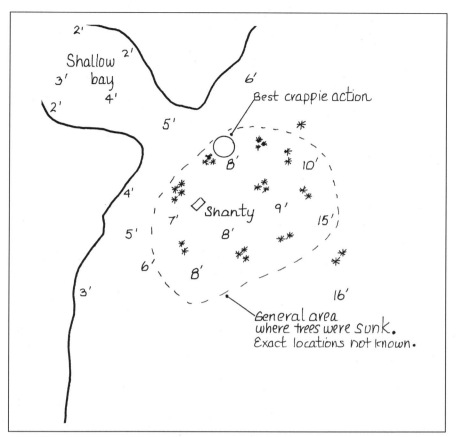

Fig. 16.7 Artificial reef

less in or at the edge of a band of natural, rooted vegetation. Finally, there is a small bay almost immediately adjacent to the tree area. In the literature on pike, a shallow, weedy bay in the vicinity heightens the possibility of any type of main-lake structure holding fish. The bay is too shallow to fish, but there certainly is every expectation that the pike feed in or otherwise utilize the bay from time to time.

It's interesting to note that pike are found throughout the tree area. Occasionally, one is taken very close to shore in water less than six feet deep. But most are caught at depths of seven feet or greater. The crappies here seem to be much more particular about location. In fact, there is one 20-foot-square area (circled) that accounts for

When the ice is relatively clear and not snow-covered, there is always a chance for some action with largemouth bass.

most of the crappies we catch here. Maybe there is a concentration of the sunken trees in this specific locale, but whatever the reason, I try to get on it each year with the jig rod.

There is another aspect to this spot. Although virtually all the yellow perch we catch are tiny, at very last ice — late March or very early April — there can be a run of extremely large yellows in the area of the trees. Some of these will go well over two pounds. Perhaps these pre-spawn yellows move in from other parts of the lake to utilize the artificial structure for procreation. Or, perhaps they use the adjacent bay during this part of their life cycle. We've never been at the lake at last ice, so we haven't had the pleasure of encountering these monstrous yellows. A bunch of them, though, have been mounted, and are displayed in the lodge at the lake's edge.

#8 MID-LAKE BASS SHOALS

During a recent dry period, we discovered some sunken islands in the middle of a large (800-acre) water supply reservoir. We went back in winter when the lake was close to capacity, and found these several adjacent sunken islands to be a prime holding area for bass,

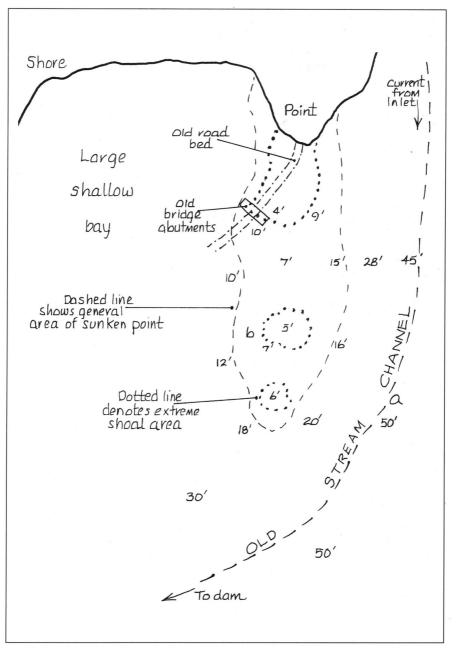

Fig. 16.8 Mid-lake bass shoals

both largemouth and smallmouth. The accompanying map shows the basic layout of the location. I think it's significant that very deep water is found all along one side of this long, mid-lake shoal area. We've always felt that a shallow bar or island located main-lake is most productive for gamefish when deep water is readily accessible.

The distance from the surface to the tops of the submerged islands varies depending on the height of the reservoir at a given time. At full capacity, the islands are down about 10 to 15 feet. One time in late February the lake was down and the tops of the islands were exposed. Now, they were true islands, poking out of six inches of black ice. We fished between and around them, and still caught bass, up to about five pounds.

We've taken some nice big yellows in this lake, but not around these shoals. Once in a while, a small white perch shows up. In the adjacent channel (a), lucky jiggers sometimes get into substantial schools of whites. Our theory is that these white perch, which we've often found deep in winter, pretty much stay in the channel, but every so often drift up onto our bass shoals.

So far, we haven't found any particularly productive part of this shoal area, although several bass, perch and even a brookie were taken at b, in very shallow water.

CHAPTER 17

Cooking on Ice

ALMOST EVERYONE THINKS that food eaten outdoors tastes better, but no one ever stops to think about why. Here's why: Because the food is eaten in a closer context of its origins. Move from the kitchen to the patio, and the soil, the wind, the sun, and yes, even the rain and the bugs become a part of the meal. Since it is these earth elements from whence the food came, eating on the patio lets us eat the food and at the same time experience part of the miracle of its birth.

Move now from the patio to the ice and you are not just surrounded by the earth elements but intertwined with them. Respect for the miracle of food, which is to say the miracle of life, comes easily after five hours spent in a minus twenty wind chill.

Cooking on the ice is not the most trivial of pursuits.

I'll be honest: Most days I just bring a small amount of food that does not require cooking or even heating. Oh, I admit I went through a phase when I had to bring, each time, the Coleman stove, a frypan, a coffee pot, bread crumbs, packets of chicken broth and beef broth and hot cocoa and on and on and on. We ate well and impressed people, but we realized at some point that we were spending more time cooking than fishing. I decided that I'd rather eat to live than live to eat, at least while living meant ice fishing.

Why, then, a chapter about cooking on ice? It's still fun to do a

Kielbasa and eggs is a wintertime breakfast few will refuse. Keep the coffee pot (or just hot water) going at a low simmer.

few times a year, when we call everyone we know and make a little party of it. It's also an excellent way to bring together a group of kids, a sportsman's club or what have you. In fact, now that we do it only occasionally, it's become even more fun, and more anticipated.

Whether or not you cook on the ice, you can bring some items from home fully prepared. We consider hot drinks to be survival gear.

I'm very fond of making soups from chicken, turkey or gamebird carcasses. I freeze it up in pint size containers, thaw it the day before the trip, and then just heat it up in the morning. A pint of piping hot, homemade broth, run through a strainer, fills my small Thermos to the brim. My partner, who comes staggeringly well prepared, always brings two Thermoses, so I usually only bring a pint. It's very important to pre-heat the Thermos with boiling hot water. Even a half hour or less of preheating will help extend the amount of time the bottle will keep the liquid hot.

My second favorite hot drink is herbal tea. I use all kinds but my favorite is Cinnamon Apple Spice from Celestial Seasonings. I make it sweet with honey, and I find that one bag in 16 ounces of water is enough, if the bag is left in there.

Third on my list is hot cocoa. I believe there are at least a couple of generations out there who don't even know what real hot cocoa is. You buy the cocoa in powdered form and then add milk, sugar, a dash of salt, and whipped cream if you have it. This genuine hot cocoa tastes worlds better than the one you make from little packets. Just read the list of ingredients on a packet of "hot chocolate" and see if you still have an appetite for it.

We drink no alcohol on the ice, but I might have a bottle of Heineken after the long trudge up to the car at day's end. Sometimes it's partially frozen and I have to thaw it out by the truck's heater.

GEAR FOR A WINTER COOK-OUT

One time I was fishing at West Branch Reservoir near my home. My partner took a brown of about 20 inches that day, but while I didn't take any trout I did take home a nifty cooking idea.

On shore were two professorial looking gents talking and kneeling over a small fire. Each had his skimmer in hand, and in each skimmer was a foil-wrapped hamburger. They were grilling the burgers over an open wood fire. They'd brought some rolls, some sliced onions and some ketchup, and when they bit into those medium rare burgers, they looked more than happy. You can use your skimmer to cook or heat burgers, hot dogs, fish wrapped in foil, breadstuffs, and other things. It's a good trick.

If you do have a fire going, you can grill a small fish on a green stick. Gut and gill the fish and take your forked stick and place it in the cavity of the fish. Now force the prongs of the stick through each flank of your impromptu lunch. Hold it or prop it up over the fire, turn it round and round as you're watching for flags, and it will be done in 15 minutes or so.

If you're a shanty fisherman, you can use your propane or kerosene stove to heat up a can of soup or something more elaborate. The beauty here is that you may need virtually no equipment or utensils. Last year, we heated up cans of soup on top of the kerosene stove in the shanty, and ate right out of the can. Of course, remove the top first, and do remember to bring metal spoons both to eat the soup and stir it.

It seems to me that a real ice fishing cook-out means just that: cooking outside in the elements. For when this inspiration strikes your fancy, you should right now put aside a box of stuff that will see you through the enterprise:

1. Camp cooking stove, gassed up at home
2. 10-inch cast iron skillet with top
3. Coffee pot, which without the guts can be used simply to heat water
4. 1½-quart pot, lid desirable
5. Spark-producing stove starter — a Godsend!
6. A little pouch with spatula, large spoon, can opener
7. In the same pouch, some silverware
8. Stove stand to support the cooking stove at waist level
9. A few small plastic (rigid) bowls and plates

This is my wintertime cooking gear. I put it in a box at the start of the season and leave it there. The wooden box fits on top of my sled-box, and comes along for the ride when I pull the sled. On the evening before the trip, I add the little things like salt, sugar, bread crumbs, cooking oil, other spices or condiments and so on. If you frequently cook on the ice, why not leave these basics in your box all the time? Finally, in the morning, I toss in whatever food there is to heat up or prepare.

Everything, all of it, is in the one box, although in the sled I might have a few extras of plastic utensils, cups, and so on.

It's not too dumb to plan your ice fishing cook-out for a day when the weather looks to be decent. Hamming it up over a stove in a high wind on a biting day is more drudgery than glamour. If the day is at hand and looks to be nasty, especially if it looks to be windy, tone the menu down so that you are more heating than preparing food when you get to the lake. Believe me, you can have most of the romance without the finger-numbing toil by simply heating up a good looking pot of vittles on the roaring Coleman stove.

Here, first of all, are some cook-at-home and heat-on-the-ice recipes that I think you and your guests might like. (The pancakes you do have to cook, but make the batter at home.)

Jim's Whole Wheat Pancakes
2 cups stone ground whole wheat four
4 tsp. baking powder
1 tsp salt
2½ T. sugar
1 T. maple syrup

6 T. melted butter
2 eggs, beaten
2½ cups milk

After much experimentation, I perfected this recipe which makes nice, dark high cakes. If you can't get stone ground flour, regular whole wheat is acceptable but might require less liquid. If possible, sift the flour. Combine the dry ingredients with the flour. Beat eggs, add 1½ cups milk. Stir in melted butter and syrup. Add this to flour mixture. Add rest of milk carefully. It shouldn't be runny. For smoothest batter, use a whisk to stir and mix. The batter keeps well for a few days, so make the day before your trip and just bring along in a plastic container. Do try to warm the batter a bit before using. You might accomplish this by placing the container of batter on a lit stove on the grate over the burner that is not lit. As an alternative to meat, try serving with some strawberry or blueberry preserves. Serves 8.

Farmhouse Cornmeal Pancakes
To one cup boiling water add a cup of yellow cornmeal, 2 T. sugar, 1 tsp. salt. Stir, remove from flame. Beat together one egg, 2 T. melted butter and ½ cup milk. Add this to first mixture. Sift ½ cup flour and add that. Bring to the ice in a plastic container. Cook like pancakes on a very lightly greased cast iron skillet or griddle. Serves 2-3.

Pasta e Fagioli
Fry two minced cloves garlic in oil. Add 1 small can tomato paste. Stir well. Add two 8-oz. cans tomato sauce and one 15-oz. can crushed tomatoes. Stir, cook 20 minutes. Add salt, pepper and Italian seasonings to taste. Sauce should be quite thin. Add a little water if necessary. (To increase bulk, add additional cans tomato sauce or one large can puree, and adjust seasonings accordingly.) Add a little sugar if desired. Dice 8 ozs. kielbasa and add to pot. Cook 30 minutes more on low flame. Add one 16-oz. can Progresso cannelini beans.

Separately, add 2 cups dry ditalini to boiling water. Cook 3 minutes, drain.

It will be best if you combine the partially cooked ditalini and the sauce mixture in the morning before you leave. Crusty bread is a necessary accompaniment. Serves 6 or more.

Tracker's Venison Soup

1 venison shank (lower part of any leg)
butter or oil
2 small carrots
handful mushrooms
1 qt. water
⅔ cup yellow turnip
1 med. onion
2 stalks celery
1 can (13¾ oz.) beef broth, or better yet, venison stock
salt to taste
dash garlic powder
dash worcestershire
dash cayenne
⅓ cup uncooked brown rice

Trim shank of excess fat and cartilage. In large pot, brown shank well on all sides in butter or oil. Chop vegetables and add to pot. Add broth and 2 cups water. Simmer about 30 minutes more. Remove shank from pot, cut off meat, and return boneless meat to pot. Add 2 cups more water and the rice. Season to taste. Cover loosely and simmer 30 minutes more. You want to end up with about 5 cups of soup. Thicken with a flour-water mixture if desired. I like to slip in a tablespoon or two of white vermouth if I have it. On the ice the next day, you should serve this with crusty bread. Serves 3.

Italian Pork Chops

2 large pork chops or 4 pcs. chicken
1 potato, sliced
½ of a large bell pepper, chopped
2 small onions, chopped
1 16-oz. can Delmonte stewed tomatoes
1 8-oz. can tomato sauce
½ tsp. dry basil
salt and pepper to taste
sugar to taste, about ¾ tsp. (or omit)
3 cloves garlic, coarsely chopped
olive oil
oregano

Sauté garlic in oil. Add chops and brown. Add all other ingredients except potato and seasonings. Cover tightly and cook 20 minutes on low heat. Add potato and season to taste. Cover, cook about another 20 minutes. Adjust seasonings as necessary. Serve with Italian bread. Serves 2.

I found that this original recipe works equally well with chicken, with no other changes. For your cook-out, why not boil up some rice or egg noodles to go with this?

Giambote

Sauté 6 sweet Italian sausages, diced, along with one large onion and one medium bell pepper, both diced. In a separate pot, parboil two medium potatoes, peeled, about 6 minutes. Dice potatoes and add to sausage mixture. Stir. Add a bit of butter or oil if too dry. Sprinkle on salt and pepper to taste, along with 1 tsp. fennel seeds and a few dashes cayenne. Add 2 T. white wine, stir. Total cooking time should be about 35 minutes on medium-low flame. Some will like this with ketchup on top. Serves 3.

Giambote with Fish

Omit the fennel seed in the above recipe. Bring the above out on the ice. Heat. Add 1½ cups cooked, flaked, fresh-caught fish. (Simmer your fish in a skillet to get to this stage.) Cook, stirring, about 4 more minutes. Serves 3-4.

THE STOVE OVEN

An ardent chef du jour can impressively augment his or her bag of tricks with a camp stove oven. This collapsible oven pops together and is made to be used directly atop a camp stove, either gasoline or propane. It measures about 12 inches cubed when set up, and can be gotten in many stores and catalogs that peddle camping gear. In summer, I bake breads, rolls and other things in it, while camping, but it takes a little while to get it up to the 350 degrees or more that you need to bake effectively. In windy, cold weather, it takes even longer to heat it up. There is a thermometer on the outside but it has no thermostat. You regulate the heat inside the oven by raising or lowering the burner on the camp stove.

In any weather, though, the oven can at least do a good job of heating up food brought from home, for example a foil tray of left-

This stove-top oven made by Coleman can work wonders out on the ice. It's shown here in summer, with a loaf of bread rising next to it.

over lasagna. If it's not too windy (wind can really sap heat from this appliance) you can use your stove oven to bake cinnamon rolls, casseroles, biscuits or muffins, a simple cake or cookies. Even with this spirited approach, it's best to actually prepare the items at home. Lots of chopping, mixing, measuring and pouring is not really what you want to be doing out in the cold, at least it's not what I want. If even home preparation seems like too much bother, you can detour to the supermarket on the way and basket some frozen goodies to heat up in the stove oven. For example, frozen cinnamon rolls already premade and ready to bake can be gotten in most stores. The smell of these baking will drive everyone near you on the ice nuts. TV dinners, Italian specialties, heat 'n' serve pies, and so on can be simply heated in the oven and eaten right out of the foil or plastic trays they come in.

Here are a few more recipes, ones for which you may choose to do some of the preparation out on the lake. A couple of these involve use of the stove oven.

Hash 'n' Eggs on English

Split two English muffins and butter them. Fry lightly in your skillet. Wrap in foil to keep warm. Heat one 15-ounce can hash in the skillet. Make 4 indentations in the hash. Break one egg into each indentation. Cover and cook until eggs are set. Break apart carefully with a spatula and serve over muffin halves. Serves 2-4.

Apache Corn
Dice one pound of slab bacon and cook on medium-low flame. Decant as much grease as possible. When bacon starts to crisp, add 1 16-oz. can kernel corn, 1 small bell pepper chopped and six eggs. Stir well, add salt and pepper to taste. Stir again, cover and cook till done. Serves 3-4.

Jim's Mountaintop Homefries
3 med. potatoes. preferably white or red-skinned
1 small sweet potato
1 med. onion
oil
butter
2 T. dried chives
paprika (about 1 tsp.)
garlic powder (few dashes)
ground red pepper (few dashes)

Bring a pot of water to the boil. Wash the skins of the potatoes but do not peel. Boil potatoes including the sweet potato for 6 minutes. Drain and cover with cold water. In five minutes, scrape away skin. Return to cold water so as to stop internal cooking process. Wrap spuds and store overnight. Bring them with you the next morning. On the ice, heat your 10-inch cast iron skillet. Add oil and butter. On low flame, cook coarsely chopped onion till golden. Add chopped potatoes. Add a little more oil if too dry. Add other seasonings to taste. Cook approx. 15-20 minutes on low – medium flame. Potatoes should have just a bit of crispness left. Serves 3.

This excellent biscuit recipe is reprinted with permission from *North Country Gourmet,* by Robert J. Titterton (The Countryman Press, Woodstock, VT, 1991).

Buttermilk Biscuits
2 cups all purpose white flour plus 1 cup cake flour
4 tsp. baking powder

½ tsp. baking soda
1 tsp. salt
3 T. butter, chilled
1¼ cups buttermilk

It seems that almost all the foods which are appropriate out on the ice should be accompanied by some kind of bread. You can make the dough for these simple biscuits at home and use your stove oven to bake them out on the lake. Sift together the flours with the other dry ingredients. Cut in the butter with two dull knives or a pastry blender. Do not overwork. Pour in buttermilk and work it in quickly with a fork. The dough should be sticky but should hold together very easily. Heat your stove oven to 350 degrees. After washing your hands at the hole, form biscuits each the size of a large egg, and bake them (on a tray) with sides just touching until golden brown, about 12 minutes. Be sure to bring some kind of baking tray to set your treats down on before placing on the wire rack of the stove oven. Makes about 10.

Tomato and Lima Casserole
Here is a delicious and simple meatless recipe that you can essentially compose at home and then just bake for 30 minutes out on the ice, again in your stove oven. Drain a 16-ounce can each of Delmonte stewed tomatoes and lima or butter beans. Place the drained vegetables in a suitable baking tin. Take 1¼ cups of the drained liquid (if you get less, don't fret) and slowly add it to a skillet in which you've first made a thick roux composed of 2 T. melted butter and 2¼ T. flour. Stir till smooth and cook on gentle heat about 10 minutes. Add salt and pepper to taste. A dash of cayenne can be added, so can the herb of your choice (try a pinch of marjoram or savory). If needed, add a bit of water, but keep the sauce on the thick side. Cool, and stir into vegetables. Next day, bring the vegetables in an ovenproof dish, and a cup of herbed croutons in a plastic bag. Sprinkle the croutons on top of the vegetables and heat for 20 minutes in your stove oven kept at 350. Goes very well with fish. Serves 3-4.

COOKING THE FISH YOU'VE CAUGHT
The ultimate pleasure and the highest form of showmanship on the ice has to be cooking the fish you've just caught. Again, think simple, and while you're thinking simple, think not too many ingre-

dients. And while you're thinking about those two things, think about what pre-preparation you can do at home to simplify procedures even further out on the ice.

It's good to have a strong bladed knife and a fillet knife. A good all around length for the fillet knife blade is five inches. The strong knife can and should be used to cut tough skin (as on a yellow perch) or bone, cartilage and fins. The fillet knife will keep its edge longer if you baby it and use it only for cutting flesh. I like to bring pliers, too, since I prefer to skin many fish before filleting them. Included here would be crappies, bluegills, and white or yellow perch.

There's nothing even remotely close to a well seasoned cast iron skillet for frying fish. Melt some butter till bubbly hot, season the fillets with salt and pepper and fry till golden but not brown. One mistake many people make is thinking that they're sautéing a tender cut of meat, which indeed should be seared initially. Fish fillets should be cooked on no more than moderate heat and don't let them get past that golden stage. Note that I'm referring to sautéing in a small amount of fat, not deep frying. Deep frying requires a higher temperature.

A coating for them? They'll be much better. Here are some choices:

1. Flour, the simplest
2. Cornmeal, superb
3. Crushed cornflakes
4. Oatmeal, ground fine in the food processor
5. Shake 'n' Bake, especially for the stronger tasting fish
6. Pancake mix (try buttermilk)

Put the coating in a plastic bag at home. If it's a type that has no seasoning, add whatever you like. I like dried parsley and dried dill, plus a little salt and pepper. Or, substitute tarragon for the dill. A little cayenne is nice in the mix. I've also used white pepper, and sometimes paprika.

Rinse your fillet at the hole, dry quickly on paper towels, and toss into the plastic bag. Shake to coat well. Let set on a plate for 10 minutes.

A more complex coating is flour, egg and then breadcrumbs. It will greatly stretch a meager catch, but it requires some kind of bowl not to mention the other ingredients. It's messy.

You really should drain your fried fish on paper towels. Bring a lemon and dole out a wedge to each diner. Nice homemade white or brown bread goes well with fried fish, but you must have some kind of bread.

A superb sandwich is fillets on grainy white bread and slathered with tartar sauce. Better yet is a fancier sauce like aioli or gribiche, which can be made at home and brought along. Even if the fish has gotten cold, perhaps due to a flurry of flags, it will make a great sandwich. If you have no tartar or other sauce, simple mayonnaise will help a lot. Can I convince you to make a homemade curry mayonnaise to bring along?

A good stick-to-the-ribs dish is a fish giambote. See earlier in this chapter.

My friends and I have never cared much for the roe of most fish, but shad, alewife herring and yellow perch are three exceptions. Perch roes are slightly stronger tasting and slightly less refined tasting than shad roe, but they're still a treat if you like fish eggs in the first place. Bacon is the classic accompaniment for shad roe, but I use bacon of a different sort: smoked pork butt, which is cured and does not require cooking. Here's that recipe, and one other, for yellow perch roe. Happily, virtually all the female yellows we catch in winter carry eggs, and the females in our waters outnumber males by about seven to one. Fish roe, like calves liver, is something that should only be eaten extremely fresh, within hours of coming out of the beast. (Preserved fish roe, like caviar, would of course be an exception.)

Perch Roe with Pork Strips

When cleaning the perch, try not to cut the egg sack. Take the roes from 4 perch and drop them into water that has just stopped boiling. Leave them in for a minute or so. Remove. Take a generous slice off a smoked pork butt, cut into small, thin strips and sauté (bacon can also be used). Drain some of the fat and then add a little butter. Add the perch roes and sauté along with the pork strips on very low heat. Sprinkle on a little bit of lemon juice. Make sure you have some good, grainy white bread to go with this. Serves two as an appetizer before a good fish dinner.

Perch Roe Piquant

Drop 4 perch roes into very hot water. Leave there for five minutes. In a skillet, melt 2½ T. butter. Turn flame to high and cook till butter is very brown but not black. Remove from flame. Add 2 tsp. white vinegar and 1 tsp. capers. Stir. Add 2 T. crumbled bacon bits. Pour sauce off and keep warm (if it gets cold return to the skillet with the roes at the last minute). Return skillet to low heat. Add a tiny bit of butter and the roes, and cook till slightly browned, about 3 minutes on a side. Serve the piquant sauce over roes. A slice off a hard roll is a good accompaniment, but any kind of bread will do. Serves 2.

If some snooty soul ever calls you down for all that frying, all that frying, be prepared with a preparation that's a bit more uptown. You do have to bring a few things from home, and you should even tell your snooty friend to bring a good bottle of white burgundy, because this trout treat will merit it.

Trout Steaks with Hollandaise

Scale, gut, and remove the head and tail of one trout (or walleye) of at least 16 inches, the larger the better. Cut into about 6 fairly thick steaks. Poach in a small amount of water in your skillet, covered, about 5 minutes. Drain off water. Add 1 T. butter. Sauté pre-poached steaks in butter five minutes to firm them up and give them some color. Take one packet of premade, store bought hollandaise sauce and prepare it in your pot as instructed. Be sure to have along the ingredients called for. Spoon over steaks, the skins of which you could remove first. Sprinkle with some dried dill. Sprinkle on a little paprika if you like it, salt and pepper, too. Serves 3 or more, depending on size of fish.

Sources of Ice Fishing Gear

All sorts of equipment is used in ice fishing, and not all categories are listed here. Card tables are found in thousands of shanties, but this listing includes no card table manufacturers. The manufacturers here make products specifically for ice fishing, though not necessarily exclusively for ice fishing.

You can tell when an activity is on the crest of a wave: Dozens of small-time manufacturers and entrepreneurs scramble for position (while the larger companies usually move in more slowly). Accordingly, many makers of ice fishing gear are small and there is substantial attrition. This list was current at press time but it is safe to say there is substantial volatility to a list such as this.

SHELTERS
    Canvas Plus
    Fanatics (Ice Fort)
    FOF Products (pop-up tents)
    Frabill (tents and Ice Shuttle)
    H. T. Enterprises
    J-Moe Manufacturing (Ins-tent)
    Mankato Tent & Awning (EZ-Set tents)
    U. S. L. Products (distribute both The Clam and The Fish Trap)
    Winter Fishing Systems (makers of The Fish Trap)
    Wydel (Hurritent)
TIP-UPS AND ACCESSORIES
    Fishing Specialties
    H. T. Enterprises (Polar, Windlass and Fisherman tip-ups)
    Handishop Industries (SWish-Rod)
    Lite Strike
    Schooley & Sons
    Sensortronics (Strike Sensor electronic bite pager)
    Solar Bear
    Strike Master
    U.S. Line
    Worth Company, The
JIGGING RODS AND JIG LURES
    Berkley
    H. T. Enterprises
    Handishop Industries (SWish-Rod)
    Jig-A-Whopper/UMM Holdings
    Johnson Fishing (Mitchell rods)
    Lake Country Products
    Normark
    Shakespeare
    St. Croix Rods
    Wisconsin Tackle
SET-LINE REELS
    H. T. Enterprises
    Heat Pack (Snap Trap)
    Lake Country Products (Rattle Reel)
ICE FISHING LINES
    Berkley
    Gudebrod

ICE FISHING LINES, *continued*
Tackle Marketing
U. S. Line
SONAR EQUIPMENT AND ACCESSORIES
Eagle Electronics
Vexilar (FL-8 Sonar)
Winter Fishing Systems (Ice Box)
AUGERS
Feldmann Engineering (Jiffy augers)
Strike Master (Mora augers)
SHARPENING STONES
Garrett Wade
Lee Valley Tools

ADDRESSES
Berkley, One Berkley Dr., Spirit Lake, IA 51360
Canvas Plus, 19900 Highway 81, Rogers, MN 55374
Eagle Electronics, 12000 E. Skelly Dr., Tulsa, OK 74128
Fanatics, P. O. Box 10880, Golden, CO 80401
Feldmann Engineering, 520 Forest Ave.,
    Sheboygan Falls, WI 53085
Fishing Specialties, 315 Short St., Auburn, MI 48611
FOF Products, P.O. Box E, Delavan, WI 53115
Frabill, P.O. Box 499, 536 Main St., Allenton, WI 53002
Garrett Wade, 161 Ave. of the Americas, New York, NY 10013
Gudebrod, P. O. Box 357, Pottstown, PA 19464
H. T. Enterprises, P.O. Box 909, Campbellsport, WI 53010
Handishop Industries, 1411 N. Superior, Tomah, WI 54660
Heat Pack, P. O. Box 7366, St. Cloud, MN 56302
J-Moe Mfg. Co., 7854 Vernon Rd. S., Clay, NY 13041
Jig-A-Whopper/UMM Holdings, Box 411, Hwy. 14,
    Dodge Center, MN 55927
Johnson Fishing, 1531 Madison Ave., Mankato, MN 56001
Lake Country Products, P.O. Box 367, Isle, MN 56342
Lee Valley Tools, 1080 Morrison Drive, Ottawa, Ontario K2H8K7
Lite Strike, P.O. Box 3107, Missoula, MT 59806
Mankato Tent & Awning, 1021 Range St., N. Mankato, MN 56001
Normark Corp., 1710 E. 78th St., Minneapolis, MN 55423
Schooley & Sons, 13700 12 Miles Rd., Greenville, MI 48838
Sensortronics, P.O. Box 509, Campbellsport, WI 53010
Shakespeare Co., 3801 Westmore Dr., Columbia, SC 292230
Solar Bear, 114 East Glen Road, Denville, NJ 07834
St. Croix Rods, P.O. Box 279, Park Falls, WI 54552
Strike Master, 411 Washington Ave. N., Minneapolis, MN 55401
Tackle Marketing, 3801 West Superior St., Duluth, MN 55807
U. S. L. Products, 3110 Ranchview Lane, Minneapolis, MN 55447
U. S. Line, P. O. Box 531, Westfield, MA 01085
Vexilar, Inc., 9252 Grand Ave. S., Minneapolis, MN 55420
Wisconsin Tackle, P. O. Box 285, Hartland, WI 53029
Winter Fishing Systems, 859 Manor Dr., Minneapolis, MN 55422
Worth Company, The, P.O. Box 88, Stevens Point, WI 54481
Wydel, Inc., P.O. Box 87, Lake Elmo, MN 55042

Index